Quaday's Quotes

70 Years on a Blue Earth River Valley Farm

Written By

Richard R. Quaday

Compiled By

Kathryn A. Husfeldt

Narrated By

Mary L. Stoffel

Innovative Order Press

Innovative Order Press
Innovative Order, Inc.
Isanti, MN 55040

©2012 Richard R. Quaday

Cover design by Amy Nelson

Printed in the United States of America by Lightning Source

Published 2012

IBSN 978-0-9844800-2-9

Table of Contents

About the Book, About the Author

This book evolved and grew over the period of twenty years and three months that Richard Quaday wrote his weekly *Quaday's Quotes* column for the Faribault County Register, in Blue Earth, Minnesota. The columns contained a wealth of material on many subjects, including the Quaday family, the history of Blue Earth, and life on the family farm from the early 1900s to the present, as well as comments and opinions on current events and modern issues.

When Dick retired from writing at the age of ninety, there was a real possibility that this personal, historical record could be lost or fade into obscurity. So two of the Quaday daughters, Kathryn Husfeldt and Mary Stoffel, decided to compile excerpts of the columns by subject and present them framed by the historical events of the times, along with the many photographs collected by the Quaday family over the years. These pictures do not have the crisp quality of modern digital photography but they accurately portray the life and times of a farm family living in a small town in the Corn Belt of America.

The memories in these columns present the good times of the growth of the agriculture industry in Minnesota, as well as the tough times of the Great Depression. Dick's farming career spanned seventy years, from working with horses on small homesteads, to renting hundreds of acres and using mammoth, self-propelled machines. This historical record portrays farming as a way of life, reflecting the values and principles this country was founded on. It clearly shows our roots, deeply embedded in the rich, fertile soil of the Blue Earth River Valley.

Introduction

Richard (Dick) Ralph Quaday was born in 1920 in Blue Earth, Minnesota, on some of the richest farming land in the world. He grew up there on the Oak Ridge Farm, later called River Road Farm, with his two brothers, Carl and John, and his sister, Marie. After farming with his dad, William Quaday, Richard assumed ownership of the home place, in turn passing it on to his son Michael and going into semi-retirement. After 68 years of farming as son, owner, and father, Richard started a new career in 1988.

He began writing a weekly column called *Quaday's Quotes* for the Faribault County Register. This contribution to the local news scene was so well received that it continued for twenty years and three months. The column reported on the doings of the extensive Quaday family, current local and national issues and social events, but also served another purpose for those missing a simpler, quieter lifestyle. *Quaday's Quotes* often gave a personal historical perspective to life on the farm in southern Minnesota during and after the years of the Great Depression. Anyone who ever called that area home could relate to the many stories brought to life by Dick's writing.

The columns were written as 'spontaneous memory' each week, so throughout the book you may see some repetition on certain subjects, because that is how the column flowed each week. 'Repeated Sequences' of events may appear when approached from a related topic.

Eventually, upon reaching ninety years of age in 2010, Dick decided it was time to really retire. Maybe. Sort of. You see, the Quaday family represents so many other families in this great country of ours. We never really stop working, or playing or living. Our heritage is that we just keep going--building, producing, and helping our own families and others as we pass along our values with the fruits of our labors. Dick's columns richly portray this scene of small-town America, relating it to a way of life that is gone forever.

So this book reflects a desire to preserve that personal perspective of those by-gone days and make it available for many others to enjoy. Twenty years of weekly columns is a lot of writing to condense into a single book and it required a joint effort. Dick Quaday authored each column, but the organization of the subjects, names, dates and pictures was done by his daughter, Kathryn Quaday Husfeldt. I, in turn, am honored to serve as narrator.

Respectfuly,

Mary Quaday Stoffel

Credits

All *Quaday's Quotes* included in this book, are reprinted with permission from Richard Ralph Quaday. They were printed weekly in the November 13, 1989 - January 31, 2010 Faribault County Register, P O Box 98, Blue Earth, MN 56013

Some of the background information on the Home Place was provided by Dick's sister, Marie Anderson in Overture to Anderson Unfinished Symphony, 1914-1942

Percival, J. F., "History of the Grain Binder," Farm Collector Magazine, September/October 1955

"The History of Ford Pickups: The Model T Years 1925–1927." PickupTrucks.com. http://www.pickuptrucks.com/html/history/ford_segment1.html. Retreived 2009-06-04

Salmon, D.E., Carman, Ezra Ayers, Heath, Hubert A., Special Report on the history and present condition of the sheep industry of the United States. US Department of Agriculture, Bureau of Animal Industry, Washington, D. C., April 11, 1892.

Several of the photographs included in this book are postcards depicting scenes and buildings in Blue Earth, MN, in the early 1900s and some of them contained a copyright date. These postcards were all published by the L. L. Cook Company of Milwaukee, Wisconsin.

In copyright law, 1978 is a key year in determining the duration of copyright. If a work was created and/or published prior to 1978, the length of copyright is not as long as works produced after 1978. There were also strict rules for renewing copyright prior to 1978. Prior to 1978, copyright on a work lasted for 28 years after it was published.

Mary Warner of the Morrison County Historical Society, Little Falls, MN, conducted copyright research on several similar postcards that were published by The L. L. Cook Company. She checked the U.S. Copyright Office for registration information on The L. L. Cook Company and found nothing. In Wisconsin, the Department of Financial Institutions tracks registered corporations, rather than the Secretary of State's Office. She checked their website and found a listing for The L. L. Cook Company. The listing showed that the company was dissolved in 1980. It also showed that the Registered Agent Office for the company was the C T Corporation System. In looking at the C T Corporation System's business listing, she found that Roger Gierhart was the Registered Agent. An address was given for Mr. Gierhart, so she mailed a request for assistance in determining who the copyright holder was for these postcards.

Mr. Gierhart's secretary called after receiving the letter and said that he had no records to help determine copyright. For these early 1900 postcards, the original copyright expired before 1978. Following strict rules, copyright could be renewed for an additional 28 years, if the copyright holder remembered to renew copyright within the 28th year. If not, the work fell into public domain. If the postcard copyrights were renewed in a timely manner, the new expiration dates were 2006 and the postcards are now in the public domain.

Mary Warner
Copyright 2002, Morrison County Historical Society

City of Blue Earth, Minnesota

The community of Blue Earth, located in the agriculturally rich Blue Earth River Valley, was organized in February, 1856. The Blue Earth River was named for the blue clay that is found high along its banks where it empties into the Minnesota River at Mankato. The stream was called Makato Osa Watapa by the Dakota Indians, meaning "the river where blue earth is gathered." The Native Americans of this area, which were the Mdewakanton Tribe of the Dakota Nation, often referred to as the Sioux, called the blue clay "mah-ko-tah" or "mah-kah-to." (The name of the city Mankato is derived from this word.) The clay is actually more blue-green than blue, almost an aqua blue color, and somewhat darker when it is damp. It is believed to be a mineral called Illite according to an analysis done by the Mankato State University.

The city of Blue Earth is the county seat for Faribault County, an agricultural community filled with deep rich black soil. The Blue Earth, Badger, and Coon Rivers meander throughout the area's fertile farm land. The city is located east of the Blue Earth River, ten miles from the Iowa State Line.

1908 Faribault County Court House

"The Blue Earth area was originally inhabited by the Sioux Indians. In 1855 the territorial legislature established Faribault County and defined its boundaries. That same year, Moses Sailor came from Iowa looking for the headwaters of the Blue Earth River. He found what he was looking for and liked it.

He built a cabin and stayed there and became the first resident of Faribault County. The next year, 1856, Blue Earth City was founded by four young men who arrived in February. It was named after the river, which was named Mahkota (meaning blue earth) by the Sioux Indians in reference to the blue/

black clay found in the high river banks.

James Dobson came to the area in 1856 and homesteaded a few miles south of the Sailor Place. Soon others settled along the west and middle branches of the Blue Earth River and the small lake (later named Woods Lake) and they named the community, and also the township, Dobson (in 1862 the name changed to Elmore).

In 1858 a log school house was built. It was called the Dobson School and was the center of much activity, serving as the school, town hall, and church."

Reprinted from "Take Me to Blue Earth", Stories and Poems by Rich Kroch. Omaha, NE: Memories and More, 2002.

This story covers not only 70 years of farming and small town life in Blue Earth, Minnesota, but goes all the way back to the early 1900s and the history of the Quaday family. I have a strong German ancestry, with Maternal Grandfather Frederick Levenick Jr., and his spouse Grandmother Mary (Willmert) Levenick. Paternal Grandparents, Charles Ludwig Quaday with spouse Pauline (Paschke) Quaday, all came directly from Germany. The German spelling of my name was Quade.

The Home River Road Farm is located on the Blue Earth Township Road, into Pilot Grove Road, to Blue Earth City, one-half mile north of school district 104. I attended my first six years in District 104, where I skipped the second grade.

The Blue Earth River

The Blue Earth River is a tributary of the Minnesota River, 108 miles long, in southern Minnesota. It is also a Minnesota Department of Natural Resources designated Water Trail. By volume, it is the Minnesota River's largest tributary, accounting for 46% of the Minnesota's flow at the rivers' confluence in Mankato. Via the Minnesota River, the Blue Earth River is part of the watershed of the Mississippi River, draining an area of 3,486 square miles in an agricultural region. Ninety percent of the river's watershed is in Minnesota.

The Blue Earth River flows northwardly in a winding course through eastern Faribault County into Blue Earth County, past the cities of Blue Earth, Winnebago, and Vernon Center, to Mankato, where it enters the Minnesota River from the south. Tributaries of the river in its upper course include the East Branch Blue Earth River, which rises in southwestern Freeborn County and flows westwardly through Faribault County to the city of Blue Earth; and Elm Creek, which rises in northeastern Jackson County and flows eastwardly through Martin County into northeastern Faribault County, where it joins the Blue Earth River near Winnebago.

The river flows in most of its course through till plains and the plain of a former glacial lake. The lower (northern) part of the river's watershed was historically covered by the Big Woods, a tract of hardwoods that has since been largely converted to agricultural use. According to the Minnesota Pollution Control Agency, approximately 84% of the Blue Earth River's watershed is used for agricultural cultivation, primarily that of corn and soybeans.

70 Years Living On The Blue Earth River

"I have spent all my 70 years living on the edge of the Blue Earth River. A lot of water has gone forever down through its crooked channels in that time. I've observed it in all phases, from raging floods to step-across drought. There have never been two years alike in my memory.

The highest water occurred in September of 1938. At that time, the blacktop southwest of town was under four feet of water for over one week. I was buying feed for my hogs from the elevator, as my first crop was still in the field. I had a choice; either drive the blacktop road, hoping it was still there, or drive my slow F-12 Farmall tractor nearly to Guckeen and come in on old 16. Being an impatient cuss, I told Dad to sit in the trailer and look way ahead to keep me on course, and I would watch close up for possible holes or washed out areas. We did very well until about 30 rods west of the bridge, there was a deeper spot. The trailer box began to rise and float, but fortunately stayed within the bolster pipes until we hit shallower water. There was a crowd at the bridge watching us.

The river had me bluffed out and I went out on old 16 on the way home to the cross road just east of Orval Paschke's place. Badger Creek was flooded in the flat east of Don Guerber's place, so we came home on old County No. 9 past the Harry Child's farm.

The low point of water in the Blue Earth River occurred in the hot, dry summer of 1934. It was only a series of pools of water with dry stretches in between. My brother, Carl, who sold cars for Howard Essler's Motor Inn at that time, offered John and I a lump sum of money to get gravel on the driveway on our farm. It is a semi-circular drive and not over 350 feet total in length. We used a big sorrel team and a high wheeled wagon with a loose plank bottom to haul egg-sized rock, clam shells, sand, and some really good gravel out of the river on the east end of the farm. There happened to be a long sand bar in just the right place for digging and still get up the bank with loads of gravel. I have no idea now many loads we hauled, but eventually we had the driveway covered to Carl's satisfaction, and got paid. By that time it was time to go threshing, so team and boys were in excellent condition with calluses aplenty.

When we lived on the Sailor Place, Neva and I took many a moonlight walk on the river in winter. We always went down there at the first freeze-up to watch the fish dart along ahead of us as we walked. Some years when the river froze up high we would cut a big hole clear across the river, throw a few oyster shells in the bottom, and with two pounding on the ice to scare the fish, and two with spears at the hole, fishing was great fun. At that time I don't think it was illegal, or if it was, everybody on the river broke the law. There were quite a few game fish in the river, as pollution was not yet worried about. The guys with the spears had to really be quick because with the first few taps upstream, the Northern Pike, if any were present, would dart through the hole like a shot. After that came the carp, and later the catfish or bullheads if there were any.

When we built our River House high above the river, we could watch the ever-changing moods of the Blue Earth River from our picture window, from the first ice breakup through flood time and back to ice again. I've never lost interest in observing the ever changing panorama."

Quaday's Quotes-partial (Reprinted with permission from RR Quaday) Faribault County Register Monday April 15, 1991

Schools

According to Kiester's *History of Faribault County*, "The first school kept in this township was a subscription and contribution school, taught in the winter of 1857-58 by W. W. Knapp, Esq., at Blue Earth City….After the organization of the first school district in 1859, the schools at Blue Earth City were the ordinary district schools and were kept in hired rooms, until the erection of the first district schoolhouse." The first building was completed about November 1, 1861 in Blue Earth City. School District No. 14, Faribault County, Minnesota, continued to grow and in 1884 a high school department was authorized by the Minnesota State High School Board. It was during the 35-year administration of Superintendent Lee R. Pemberton, 1923-1957, that the present buildings were erected. During the period from 1951-53, the Blue Earth district expanded to include many of the surrounding rural districts, as they could petition to be attached to an existing school district with a high school. As a result of this movement to the city schools and the consequent closing of rural schools, the Teacher Training Department of the Blue Earth School, which had prepared students for rural teaching since 1910, was discontinued in 1948.

1908 Blue Earth Teacher Training Class

Taken from the Blue Earth School Centennial Book. Blue Earth, Minnesota: Tuff Publishing, Inc. 1986.

Country School

"My Mother never had a chance to attend high school, but was smart enough to pass the entrance exam to the Blue Earth Normal Training course. She graduated with a certificate to teach students in grades one through eighth in the one-room country schools. While teaching for two years in the District 104 school, she met my Dad. The school board in District No. 2 offered her $10 per month more pay, so she taught there for two years. The school board of District No. 29 in Pilot Grove had two teachers who quit in one year, so they asked the county board to recommend a good teacher--one who could handle a tough bunch of boys they had, some of whom were 18 and 19 years old. Lorena Levenick, her maiden name, took the job.

She was a tall, good looking young lady, the kind of a teacher Pilot Grove boys were not used to. The two previous teachers had been men, but they

5

had a hard time disciplining these elderly boys who would spit tobacco juice through the knot holes in the school house walls, among other forms of rebellion. Mother didn't try to enforce discipline by force--instead she charmed them. She was highly successful and wound up teaching there two years. After six years of teaching in the rural schools, Mom and Dad were married by Reverend Ketchel in the Salem Evangelical Church, across the street from the Etta C. Ross Memorial Library.

I would suspect that the tough boys from No. 29 had somewhat the same experience when Mother taught school there that I had with the beautiful Miss Leona Erickson. Years later, when those old-timers found out who I was, they would tell me, "Your Mother was one of the best #$"*&% teachers we ever had."

Quaday's Quotes (Reprinted with permission from RR Quaday) Faribault County Register Monday December 22, 2008

The Blue Earth Original Swinging Bridge

School District 104

The original Swinging Bridge on the Blue Earth River, located below the District 104 school house, was built with two inch cables woven into guide wires, with rough lumber girders, planed one foot by twelve inch boards, using the giant Oak trees as

6

anchors on the West side and dead man concrete anchors used on the East side. The bridge was a favorite trysting spot. The builders of the bridge, Curt Swift, Maynard Sailor, and Clarence Dobson, built it for their children to use to cross the river to attend school, and to be able to use the pasture land on the other side of the river for their livestock.

Swinging Bridge, Quaday's Barking Dog Was Family's Signal Lover's Lane On River Road Was Getting Busy

"One of the more famous attractions out on the River Road was the old Swinging Bridge. It was built by the late Clarence Dobson, Maynard Sailor and Curt Swift.

The two families on the east side of the Blue Earth River, the Dobsons and the Sailors, were farming in School District #104, which was on the west side of the river. Swift lived on the west side, so it was to everyone's advantage to have a bridge to get children to school and also get cows home morning and night.

When I attended 104, we always had a day-long picnic at the Swinging Bridge on the last day of school. By then the Sailor children went to town school and the Dobson children were grown up and gone from home.

We had games and races and always all one could eat for dinner, but the big attraction for all of us was "The Bridge."

We would watch our chance to catch a few girls out in the middle, have one little rascal on each end and start the thing swinging. The peace was then disturbed for miles with screams, usually of mock fear. I'm sure some of the fear was genuine, but they always seemed to go back out there even though they knew what was coming.

In later years it fell into disrepair, so only one side was left. Then only two 12-inch boards were laid out on two cables stretched across the river.

It was about this time that I did one of the most foolish things ever. We had bought the old Abel Sailor farm on the west side of the river. Most of the pasture for the milk cows was on the east side, so when the dog didn't bring the cows home, I used the bridge during the high water.

One big black cow was due to calve and decided to do it during a severe thunderstorm in June, after some heavy rains. Of course, she did so under a big tree on the east side.

When I walked across to get her, the water was about three inches under the boards. Lightning had struck the tree and the calf looked alright, but could not walk. I put him over my shoulders and headed for home across the bridge.

With the added weight on my back, the bridge out in the middle hung in about two inches of water. Once out that far there was no turning back, so I sloshed across. By the time I got home, the calf was bleeding out of his ears a little. Then I realized that the lightning strike had damaged him beyond repair. The next morning he was dead, so it all went for naught.

You know where I thought most about not knowing how to swim? Right out in the middle of the bridge, that's how thoughtful youth is sometimes. The water was about 10 feet deep right there and moving swiftly.

On better days and nights the bridge was a favorite trysting spot, and many a young couple spent happy hours by the bridge.

The bridge was anchored at the east end by two giant oak trees and on the west by two oak posts, with the cables tied to cement anchors sunk in the ground.

Oak wilt killed the trees on the east end and the late Herb Schwen agreed to let it be moved down-stream to the old Sailor place, then owned by my Dad, Bill Quaday, and leased to Russell Golay.

Golay rebuilt the bridge directly below the old barn. The local kids and our kids continued to use it and play on it until the Reinen Bros bought the acreage. By then it was starting to deteriorate again and the Reinens were afraid someone would get hurt on it, so they let the cables down, probably forever.

The cables were made of good copper-bearing steel, so maybe someday someone will dig them up and rebuild "The Bridge." It will always swing in my memory.

One thing that never changed much out on River Road was, at the first onset of the warm evenings of spring, young couples began to use our road and our driveways for a lover's lane.

If old Bob, our collie dog, started to raise the roof around ten pm, Dad would say, "they're starting a little early tonight." Mother would smile and say nothing, no doubt thinking back to their horse and buggy courtship.

Mother, who taught school in District 104, wouldn't have cared to give any of her students cause for comment either.

During the 20s when prohibition controlled the drinking of alcoholic beverages, many times we school children would see the evidence to the contrary walking to school the next morning. Good pop bottles sold for two cents each at Nate Gendler's store, so we liked the advent of spring for a few chances at pocket change. With the demise of prohibition the bottles discarded along the right of way changed to the beer variety, so we could sell both kinds of bottles.

One could always tell whether the lovers were city or country dwellers because, if the driveways into lanes or woods happened to be fenced, the city guys would many times leave the gate open when they left. The country boys, fearing reprisals, always closed the gate when departing.

One of the most popular trysting spots was the Swinging Bridge about a mile south on the River Road and down a river driveway through the old "Dobson Place" now owned by the Schwen Estate and farmed by Dick Paschke.

The bridge was located at the base of "Devil's Cliff" as our kids called it. The cliff seemed awfully high and steep to young children, as it rose straight up for about 35 feet above the river. Russell Golay, who was quite an engineer, rebuilt the Swinging Bridge about a mile downstream from its original position. He then lived on the Sailor Place, owned by my Dad at the time. Our younger five children had many a pleasant afternoon with Russell's version, but it never attained the notoriety of the former years."

Quaday's Quotes- partial (Reprinted with permission from RR Quaday) Faribault County Register Monday April 27, 1992 (and) Faribault County Register Monday, February 12, 1990

The schoolhouse was about 1/2 mile south of our house and stood on a bit of ground that had been donated by one of the pioneer farmers living adjacent to it. The school yard was surrounded by open fields and had no trees of any size on it. The barbed wire fence around it had a good stand of poison ivy underneath it and during school months--September through May--the playground was either covered with snow or mud, since it was discouraging for any grass to grow when it was trampled on regularly.

Toilet facilities were provided in two little buildings--one for the boys and one for the girls. The ground on which these buildings stood was continually excavated by gophers which made big holes around the bases of the frameworks thus letting the frigid breezes in the winter freely circulate up through the holes provided. Needless to say no one loitered any longer than necessary.

The schoolhouse itself consisted of one large room containing the desks for the children, arranged in rows, and the teacher's desk at the front. There were blackboards on two sides, a large coal-burning heater surrounded by a jacket at the back, a crockery water container with a spigot in one corner, and, believe it or not, a huge grand piano of ancient vintage in one front corner. This piano was usually tightly closed and used as a table for piling books, papers, etc. At the entrance of the building there was a small hall, with a cloakroom for the girls on the right and on the left a similar room for the boys. The building actually had a full basement in which the supply of coal for the heater was stored, as well as storm windows, screens, wood for kindling, etc. Such a basement should have helped in keeping the floors of the schoolroom warm in winter, but batted balls and thrown stones always seemed to find their way through the glass so that the breezes were usually free to blow through no matter how often the glass was replaced. Being situated in the open field with absolutely no protection by trees or other buildings from the winter blizzards resulted in a very cold room in which to try to sit still and study. Mother knitted heavy wool stockings for us and Dad bought moccasins made of sheepskin to wear over the wool socks. But still our feet turned numb and the teacher, whose feet were probably colder than ours because she had to stand most of the time, let us go to the back of the room and prop our feet up against the heater jacket while we studied. As the toes started to warm up they also began to hurt and itch because we had developed chilblains. We couldn't decide which was worse--to have numb toes or itching, aching toes!

There was no well on the grounds so each day two of the boys (taking turns) walked to the nearest neighbor's and carried back a large pail of water. In the winter, if they happened to spill any on the floor as they poured it into the water jar, the spilled drops turned into balls of ice as we watched.

We carried our lunches to school in 2-qt. tin syrup pails which had tight-fitting covers. Mother quite often put in jelly or jam sandwiches so by lunch time everything in the pail had the aroma of jelly or jam. At one point, the county superintendent of schools recommended that all the country schools make an effort to provide hot lunches for the students. The parents decided to take turns bringing soup, etc., which could be heated up at noon. These arrangements didn't work out very well though, for several

10

reasons. The kids refused to eat what was furnished by another family or the teacher forgot and let the stuff boil over or it burned on the bottom and had a scorched taste. And in some cases it didn't even need that type of treatment to make it inedible.

The day's schedule called for two 15-minute recesses (morning and afternoon) and an hour free time at noon. This gave us quite a lot of time to play and fight (most games ended in an argument over who was cheating and how). In good weather we were all outside playing baseball (with a regulation baseball--no soft ball for us), prisoner's base, pom-pom pull-away, what's your trade?, kick the can, hide and seek; and when it was too rainy or cold we stayed inside and entertained ourselves with hangman, cat and mouse, feather volley ball and writing on the blackboard--if the teacher would let us.

The day always started with the salute to the flag and singing "Star Spangled Banner" and then the teacher read to us for a few minutes. Then came the recitation classes. Starting with the lowest grade represented, each class came to the front of the room and read or answered questions as called on. While this was going on, the ones in the other grades were supposed to be studying their assignments.

One of the big disadvantages of the country school of that time was the scarcity of books other than textbooks. Our "library" consisted of one shelf 3 feet wide filled with books which were supposed to satisfy the reading desires of all eight grades.

However, there was also a big advantage in having all the grades in one room. When younger students finished their lessons they could listen to those in higher grades going through their grammar, history, math, etc. recitations. By the time they came to those grades they already knew a good bit of the required material.

Taken from Overture to Anderson Unfinished Symphony, 1914-1942, written by Marie Anderson.

Remembering the Country School House

"The year was 1925 and I was privileged to enter first grade that year because my birthday came on September 2, and Labor Day was on the fourth. There was no kindergarten in country school at that time. My teacher was Miss Sophia Schneider. She walked to District 104 every day--a distance of two miles, one way, from Blue Earth. Miss Schneider walked rain or shine, spring or fall, five days a week. I don't recall her ever carrying an umbrella on rainy days, but she did wear a dark colored rain coat. She walked past our River Road Farm promptly at 8 am each morning. School opened at nine, giving her a chance to do janitor service before ringing the brass bell

11

and signaling the start of classes.

Our first grade in 1925 was the beginning of education in public school 104 for Helen Plocker, Caroline Dobson, Gertrude Swift, and myself. All eight grades were represented with four Swifts, four Dobsons, three Severtsons, Helen Haden, Helen Plocker and my brother John and I--a total of 15 students. Miss Schneider handled the janitor work and operated a big pot bellied stove in the winter. All this effort was expended for the monstrous wage of $25 a month--and she had to furnish her own room and board. For whatever reason, Miss Schneider had a conference with my folks and it was decided I was going to begin third grade in 1926. My brother Carl, sister Marie, and older brother John, had all skipped two grades but I was only allowed to skip one because of a new state rule, making me the black sheep of the family. We were lucky, living only a half mile from school; the Dobson kids lived a full three miles away on the Neuhalfen farm, too far for little kids to walk during rough weather. I can remember Orville Dobson hauling the younger ones to school in his 1924 Ford Model T Roadster and Hallet, their Dad, with a team of horses and bob-sled in winter. Years later, Mrs. Fred Lange hauled the Lange kids in the Willys-Knight touring car. The kids sometimes drove a team of horses on a buggy, stabling them in the barn of the Sailor Place just north of school. John and I would go along with Burdette Lange to feed and water the horses at noon lunch period, going through the woods and chasing rabbits on the way.

Maynard Sailor's three sons, Sidney, Maynard Jr. and Merit were in our school district but would have had to cross the Swinging Bridge over the Blue Earth River, so elected to pay tuition and attend town school. Later on, the Oliver Wendt family and the Walter Plocker family also sent their kids to town school. I attended town school for eighth grade because my sister, Marie, was hired to teach 104 and I was not about to go to school with her as my teacher. For me it was a good move, integrating me into junior high with several different teachers. I also began to get some entry into music education, which I loved. I had excellent arithmetic, grammar and history teachers: Miss Askdahl, Miss Garry and Miss Olson. I needed some catching up in arithmetic and Miss Askdahl spent extra time and effort getting me caught up with my class. According to my country school grades, I was dumped into the "A" class and they were a super-smart bunch to keep up with. When our class entered the Blue Earth High School we lost--or flunked out--13 students before graduation, making it a very small class of 53.

I was not allowed to take any 'easy' subjects in high school, with Latin and Algebra my first two electives. I was not too enamored with either one, as my only D grade--ever--came in Latin. My grade was later made into a B with extra work. Our first Latin teacher, Mrs. Protexter, came down with health problems and we missed classes for a few weeks before a new teacher, Miss Krinkie, was hired--hence the incomplete grade. I didn't care much for Algebra either, always feeling it was too abstract. I really liked Latin after getting into Roman history and am eternally glad my Mother, who was a country school teacher, forced me to sign up for it.

When I was a sophomore, I was third from the shortest in the gym Phy-Ed lineup. When we were seniors, I was third from the tallest and oh, so proud of it. I had become the tallest in our family at 6 feet, 1 inch. Age and farming have removed an inch now. Possibly hard times took a little off as well."

Quaday's Quotes (Reprinted with permission from RR Quaday) Faribault County Register Monday September 8, 2008

School Picnics Fun - Presidential Election Not

"The first part of June always reminds me of "The Last Day of School," in my seven years of study at the institution of lower learning out on River Road. We always closed the school year with a picnic down at The Swinging Bridge. I am positive that we had a wonderful sunny, warm day for this event--just as if we had ordered it--on that particular day. We could be sure of one other thing. The driveway down the river bank to the picnic grounds went through Curt Swift's yard, so we had to open the wire gate into the pasture. The Swift milk cows also used the pasture, so we had to be somewhat careful where we stepped. One other thing that was a given; the Swift family never attended the picnic. All the other families did, even though it came on a Friday, a working day.

The pattern did vary some years according to the whims of the current teacher. The food was always heavy on fruit salad, potato salad and baked beans. There was always a five-gallon drum of Schwen's ice cream for dessert, with the last of it dished out as cones before we headed for home, after the games were over and the kids were tired out from running up and down the steep hill on the east bank. Of course the boys had to catch some of the girls crossing the Swinging Bridge and gave them a bouncy, and sometimes scary, ride out in the middle.

The tenants of the D.D. Murphy farm had pasture on both sides of the river and used the bridge to bring the cows home for milking. Curt Swift kept the bridge in good repair when he lived there, with 1½ inch cables stretched between two oak trees on the east end, and two big round oak posts anchored with concrete deadmen on the west. Two-by-fours were clamped to the cables every eight feet, and two rough foot boards 16 feet long, were nailed to the two-by-fours, making a sturdy deck with good traction. Two-by-fours were bolted upright on each side, with woven wire stapled to them making side handholds. It was quite an engineering feat.

In later years, with other tenants on the Murphy farm, the bridge was allowed to deteriorate to the point that it had only one foot board and no wire sides. It still was navigable, if one had good enough balance. It was a little scary when the river was high enough to lap at the bottom of the foot boards, out in the middle of the river. That was the situation and condition of the bridge many years later when Neva and I owned the Sailor Place, the farm adjoining the Murphy farm on the north. By that time Herb Schwen owned the Murphy farm and the Potter Place on the south, where Fred Paschke lived.

When Russell Golay rented the Sailor Place from my Dad, the bridge lay in the river with west end posts pulled out by an oversized flood. Russell had milk cows, so he salvaged the cables, moving them downstream about 60 rods. We had traded 80s with my Dad, and our kids were eternally grateful to Russell for rebuilding the Swinging Bridge, as that was their playground in the summer. They played up and down the river, as far south as "Devil's Cliff," where the river had washed out the east bank. Our kids sat on the bridge and fished. At that time there were walleyes and they don't live in polluted water."

Quaday's Quotes -partial (Reprinted with permission from RR Quaday) Faribault County register Monday June 22, 2009

Final School Picnic Before Summer

"The last day of school out in district 104 on River Road was a joyous occasion. The teacher was relieved to have nine month's grind come to an end. The children were happy to have three months to lay the books aside and have a complete change of schedule for the summer.

A noon picnic was always held down by the Blue Earth River at the Swinging Bridge. The Swinging Bridge was built for quite a number of reasons. District 104 included land on both sides of the River and driving clear around the south way on all mud roads, was very time consuming with a horse and buggy during the spring.

I entered first grade at 104, one day over the age of six, and my teacher was Sophie Schnieder, who taught me for my first three years. She was an excellent teacher, who insisted on strict discipline during actual school time, which ran from 9 am to 4 pm with two recesses of 15 minutes. The noon lunch hour was just that, one hour. The recesses were pretty necessary as giving each child a chance at the outdoor two holers eliminated having to raise one's hand for a "biffy call" during classes; for some children, this was rather embarrassing.

In 1926 our River Road was still un-graded, without a stitch of gravel. After the First World War boom had subsided, hard times simply did not allow for the upgrading of township roads.

Most of the land near the River was used for pasturing of cattle and quite a few farmers had land on both sides, so if a tree didn't fall across the river in the right place, one headed for the Swinging Bridge to fetch the milk cows home. At the time I attended 104, D.D. Murphy owned the farm where the bridge was located, which was farmed by Curt Swift. We always had to open two gates to drive through the cattle yard and down the steep hill, in Model T Fords and four cylinder Chevys, to the picnic area. It was pretty scary, with the road within two or three feet of the river bank, and water over 20 feet below. Sometimes after a severe flood, the driveway had to be dug over into the hill another three feet. Nobody ever drove over the edge, that I know of. The Model Ts had a tough time getting back out of the area, with a climb of some forty five feet, and quite steep.

We always had running races, sack races, and three-legged races, with high jumps and broad jumps, for prizes furnished by the school board, and our teacher always gave each child some small trinket to remember her by. The food, of course, was fantastic, as each mother would bring her specialty, trying to outdo each other. The school board bought a five gallon drum of ice cream, so there was no limit, except what one could comfortably hold. There was enough for cones after the kids had run and jumped to their heart's content. The most fun for the boys would be to start swinging the bridge while it was full of girls. The girls always pretended to be scared

15

half to death, with screaming that could be heard for miles. Maybe they were, but it never kept them from going back on the bridge. The last day of school picnic broke up at chore time, 4:30 pm, because even on such a holiday the farm families had to get home to tend the livestock, which all farmers had in those days. The better the livestock was taken care of, the better the family lived; it was as simple as that.

It was a wonderful time to be a child in country school; no one had any money, but we ate well and always got a new pair of bib overalls to start the school year."

Quaday's Quotes -partial (Reprinted with permission from RR Quaday) Faribault County Register Monday May 31, 1999

Politics at Country School

"As the presidential election campaigns begin to heat up, I have to think way back to the election of 1928, when I was a third grader in country school district 104.

We started school the day after Labor Day and just a few days later, Hilda Plocker brought Helen to school, telling Miss Sophie Schnieder, our teacher at the time, she had some Hoover buttons for the kids to wear and flyers for them to take home for the adults to read.

Miss Schnieder seemed a bit cool about it at first, but acquiesced, thinking it would be a good lesson in citizenship for her pupils.

My brother, John, and I proudly wore our Hoover and Curtis tin buttons home with some larger ones for our folks. My Mother, who was a staunch Republican all of her adult life, wore her button wherever she went--even to church. Dad, on the other hand, threw his in the dresser drawer and promptly forgot about it. I must mention that these were prohibition times, when the consumption and distribution of alcohol was forbidden by law. The mayor of New York City, Al Smith, ran on an anti-prohibition ticket, promising to bring back beer and spirits to the public. Herbert Hoover ran strongly prohibition.

The next school day a sharp division of opinion appeared at 104. Clarence Dobson, who lived across the Blue Earth River but lived in District 104, was just as Democrat as my Mother was Republican and handed Smith buttons to the Swift and Severtson children to wear to school. The Hallet

16

Dobson family including Joe, Mary and Caroline, also wore Smith tin buttons. The Perry children, who lived on the Murphy farm which straddled two school districts, didn't wear any buttons.

From September to election day many hot arguments and occasional fisticuffs occurred.

On election night everyone who had a battery radio had them charged and running. Those without radios were invited to farms that did and, as the results of the vote count came in, it became apparent that Hoover and Curtis had won. That didn't end the arguments, but they did dwindle after a few days.

The communications were not so speedy in the 20s and 30s, but the big cities on each coast, along with Chicago, had their votes counted and tabulated by around 3 am and telegraphs dotted and dashed the news shortly thereafter.

In 1932, Agnes Bleess was our teacher, and we had a decidedly different arrangement of families in 104. The Plocker, Wendt and the Sailor children all went to Blue Earth City School. The Lange, Anderson and Paschke families replaced the Swift, Dobson and Severtson families, and every child got to cast a vote in the school election. Mr. Hoover had preached prosperity 'Just around the corner', but the country didn't know which corner he was talking about. The world was in the depths of The Great Depression and was ripe for any kind of change.

Franklin D. Roosevelt won the election in a landslide and 'happy days are here again' became the theme song of the day, even though The Great Depression hung on for six more years. At least the alcohol drinkers could drown their sorrow in 3.2 percent beer, which sold for between 5 and 15 cents a glass, depending on where one lived.

When I attended Blue Earth High School, we held a straw vote in our citizenship class and FDR won easily, as his 'fireside chats' captivated the imagination of the country and his forward-looking social programs gave the country new hope--something which had been absent for so many years of the Depression.

His theory that "The only thing we had to fear was fear itself," had taken hold. Men were going back to work and taking home paychecks, even though they were small, banks were open again, and a general feeling of hope and prosperity slowly came back in our country.

I'm sure that elections for President were still hotly contested in some areas, but here in the Midwest, they didn't raise temperatures as much as in my country school on River Road farm."

Quaday's Quotes (Reprinted with permission from RR Quaday) Faribault County Register Monday September 13, 2004

Remembering County's Country Schools

"When I was attending Country School District 104 out on River Road, from 1925-1932, many of the country schools in Faribault County were still in operation. A few of those closest to towns had closed, with students entering elementary school in the city schools. It was a time of prosperity on the farms around the Corn Belt, with good prices for farm produce after the end of the first World War. The devastated countries of Europe were importing all the food grains that we could raise, and farm production costs were low, due to horses furnishing practically all the power needed. Feed for the horses was raised on the farm and consisted mainly of oats and hay.

The traditional country school social and athletic events held in the middle of May after a long, hard winter were still being observed by the school in our area. We practiced nearly every day for spelling contests and the athletic event held on separate Saturdays in May. A Declamatory contest was held immediately after the spelling contest, with students reciting poetry, essays and sometimes, in the larger schools, a one or two-act play. The athletic events consisted of running races, with the hundred yard dash being the most popular for both boys and girls. I can remember doing pretty well at our school practice sessions and being quite proud of my running ability--but ending up in the dust at the Play Day (as the event was called) beaten by a little girl who was faster.

The high jump and the broad jump (now called the long jump) were hotly contested, with the winners receiving red, white and blue ribbons for first, second and third place. I was always long-legged, tall and skinny, so I did well in the high jump and broad jump. In between events, and while prizes were being awarded, some smart talk, and occasionally a fight, broke out and had to be squelched by the teachers or some of the parents who came to watch. I got into one myself, with a boy from District 58--known as the Gartzke School--and had to take a fence post away from him to keep from

18

getting clobbered with it.

The spelling contests were my best performance, where I usually ended up first or second. I read poetry and recited speeches by great orators, but never made much of an impression on the judges. The County Superintendent, Miss Jones at the time, was always one of the judges and carried the most weight. I had a light, tenor voice and my voice did not carry well in a crowd. There were no microphones, yet, in country school at that time. Billy Haase, who years later starred in our junior and senior class plays, always won the Declamatory contests with perfect recitations of poetry and speech. Alice Paschke, of 104, was often a winner at poetry recitation.

After the students had finished performing and showing the talents they had acquired during the year, a basket social was held because by then everyone was hungry after a hard day's work; planting corn or gardening, and listening to seemingly endless performances by their children. They undoubtedly had heard most of the material practiced at night, with lots of guests. Every lady who attended the contests had to bring a lunch basket to be auctioned off, by either one of the school board members or a volunteer auctioneer, usually a professional who needed the practice or the advertising. The proceeds were earmarked for buying much needed books which were expensive, or sporting and playground equipment, which was almost non-existent.

If the school teacher was young and good-looking, all the hired men and some bachelor farmers would eagerly bid the schoolmarm's basket sky high, to get to eat with her and possibly make a few points. At that period, if the school teacher got married she was all through teaching school. There was much competition for the rural school teaching job, even though it was a very tough occupation with low wages and endless work, janitor and all. Very few school teachers had their own car, so they had to walk to work or sponge a ride with someone who worked close by. Sometimes the bachelor farmer in the district would be courting the teacher and haul her back and forth to work. Many a country school teacher married a rich farmer, in those days.

It was a time in the development of our country that had established a unique system which worked well to educate country kids, who otherwise would have had to be home schooled or go uneducated. Some of our greatest statesmen received their early education in a country school, and were always proud of it in later life."

Quaday's Quotes (Reprinted with permission from RRQ) Faribault County Register Monday May 25, 2009

Country Schools Were A Great Place For Education

"In country school District 104 out on River Road, we didn't have kindergarten, but had a distinct advantage by having very small class sizes; not more than four or five per grade, so the teacher could give special help to the children with a problem in the reading department. We all had to learn to read out loud in front of the entire school by the third grade, or whenever the County Superintendent visited our school. I'm sure the Blue Earth City School didn't have such a requirement, as their class sizes in the elementary grades ran from 20 to 25, and time would not allow that many children to be reviewed. All education actually depends on being able to read and interpret, and remember the message in the book or paper.

The problem with many children, of course, is the parents, many of whom never learned how to read well and so didn't read to their children at the age when it would have done the most good. Learning to read aloud is much more difficult than silent reading, which is why country school teachers usually read story books or newspaper articles of current events to their students, to hold their attention while teaching them to read. The big city schools are having problems with the "No Child Left Behind" laws and rules, mainly because they haven't installed the pre-school system to have the students properly prepared for kindergarten and first grade.

Back in the days when we milked cows by hand and did chores before breakfast, a farm news commentator named Maynard Speece did his diatribe from 6:30 am until 7 am, while we were milking. At about the time back then, when much discussion in the city and consolidated school was about teaching sex education in schools, one of Speece's comments to city parents was; "The best way to teach children all about sex education was to send them to a country school." The boys and girls all had to walk to school together, or drive a team of horses on a cart or buggy and ride together. They had to learn to play the same games, or cooperate on a teeter-totter. In District 104, our teachers could hit a softball just as far as the 16-year-old eighth graders (yes, we had some of them).

The three Lange children, who lived on the Neuhalfen farm, drove a team and buggy the three miles to school, stalling the team in the barn on the

20

Sailor Place which was unoccupied at the time. That farm straddled the township line between Elmore Township and Blue Earth, so the children could go to 104 or the "Pitcher School." The Dobson children went to 104 when they lived there too. When the three Perry children lived on the Murphy farm, which had land in three townships, they opted to attend 104 and Carl or Mrs. Perry hauled the kids to school in their Model T Ford touring car. Harold and Donald had no trouble changing school, but their older sister missed her friends in another district so much that she cried in school and wouldn't join in any games for nearly a whole year. She was either in seventh or eighth grade, and the move was very traumatic for her.

Most of the time, we carried our lunch in a dinner pail or a brown paper bag. A hot lunch program, with a rotation of prepared soup or hot dish, was tried for a year or two, but some of the children didn't like the macaroni tomato hot dish furnished by one of the ladies and went home for lunch, so the program failed. The kids only lived 1/4 mile from school. After that, my Mother bought us Thermos jugs and we had hot soup and sandwiches for lunch, or cold milk with sandwiches when the weather was warm. When District 104 students numbered only eight, the School Board decided to merge and consolidate with Blue Earth District. By then I was treasurer of the board and hated to see it happen. But we thought the change was for the better."

Quaday's Quotes -partial (Reprinted with permission from RR Quaday) Faribault County Register Monday November 1, 2010

Books, Spelling and Beyond

"When I attended District 104 Grade School out on River Road, we had one bookcase with four shelves in the front of the building. It was about four-and-a-half feet high and four feet long with glass doors on the front. The framing was light oak, shiny, and the case was very heavy to move. The glass stayed clean for a long time because hardly anyone ever read books from it. The titles were definitely not interesting to kids under the sixth or seventh grade. I went there for seven grades, so I did not read many books during that time. I remember one book that I did read, titled "Abraham Lincoln." There was a book about Indian tribes in Minnesota that I read while in fifth grade.

We had a globe of our world mounted on a cast iron frame with different colored countries and blue bodies of water which we could rotate to the countries being studied for geography class. I loved geography--a subject hated by most students--because it told interesting stories about exotic places like Tibet and Italy while listing customs and products raised in each country. Pictures of the capital cities, mountains, lakes and rivers were very interesting to me. I still could pass almost any geography test and it amazes me how little today's students know of the planet we live on. Many can't even tell which states border their own.

About once a month, we had an all school spelldown when the students lined up across the front of the room and took turns spelling words they had studied and were supposed to know. The eighth graders stood on the left side and down on to the second graders. Our teacher took care to give each grade only words in their category. I can't ever remember losing a spell-down. The neighboring districts also had a spelling contest along with a Declamatory contest every year where students were given a chance to show their talents reading poetry or dramatic readings. I tried my best to get into the spirit of drama, but failed miserably. I never won a spelling contest on this level, as there were always some really sharp eighth graders from other schools.

I plugged along in arithmetic, as it was called then, hating every minute of the problem solving, although remembering the multiplication tables and measurement figures was easy for me. I didn't really get into arithmetic until I attended eighth grade in Blue Earth. My teacher for the subject was Miss Askdahl and she was wonderful. She sensed right off that I was struggling with numbers and problem solving and took extra pains to get me interested in her subject. I began the year with a C-, but because of her teaching ability, I ended the year with a B+. The school management took one look at my report card from country school, and put me in the "A" class. We had A, B and C classes at that time. I soon found out that I had work to do to keep up with that A class.

The school library, located down in the 1928 building, right next to the main office at that time, was most interesting to me, and any time I had my work done and had studied for the next day, I took a pass to the library. The great variety of novels, history books, and up to date periodicals, were all most interesting material for this country boy. I had a great teacher for eighth grade grammar. Her name was Miss Margaret Garry and if a student didn't learn grammar as it should be used, they stayed in her class until

22

they did. I still thank her for making it easy for me to form sentences and paragraphs correctly, using the best English, combined with colloquial terms used in the area where one lives.

1908 Etta C. Ross Memorial Library

The Etta C. Ross Library, across from the 1928 school building, was a treasure trove for me. Alta Cummings, and later, Hope Cummings, always took an interest in kids who took out "learning" books instead of frivolous "best sellers," and were a great help to me, many times guiding my selections for reading. Having an old rural school teacher for a mother helped a lot in my learning process. We had very few books in our family library. The Bible, Ben Hur, David Harum and a home health book of remedies for common complaints were all I remember.

We had a black covered set of encyclopedias and a Webster's Dictionary that Mother used when teaching country school. I still use our wonderful public library whenever I have slack time. Our daughter, Pauline Siem, manages the Faribault County Library, so I know it is well run."

Quaday's Quotes (Reprinted with permission from RR Quaday) Faribault County Register Monday November 11, 2002

I attended Blue Earth Public School, from grades eight through twelve, graduating in 1937. My extra-curricular activities included Boys Glee Club, mixed chorus, Quill and Scroll charter member, and business manager of The Mah-Ko-Tah, the school newspaper for two years. I was the stage manager for my Junior and Senior Class plays, while still maintaining a B average and Honor Roll. Occasionally I would make the A Honor Roll. I was a Boy Scout for one year.

Class of '37 Publishes A Newspaper

"I have always wondered what happened to the Blue Earth School paper, The Mah-Ko-Tah. This monthly paper, written entirely by the students, was a very lively and entertaining periodical. It was started in about 1934 or 1935. Miss Lillias Davis was the faculty member who master-minded the production. No one took my writing talents seriously so I became the business manager for my junior and senior years on the staff. We sold advertising to local merchants and to Josten's, who always got the class ring contract. The Mah-Ko-Tah sold for 5 cents and we always had enough money to pay the Blue Earth Post (forerunner to the Register), for the printing of the paper.

1937 Mah-Ko-Tah Newspaper Staff

We had some really talented writers in the 1936 and 1937 classes. Fern Stier, June Henke, and Helen Houghtaling did the bulk of creative writing. I believe Kenneth Meyer wrote most of the sports, and Betty Robertson and Elaine Larson did the columns. Interest remained high all through my tenure as business manager and we almost sold as many copies as there were students in senior high.

The 1938 class placed a goodly number of writers on the staff also. Marjorie Bassett, Shirley Lein and Opal Johnston carried the load after we graduated. Janet Bassett did the art work, and Elvira Martin, I think, helped with the circulation.

The spring I graduated, Miss Davis encouraged us to start a chapter of Quill and Scroll which is an organization of high school journalists throughout the world. I still proudly wear my gold Quill and Scroll pin. It would be fun to have a meeting of the old Mah-Ko-Tah staff. I believe practically all of the 1937 class Scroll members are still alive and well."

Quaday's Quotes -partial (Reprinted with permission from RR Quaday) Faribault County Register Monday November 25, 1991

Remembering His Good Old School Days

"When I was just a skinny kid growing up out on the River Road, any contact with a female my age was severe trauma for me. I guess the word bashful would best describe my failure to appreciate the opposite sex. That attitude began to change with the entrance into my life of my first really beautiful school teacher in the eighth grade of the Blue Earth City School. Her name was Leona Erickson and she was a tall, blonde Swede, with a traffic-stopping figure--which had to be near perfect to even be noticed by a twelve-year-old boy.

Farm kids, during that period of history in the Corn Belt country, were not the most popular in the town school. Miss Erickson didn't seem to mind whether we came from town or the farm, even when we came from physical education (gym class) sweating and smelling like the farm. She was so charming one just felt he had to behave himself. We were seated alphabetically in Assembly, so I thought, "How lucky can I happen to be, to get to have the back seat and get to turn in the attendance slips twice a day." Had I been above teenage, I suspect I would have suffered the first pangs of love.

During The Great Depression, it was a victory just to have a job, any job, and to receive a pay check--though meager--every month. School teachers were cheerful and upbeat in those years, because their checks were always good even though not large, and they lived much better than a great many other wage earners. I never could figure out why, but many school teachers in those days married one of the local farmers. Possibly they came into the teaching profession having been raised on a farm and right out of teachers college, or in the case of rural school teachers, a Normal School Training two-year course."

Quaday's Quotes (Reprinted with permission from RR Quaday) Faribault County Register Monday December 22, 2008

1930s Blue Earth High School

Dick's High School Days

"I always read with interest about the success of our various athletic teams put in play by the Blue Earth Area High School. Also, I cannot help but compare the present system to the way things were handled during the Great Depression, while I was making my way through Blue Earth High School.

I believe the Baldy Haase Era began in 1934, when Mr. Haase came here from Mandan, ND, to take over the athletic department from Harold Harm, who moved to the Twin Cities. Mr. Harm, and his wife Edna (Merrick) Harm were the physical education teachers, the athletic team coaches, and the Drama coaches for the whole school. All boys and girls were required to participate in physical education classes three days per week, and it took a very real disability to be excused from class.

Things changed dramatically when Baldy Haase took over the Phy-Ed and athletic departments. He coached the football, basketball and track teams, with only Venzel Peterson, as his assistant. We had great teams in those years with Mankato, Mason City, Iowa and Sioux Falls, besides the local county teams, as competition. Baldy taught Modern History in addition to his coaching duties. He was an avid hunter on weekends, when he could get away. It was his hunting enthusiasm which caused the fatal shooting of his wife, while cleaning his gun in the kitchen. That accident changed Baldy forever. He could never again work up the enthusiasm in his teams, and promote the drive of his former days.

1937 Class Play Cast

Edna Harm ran the Drama department when I was a junior in high school, and of course, I tried out for the class play, which was a great event. I failed to project enough voice to qualify, losing out to Billy Haase (no relation to Baldy) for the part of Huckleberry Finn, in the play Tom Sawyer. I did

27

become stage manager, so I got in most of the fun without the stage fright. Now that I think it over, the play's name was Huckleberry Finn.

In my senior year, Esther Mace Stahl was the drama coach, and a professional she was. I again failed to be an actor, but stage managed that play also, with a lot of help from Nate Sydow, who ran the complete engineering department with the help of two high school students. Our Superintendent, Lee R. Pemberton, had a marvelous bass voice, which could be heard from one end to the other when he hollered for "Nate" to come and correct some deficiency in the plumbing or heating.

In sharp contrast to our hands-on-system of my high school days, our school now has ten or twelve coaches, with many more athletic teams, for both boys and girls. We had no girls' athletic teams, except intramural competition, no wrestling, no volleyball, no baseball or softball teams in inter-school competition. In my day, we had one music teacher, who was expected to teach grade school music classes, conduct the orchestra, the glee clubs, and even put on an oratorio, the Messiah, when I was a junior.

I sang first tenor for that production, and it was a high point of my high school era. I still get goose bumps when I hear selections from the production on TV or radio, to this day. Miss Flagstad was the overworked, but 100 percent efficient music department head, during my time in high school. She married Fred Pickett, who at that time managed the JC Penney store here. I believe they still live in Austin. She came to our class of 1937 reunions many times years later. The 1928 (new) building at that time had a dining room, but no school noon lunch program. We carried our noon lunch, some in brown paper bags, some with dinner pails. If one wanted to be mean to a school mate, they hid his dinner pail. The best part of the day was the five-minute lunch, the 55 minute basketball game in the '28 gym, the shower, and then being 10 minutes late to the first class after dinner. We were invariably late, called down for it, but nothing was ever done about the problem. Some of the kids would sweat through a basketball game and neglect to shower, but the teachers didn't like that either.

Miss Foss, from Minneapolis, was our Social Science teacher. She had a habit of calling her students desultory names, when they didn't pay attention in her class. One day she called me a "Hayseed", which I didn't feel I had coming. That was my only trip to Mr. Pemberton's office, a dreaded event. I walked out of Miss Foss's class, straight to the office. I told my story and waited for results. Surprisingly, I didn't get a going-over, with Mr. Pemberton agreeing that Miss Foss shouldn't be calling such names, and he would take care of the matter. I was satisfied, had my say, but I'm sure nothing was ever said to Miss Foss, as things continued on the way they always had."

Quaday's Quotes (Reprinted with permission from RR Quaday) Faribault County Register Monday February 28, 2000

Since there was no extra money, there was no High School Class of 1937 picture taken, so our class was not represented in the 1928 school building hallway. My classmates didn't have individual photos taken, so we had to organize a photo hunt to assemble our class picture. In 1980, we used Army and Navy photos and other individual special photos that were submitted as a project for a Class Reunion, to have a compiled picture of our class to hang in the halls of the Blue Earth High School.

1937 High School Class

Dick Recalls Class Reunions

"Blue Earth High School graduating classes, and I suppose, most other small town classes, tend to get together for class reunions. The schedules vary from every year to 25 years, the period of time which went by before our class of 1937 had their first reunion. It was a gala event held at the Riverside Town and Country Club with many of our teachers joining us. Lee R. Pemberton, Coach Baldy Haase, H. Milton Anderson and our music instructor, Sylvia (Flagstad) Picket attended. Our commercial teacher, Miss Lillias Davis (I don't remember her married name) who was our Mah-Ko-Tah High School Paper advisor, was also present. Clarence Cherland, our class president, was toastmaster. He had become a Lutheran minister and was stationed up on the North Dakota and Canadian border. He loved the thought of sermonizing his former classmates, I'm sure, because it took him over half an hour."

Class of '37 Reunion, class members attenting as follows: (In the order in which they appear in the picture.)
Sylvia Flagstad Picket, Janet Buscho Lee, Vivian Coulter Laue, LaDonna Gaard McDonald, Hazel Dagen Greiman, Gertrude Keller Arends, Helen Houghtaling Peterson, Elvera Martin Kabe, Bernice Skogen Vinje, Gladys Sandness Johnson, Clara Nimz Wells, June Henke Shiffler, Lorene Kark Clark, Helen Funk Anderson, Audrey Ankeny Pettinger, Sidney Sailor, Pauline Mundale Sailor, Phyllis Welk Owens, Ruth Mensing Eder, KKenneth Bottleson, Elaine Mensing Hagedorn, Casper Hanson, Richard Quaday, Wayne Rorman, Helen Kennedy Seath, Kenneth Meyer, Venzel Peterson, and John Ginn.

Baldy Haase, never at a loss for words, held forth for quite a while. Mr. Pemberton, bless him, had the very shortest speech; having been to many such affairs, he realized the importance of brevity.

Our 50th reunion was held at the Blue Earth Legion Club and was also well attended. Again, Mr. Anderson, Venzel Peterson and Mrs. Pickett were present. The Rev. Cherland had passed away as had about seven other class-mates. At this affair, our promised emcee called shortly before show time to tell us that she could not be present. The fact that I was drafted for the task shows how close we had come to the bottom of the barrel. Being the youngest member of our class did not merit much respect. However, being a District Deputy for the Knights of Columbus for four years had decreased my fear of microphones to some extent, and I had accumulated a number of gutter jokes which I tried to clean up. I remember one which only Dr. Paul Eder thought funny, with the rest of the audience sitting in stunned silence. Doc had been my vet for 30 years or so and we understood each other's sometimes weird sense of humor. Many compliments were paid to the Blue Earth School, with some of the college grads telling how they came to college far ahead of young people from other areas, and other schools. School spirit ran deep in Blue Earth and many of the urban people let it be known how much they envied the folks retired and living in the home town."

Quaday's Quotes-partial (Reprinted with permission from RR Quaday) Faribault County register Monday August 10, 1992

Education - Then And Now

"Our family has been quite education minded. Mother was a country school teacher in three country school districts: District 104, No. 2, and District 29. When a district had trouble with their teachers and student discipline, the school board came to her and offered her more money to teach their children. Most country districts tried to elect land owners to the board in order to have continuity to their programs and hire the best teachers available. Most country teachers were young, single girls; graduates from Miss Marian Drake's Normal Training School, located in Blue Earth, for Faribault County--when I attended District 104 a half mile south of our River Road farm.

That system began to change when Mankato, Winona and St Cloud built teacher training courses into their college curriculums. My sister, Marie, graduated from Winona State Teachers College with a four-year degree, and taught District 104 for two years before moving to No. 2--following in my Mother's footsteps. She then taught sixth grade in Blue Earth Public School, under Superintendent Lee R. Pemberton, for four years, before going to the University of Minnesota to earn a higher degree in teaching and library science. After her marriage to Don Anderson, she worked in a research laboratory in New Jersey, where they developed detergents for automatic washing machines, in order to finance Don's way through Columbia University in New York for his master's degree in music education. She ran libraries in Fosston, Dubuque, IA, and Crookston before retiring.

My brother John left the farm for good, entering Winona State at age 16, studying to teach mathematics and science courses. He attained his degree in four years and was hired to teach and coach at Red Wing, which he did for two years. He taught math and Phy-Ed at Wahpeton, SD, for two years. When the Second World War broke out, he enlisted in the Army, knowing he would be one of the first draftees from our county. He spent four years behind George Patton's big guns, as a range finder. This was all done mathematically before computers were invented, and with eight years of high school and college math, he was a shoo-in for that job. He went in as a buck private and was doing a captain's work when discharged.

After teaching and coaching at the University of North Dakota, Grand Forks, for four years he used his Army Education Grant to get his doctorate degree in Phy-Ed at the University of Illinois, sold his house in Grand Forks and moved into a barracks with his wife Stella and four kids. After two more years of school he moved back to Grand Forks, teaching and coaching in the UND. Two of his golf students made the pro tour and got wealthy for a few years. He retired after 36 years as a professor at the UND. He and Stella sold his big house on the Red River, and moved to Grand Rapids buying an acreage on Wabana Lake.

He built a new house there, doing all the work himself. He had a good teacher. Our cousin, Roger Quaday, is a self-taught contractor and the two of them built the new house in Grand Forks from the ground up, and everything worked to perfection until sold. John cut the trees, sawed the lumber, dug the footing, laid the block, did the plumbing, wired the house, tiled the baths, laid the hardwood floors and painted the house and two stall garage. It took him forever, but he said he enjoyed it so much he didn't care if he ever got it done. All my Mother's pushing for education did eventually pay off, one way or another.

I keep seeing articles in our Minnesota daily papers about the latest ratings of our public schools, and how they have fallen when compared with other states here in the United States and other countries. The "No Child Left Behind" legislation by Congress and the W. Bush Administration apparently led some states to upgrade their public schools to conform to the higher standards and regulations. Our state has lowered our rating in the last six or eight years. We had been carrying on with our school rated at--or near--the very top for most of the Twentieth Century."

Quaday's Quotes - partial (Reprinted with permission from RR Quaday) Faribault County Register Monday October 4, 2010

I farmed three years to make enough money to attend the School of Agriculture, at the University of MN, St Paul Campus, in the winter of 1940. Dad did the chores, while I did eighteen credits of work. I participated heavily in intramural sports. I played on three Championship basketball teams, playing the position of center--the Dining Room, The Junior Class, and the All School teams. I took second in the Ping Pong tournament and second in the indoor track tournament high jump competition, since I was six feet, four inches tall.

I participated in the Literary Club and won the essay contest. It was my habit to throw all of the 'guys who wanted to shoot the bull' out of my room, so I could study. I was the only student who was able to keep a car on campus. I kept it at my sister Marie's house, to avoid the strict parking rules at the UMN. Marie worked for Dean Blitz, on the main campus. So I was able to take the street car when I needed to travel.

"As a graduate of Blue Earth High School at the age of 16, in 1937, Richard Quaday began farming in Faribault County. After working the land for three years, he attended The School of Agriculture under J.O. Christianson, a well known Norwegian in the farm circles, completing 18 credits, with four A's, a couple of B's, and one C. He purchased his first tractor, an F-12 Farmall, and pulled a single John Deere plow, and a 10 foot disc Harrow. He married in 1942, and purchased his first 80 acres for $65 an acre. It was the first deeded land in Faribault County. From this meager start, Richard and Neva farmed for 46 years. When they retired from farming, they were operating a 750 acre farm, had 2000 lambs, 100 head of cattle in the winter, and 150 head of hogs in the summer months. They had milked cows, raised chickens, raised sheep, fed cattle, and raised hogs. Green Giant harvested corn or peas on the River Road Farm for 44 consecutive years.

In addition to his agricultural success story, Richard and Neva raised nine children, 6 daughters and 3 sons, all of which had an opportunity to a higher education. They retired in 1984 and moved into Blue Earth in 1986. Richard, at age 69 began writing a column, *Quaday's Quotes*, for the Faribault County Register.

Corn Talk will feature Quaday's Qorn from time to time, printing his stories of the trials and experiences of the early farming days in Southern Minnesota, beginning with this issue."

CORN TALK, Monthly Newsletter for corn producers who are members of the Minnesota Corn Growers Association, Vol. 14, No. 4, April, 1994.

1920s Blue Earth Main Street

Special Memories of D.D. Murphy

"In the 1920s and 30s, when I was growing up on our River Road Farm, the largest automobile and farm machinery firm in Blue Earth was the D.D. Murphy Co.

We always came to town on the Pilot Grove Road, which led into South Main Street. It was always fun to count the shiny, new Fords in the show-room and lined up on Main Street. The John Deere Agency, with its bright green and yellow colors, occupied the south end of the building. The Fordson line of machinery was also sold here, along with small gas engines, pump jacks and various other implements used around the farms of Faribault County.

The Jack Lattin Blacksmith Shop was located at the south end of the block, and the D.D. Murphy Co. building covered the rest of the block. The First National Bank is now located on the place where the office and the parts department were.

At the time, my brother Carl worked for D.D. Murphy Co. I was too young to own an automobile, so never had many car dealings with them. Much later, when I began farming on my own, I owned quite a number of John Deere implements: corn planter, plow, and manure spreader. Sometimes when Dad was busy in the field, or on Co-op business, I would wait in the showroom for Carl to head home; in that way I didn't have to walk home from school.

In this way, I became well acquainted with Vincent and Cyril Murphy, and John Kopplin, who was the bookkeeper at that time. Bill Merrick was a long time employee, who sold many cars yet never owned one. When I lived on the Sailor Place and had no electricity, I bought about the last pump jack that The Murphy Co. handled from Bill. Most water was pumped with electric motors or windmills by then."

Quaday's Quotes (Reprinted with permission from RR Quaday) Faribault County Register Monday February 15, 1992

A Second Look At D.D. Murphy

"In my youth, during the 20s and 30s, it was a foregone conclusion that D.D. Murphy, who started The Murphy Co., was the richest man in Blue Earth.

He owned the Ford and John Deer agencies, a beautiful residence at 6th and Nicollet, several business buildings, besides farm land totaling around 4,000 acres.

He had started his business with a great faith in the farm land surrounding Blue Earth. Faribault County had never had a crop failure, and with some of the most productive land in the world, Dan looked forward to many years of good business here.

He started The Murphy Co. with a $500 loan from W.E.C. Ross, who was

1927 Motor Inn

the most daring banker in town. The note had to be signed by Dan's father. The time was St Patrick's Day, 1890, and Dan, who was completely Irish, always considered it his lucky day. Dan was 24 years old when he started the business.

In 1908, the Ford Motor Co. signed an agency contract with D. D. Murphy, and he stayed with them through all his business years. He took on the Firestone Tire Agency, and both proved to be good business propositions. The Murphys had two sons and two daughters, all of whom, after college, were active in the business.

Vincent ran the Ford Agency in Bricelyn, and Cyril ran the Ford agency in Winnebago. The daughters, Ayleen and Leone, worked in the office until their marriages. By the 1930s, during The Great Depression, the banks were in such bad shape that they didn't dare loan much money on farm machinery or autos, so D. D. Murphy did most of his own financing, with Harry Pfeiffer doing considerable auto finance business.

Farm prices were so disastrously low that many farmers were losing their farms. Dan Murphy made a vow he would support the price of farm land as best he could; buying up many farms to keep the proprietors from going through bankruptcy. He rented these farms out on grain share arrangements; three-fifths to the farmer, two-fifths to the landlord.

During this time, only the best and luckiest farmers were able to borrow enough money to pay interest and taxes. It is a tribute to the business acumen of D.D. Murphy, that he survived that depression in fairly good shape.

After acquiring quite a number of farms, Dan began studying the tax structure in Minnesota. He felt farmers were being taxed unfairly, and decided to do something about it. He won Faribault County's state senate seat, and made his presence known at budget and tax hearings in St Paul. He became known as a very conservative Democrat, which is an unknown quantity these days.

I attended the gala 50-year celebration, on March 17, 1940. The whole town helped Dan with the party.

There was a parade and free lunch, with a free movie later. Bigwigs from Deere and Weber, and the Ford Motor Co., came to Blue Earth for much handshaking and picture taking, with probably the most toasts enjoyed later in the evening.

It proved to be Dan's last great hurrah. He declined to run for the Senate, after two terms, and passed away December 4, 1944, one of Faribault County's all time great men."

Quaday's Quotes (Reprinted with permission from RR Quaday) Faribault County Register Monday February 22, 1993

Remembering The Car Dealerships

"When I began to attend eighth grade in Blue Earth School in 1932, there were five active automobile franchises in our town. They all had at least one mechanic and were all making a good living. The Motor Inn was located on the northeast corner of Fifth and Main and they sold Buicks, Oldsmobiles and Chevrolets. The D.D. Murphy Company, located on the southwest corner of Eighth and Main Streets, sold Fords, Lincolns and John Deere farm machinery. Oscar Lehman and son, Ferd, located on the north side of Sixth Street, across from the Sandon Theater, sold Durant, Hudson and Lafayette autos. J.F. Barnes, located on the northwest corner of Fifth and Main, sold Dodges, Pontiacs, Whippets and Plymouths. Earnest Franklin, located on West Seventh Street, sold Studebakers and Erskines.

Automobiles were cheap in those days, costing between $500 and $1000. Those prices remained in effect through the Great Depression and until after the Second World War. The county roads were nearly all graveled, but a

37

1940 D.D. Murphy and Sons

great many of the township roads in Faribault County were still dirt--mud in wet weather. The cars, many of them using 'Body by Fisher,' had a lot of wood framing which didn't stand up well with rotting door posts. In our moisture-laden climate, all of the General Motors cars had dragging doors. Henry Ford, who made the Model T Fords (Tin Lizzies), foresaw that problem and made frames of steel, which rattled like everything but stood up well. It is hard to understand why, with new automobiles selling for over $20,000, Blue Earth can't support a new car franchise.

We lived on a township road and received our first coat of gravel in the summer of 1934, and what a relief it was to be able to travel our hilly River Road after a heavy rain without putting on the chains. After the gravel, which was trucked from Kiester in 3-cubic-yard gravel trucks, we used chains on our Model A Ford only in winter when the snow got deep. We had Fords when my brother, Carl, sold for D.D. Murphy, but switched over to Chevrolets in 1934 when he hired out to Howard Essler. Bernie Buggy, who had been a partner in the Motor Inn, was killed in a car accident in the late 1920s.

When we had all these car agencies, we had enough filling stations to keep the cars on the road. I can remember 14 operating gasoline stations in 1937 when I bought my first real car, a 1929 Erskine Sedan, formerly owned by the Trinity Lutheran pastor. The manufacture of Erskines had stopped due to poor sales, so the Erskine was considered an orphan, and nobody figured they would be able to buy parts to keep them running. The car had only

35,000 miles on the odometer and I bought it for $25. The interior was just like new and it had a Carry-Keen trunk, which was not standard equipment and cost much more than I paid for the whole car. I had to crank it in winter, because it had only a 6-volt battery. I drove it for a year and sold it to Lyman Moberg for $35 when the battery went dead.

That was the beginning of my used car operation. I had used the money from my bicycle shop, which I had run while in high school, to buy the Erskine. While farming our 160 acres, I had some time to fool with used cars, so I would buy one at a time--clean it up, fix what was needed, paint it if it needed it, put on good used tires and drive it until someone wanted it more than I did. I always was well paid for my work. It was an interesting sideline and I learned a lot about cars, dealing, repairs, and maintenance. The license bureau at the Court House must have gotten very sick of me trading cars and titles during that five years; I must have owned 30 or 35 cars during that time. I always made a few dollars on each one that I owned. My brother, Carl, encouraged the operation.

My Dad finally got sick of my spare time being spent on the used cars and didn't really want me to become a used car jockey. He wanted me to be a full-time farmer and concentrate on that and learn enough to support a family when I got married. When my appointment to Annapolis fizzled out because of color blindness, I did settle down into full-time farming. I spent my own money to attend the Farm School in St Paul and took the courses I figured that I would need to fill in what I hadn't learned from little on up, handling livestock. The crop yields, at that time, were unsatisfactory and the experiment stations were making good progress in that regard. I wanted to learn and use the latest techniques in crop production.

The machinery, cars, trucks, and bicycles, at that time were relatively simple, so even a farm kid could tear them down and reassemble them with a few wrenches and a pair of pliers. At present, one would need thousands of dollars worth of sophisticated equipment to even start an overhaul job."

Quaday's Quotes (Reprinted with permission from RR Quaday) Faribault County Register Monday April 19, 2010

A Memorial Tour of Two Historic Local Buildings

"We had a wonderful Memorial Day weekend. Our daughter, Jeanette Jorgensen, visited us. All the holidays she and Chuck were married, they went to Lake Sylvia and enjoyed fishing, swimming and boating with Chuck's children, Jeff and Jennifer and their families. They had a beautiful three-story new house which replaced the smaller two story one that burned five years ago. They had a pontoon party boat, a bird sanctuary with humming birds, and orioles just thick in the woods around a screened-in porch. The home was situated on a bay, so storms very seldom caused much damage. There was an attached two-stall garage with a black-topped driveway. Why wouldn't they go to the lake?

That all changed when Chuck passed away last fall after a fatal stroke. The estate is nearly settled, with the family selling Shangri-La. The price and taxes on lake property have skyrocketed in the last few years. Three generations of Jorgensens had owned and enjoyed the lake home and knew all the people there. Mr. Schwebel, the lawyer, owned the next door property and they were good friends of the family.

Jeanette had never toured the Wakefield House and neither had Neva, so she called A. B. Russ, who is very involved in the Faribault County Historical Society, to inquire about obtaining a visit. Mr. Russ volunteered to open the house and even gave us a guided tour. Neva and I are lifetime members, thanks to our daughter, Pauline Siem, who gave it to us as an anniversary present on our 65th. I have always been a history nut and would rather read history books than best sellers or mysteries. Many of the antique displays were identical with the furniture and furnishings Neva and I started housekeeping with when we bought the Sailor Place on River Road.

The cook stove, kerosene lamps, home-made quilts, and tables and chairs all brought back a lot of memories of our six-year tenure there. During our tour of the Wakefield House, A. B. asked if we had toured the Episcopal Church of the Good Shepherd. Neva had been inside one time, but neither Jeanette nor I had. We enthusiastically said 'yes' to a tour so Mr. Russ said, "Let's go!" I have read many newspaper articles about the 'church' when it was built, how many members worshiped there in the early days, and how Mrs. George Washington Holland donated the later addition. But I was not prepared for my first view of the gorgeous front stained glass window.

I stood in awe during my first glimpse for at least five minutes, taking in the overall picture before walking closer and examining the perfection of the detailed work on all three windows. The shepherd and the sheep are stained glass perfection with wonderful coloring. The windows are all imported from different countries in Europe and the saints' names are printed in Latin under their pictures. I took two years of Latin at Blue Earth High School, so I could read them, but didn't take notes so I couldn't tell you the names.

I would strongly recommend a trip to the church if the opportunity arises, even if it's just to view the windows. The pews are not the most comfortable in the world but are well made and solid. The pews are assembled with wooden dowel pins and so perfectly fit that they have stood the tests of time and squirming children. I understand part of the foundation of the church is deteriorating and must be repaired or replaced. The old part had Kasota Stone and the new cement block. A considerable amount of dirt must be moved by hand. Volunteers anybody?"

Quaday's Quotes -partial (Reprinted with permission from RR Quaday) Faribault County Register Monday June 2, 2008

Memorial Day and Organic Farming

"The town of Blue Earth has done a wonderful recognition for the veterans of all the wars our country has fought through its history, whether they were fought for conquest, resettlement, expansion, or to save our allies. Blue Earth has always maintained one of the most beautiful cemeteries in the area and holds the Memorial Day program there, in an outdoor setting, with present day Veterans in charge and the Blue Earth Area High School contributing to the program, along with the town's Boy Scouts.

Down through the years our family has been proud to furnish servicemen and women for our armed forces, serving in the army and air force: seven uncles in the First World War, my brother, John, in the Second World War, and grandson Joe Lacher in the Air Force. Our daughter served in the Army for four years. Pauline was a Private First Class. Had I been able to pass the color blindness test, I would have been in the middle of the Second World War as a Navy officer, newly commissioned, graduating from the Annapolis Navy Officers School. The world was in turmoil already in 1938, when I received my appointment for Annapolis. I would have cut my Navy eye-teeth in the Great War, graduating in 1942. It didn't work out that way, so I'm still alive and well nearly 70 years later."

Quaday's Quotes -partial (Reprinted with permission from RR Quaday) Faribault County Register Monday May 8, 2000

41

The Home Place

Oak Ridge/River Road Farm

My Mother, Lorena Mary Levenick, was born September 21, 1882 in Blue Earth, MN, daughter of Fred and Mary Levenick. She attended Blue Earth school and for a number of years taught in the rural schools of Faribault County. On September 20, 1906 she was united in marriage to William H. Quaday, also of Blue Earth, MN.

They resided on farms south of Blue Earth, continuously, with the exception of 3 years spent in California. Shortly after returning to Minnesota in 1914, my parents bought 80 acres of land located about 1½ miles southwest of Blue Earth on the west branch of the Blue Earth River. This became the Home Place and they named it "Oak Ridge Farm."

I have been told that the house was known as "the Pitcher House" (for the family that had previously owned it) and was just barely habitable when they moved in. There were thousands of Burr Oak and Red Oak trees on the farm at that time, but the drought years of The Great Depression decimated a great many of them.

Later, the name of the Home Place was changed to River Road Farm. In 1948, they retired from the farm and moved into the town of Blue Earth, residing at 415 South Moore Street.

Grandpa Charles

"When I was a very young lad on our River Road Farm, Thanksgiving Day always was celebrated by a table groaning array of home grown food. Mother worked out an arrangement with Aunt Bertha Neuhalfen and Aunt Lizzie Baum, so that the Thanksgiving Day host did not also host the Christmas celebration in the same year. There was also a concerted effort to have all the corn picking (all by hand) done by Thanksgiving Day, but it didn't always happen.

In those days, a day or two one way or the other getting done picking corn, didn't make that much difference, unless the Old Farmer's Almanac forecast an early winter. My Grandfather, Charles Quaday, religiously bought and read the Almanac from cover to cover, always planting according to its best phase of the moon. He was not able to ever be a good corn picker, as that is strictly a two-handed occupation, and he lost an arm in a horse-powered threshing machine when he was 23 years old. However, he was real good at giving advice to his sons, my Dad (Bill), Jule, Fred and Herman; hurry up and get the fall work done early if his Almanac told of dire weather.

Grandpa had a German Bible, which was well worn, with leather binding and formerly gilt edged pages. There were quite a few pictures of a Religious nature to interest us kids, but we never learned to read German with the exception of my brother, Carl, who learned German and English both before going to country school.

Grandpa, who came from Germany when he was 12 years old, felt strongly that the United States should never have entered The First World War. He said, "Our boys will be fighting their brothers and cousins," over there. He had a born-in distrust of France and England, because of the almost continuous wars during his youth in Europe. His parents had seen firsthand the devastation and famine that always followed war. This is why they made arrangements with relatives to have grandpa hired on a cattle boat hauling Holstein breeding stock to Wisconsin. Military conscription was mandatory in Germany at age 13, so grandpa left his homeland at age 12."

Quaday's Quotes -partial (Reprinted with permission from RR Quaday) Faribault County Register Monday November 20, 1995

Grandpa Farmed With Just One Arm

"My grandfather, Charles Ludwig Quaday, was a German immigrant. By the time he was 13 years old, he had already experienced many things that most people never have a chance to do in a lifetime. His parents, who lived in Posen, Germany, didn't want him to be drafted into the army, because Germany, at that time in history was continually at war, and the casualty rates in European wars were always very high.

Charley fed Holstein cows and scooped manure overboard for his passage to America; specifically to a dairy farm in Wisconsin, where relatives put him on a train to Blue Earth. He had already taken a voyage across the Atlantic Ocean on a new-fangled steamship, with no other relatives aboard to look out for him. He had gotten through Ellis Island without knowing ten words of English and traveled thousands of miles to a completely new World by himself, at age 12.

1942 Charles L. Quaday at Oak Ridge Farm

He had already learned to pay his way by hard labor wherever he went. Grandpa Krinke, (according to our daughter Kay's genealogy records, his name was John), expected Charley to herd and milk cows to earn his board and room, and also pay his train fare from Wisconsin to Blue Earth. He also was expected to go to the country school district and learn English, so he could gain citizenship in America.

There were several Quade families in that school district, and to distinguish between families his teacher changed his name spelling to the French version, Quaday. The Krinke family was generous in some respects, but not with money; at his death, Grandpa Krinke owned several farms, all good land northeast of Blue Earth.

The Krinke Family attended the East Evangelical Church, which held camp meetings each summer for a week or two, to freshen up on their religion and so that their children would get acquainted with each other, and hopefully, fall in love with and marry one of their fellow members. The camp meetings were held in a thickly-wooded area southwest of the church with giant oak, maple and ash trees, in late summer or early fall --when the mosquitoes didn't bother so much. A visiting minister conducted religious education classes for the young people and the church ladies chaperoned and did the cooking. It was virtually a tent city for about a week, and was enjoyed by all of the congregation.

It was at one of the camp meetings that Charley met--and fell in love with--Pauline Paschke, who belonged to one of the prominent farm families in the congregation. They married young, as was the norm in those days.

1942 Charles L. Quaday Family at Oak Ridge Farm

The threshing of small grain, (oats, wheat, and barley), was done with a horse-powered threshing machine owned by one of the Fenske families. They did have binders, which tied the straw in bundles with twine. It was an accident with the horse-power that cost Charley his right arm. The horses were stopped to rest and he was greasing the gear mechanism when someone started up the horses, grinding his arm into the gears. It took nearly two hours to take the horse-powered machine apart. By the time he was taken to the doctor it was too late to save the arm, with only a six inch stub left up to his shoulder. He was only 23 years of age at the time.

Charley and Pauline went on to buy a farm and raise a family of eight children: four girls: Bertha, Elizabeth, Emma, and Alice; and four boys: William (my Dad), Julius, Frederick, and Herman.

With only one hand he was too slow milking cows, but Charley did it when the occasion demanded it. He always said, "I milked too many of them when I was young." He specialized in raising hogs and was very good at it, calling them, "The mortgage lifter." His farm, near the south end of River Road, sported a state-of-the-art hog house for its day, and a Faribault County tile down below the hog house furnished clean running water, year-round, free.

Sadly, just about the time everything was going too good to be true, for Charley and Pauline, Pauline developed a case of tuberculosis and died, with Emma and Alice also dying from the disease. At that time there was still no known cure for TB. Pauline was a lover and trainer of horses. After Pauline's death, Grandpa lived with Uncle Jule during the summer, spending his winters in Long Beach, California. Jule never married and became an excellent cook; he and Grandpa got along very well.

Neva and I named our first son Charles after Grandpa but he calls himself Charlie. Whatever works, I guess."

Quaday's Quotes (Reprinted with permission from RR Quaday) Faribault County Register Monday August 23, 2010

One-Arm Charley Still Out-Scooped Most

"My Grandfather, Charles Ludwig Quade, was born in the province of Posen, Germany, in 1861. This area would be in East Germany at present.

Charles' last name was spelled Quaday by his first school teacher to distinguish him from the other Quade families. Incidentally, my professors at the U Farm all thought I was French because of the spelling.

Charles and Pauline Paschke were married at age 19 and farmed east of Blue Earth. At age 23, he was greasing the horse power on a threshing machine when the horses started up, grinding his right arm into the gears. The others had to take the power unit apart to get him out, but the arm was so mangled that it was amputated six inches from the shoulder. After that, he was known as "One Arm Charley."

It was amazing how much work granddad could accomplish with just one arm. When my brother, John, and I were growing up, he would come over and help shock corn fodder or scoop corn. We couldn't keep up until he got well past 70 years of age.

In the early 1900s, Pauline and two of her daughters, Emma and Alice, became ill with TB and all three died. My Father was afraid he would also contract the disease, so he and my Mother sold the farm, now owned by Gilbert and Ramona Ehrich, and moved to California with Carl, their oldest son. Grandpa went to California every winter for 24 winters. He pitched horseshoes and played dominoes."

47

1925 Charles L. Quaday Pitching Horseshoes in CA

Quaday's Quotes (Reprinted with permission from RR Quaday) Faribault County Register Monday, March 5, 1990

I was born on September 02, 1920 on the River Road Farm, 2 miles southwest of Blue Earth, MN. The Blue Earth River ran through the farm, and we had many huge oak trees, and twenty-four varieties of apple trees. I was the youngest of the children: three brothers, Francis, who died at birth, Carl Frederick, and John Leon, and one sister, Marie Pauline. The farm site was all white buildings, including the barn, hog house, chicken house, brooder house, garage, and house.

Dick Recalls His Mother's Simple Life

"I am the youngest of William and Lorena Quaday's family so I must rely on hearsay and documented family history, for a word portrait of my Mother.

When my parents were married, I'm told Dad knew of Lorena's intense dislike for alcohol and saloons so he respected her feelings and drank no strong drink. Having consideration for her city upbringing, he never expected her to participate in the heavy work on the farm. Mother could drive a team of horses hitched to a buggy or hay-rope.

My brother, John, and I coaxed Mother into going out in our 40-acre pasture, where we attempted to teach her to drive a Model T Ford. She was an eager learner but never developed enough confidence to venture out on the road. Fortunately, Mother was a home body who cared very little for travel so Dad had less taxi time.

1900 Lorena Levenick and Minnie Willmert

My Mother, Lorena, was the only daughter of Fred Jr. and Mary (Willmert) Levenick. Mary died when Lorena was 10 years old from an inoperable brain tumor. Fred Levenick Jr. later married Lydia Fenske and this union produced eight boys and one girl.

Lorena's grandmother Willmert was not happy seeing Lorena drop out of school to tend children. She took steps to help Lorena finish her schooling and qualify for a teaching certificate for country school. Lorena was an instant success and taught in District 104, District No. 2, and District 29, before her marriage to Dad. She was a born teacher, seeing to it that her children got every bit of education the family could afford. Later, Lorena continued her efforts by teaching Sunday school in the Salem Evangelical Church. She took every opportunity to teach her grandchildren by making learning fun and charming them into greater efforts.

Bill and Lorena Quaday purchased a farm on South River Road known at that time as "The Engels Place." Gilbert and Ramona Ehrich now own the farm located directly across the township road from the William Pitcher Stock Farm. They and the Pitchers became lifelong friends and Dad sometimes helped Mr. Pitcher tend his purebred Hereford cattle at shows and fairs.

When Dad's mother, Pauline, and two of her sisters died from tuberculosis, the folks sold their farm and moved to California for three years. Lorena hated the west so when the tuberculosis scare was over she and Dad moved back to Minnesota and purchased 80 acres on River Road from Steven Pitcher, William Pitcher's father.

In 1949, Dad and I traded 80s and the folks moved to South Moore Street in Blue Earth. They lived in the house now owned by Tim Malally until Dad's death. Our children used Grandma's house for a home away from home, stopping in after school or staying there during a blizzard. Mother always saw to it that they were well fed and when Neva and I were gone for a few days, she babysat and loved every minute of it.

My parents never played cards, drank alcohol, smoked, chewed or used profane language, nor did they dance. They belonged to Salem Evangelical all their lives. Mother taught Sunday school for many years and worked in the kitchen for Ladies Aid dinners in the church basement. She was a member of the missionary society and was always available to help serve funeral dinners.

Dad and Mom belonged to a couple's Birthday Club which met at least once a month. The Emil Henkes, the Walter Oelkes, the William Schandels, the Julius Mittelstadts and the Sam Bankers comprised the club. One might ask, "What do they do?" They honored birthdays that occurred during the month, had supper, washed the dishes, showed any new pictures and visited until around 9:30 pm, said their goodnights and went home. Believe me, the conversation never lagged and any time I listened in, it was very interesting.

Mother never liked to travel so a three-day trip to Grand Forks, ND, to visit John, or to Crookston, to visit Marie, my sister, was about the extent of her little sphere. She was content with her circle of close friends, and led a simple, yet rewarding life, passing away in her sleep at St Luke's Lutheran home at age 99."

Quaday's Quotes (Reprinted with permission from RR Quaday) Faribault County Register Monday May 11, 1992

William Quaday Farm History

"When my grandmother, Pauline (Paschke) Quaday, died of tuberculosis back in the early 1900s and my two aunts, Emma and Alice, also died of the disease, my Dad became alarmed about his health. There was no cure for tuberculosis in those days except a sanatorium or death.

He and my Mother were still newlyweds and my brother, Carl, was an infant. They sold their farm on south River Road, where Gilbert and Ramona Ehrich now live, and migrated to California where people in the early stages of TB--or worried about getting it--went for the dry climate, which they thought would help.

Dad worked for a truck driver for a time before buying a forty-acre orange grove at Long Beach. He operated the orange orchard for two years, but when Mother became homesick for Minnesota (she hated California), he sold the 40 acres and came back to Blue Earth. Actually, he lived all his adult life on River Road, except those three years at Long Beach. He kept the orange grove a few more years until oil was discovered.

We would be billionaires, as the real estate out in that area now sells for a million dollars a front foot on the ocean where they were. Oil pumpers stand as thick as trees in the forest.

They bought 80 acres from Steve Pitcher, the second place south of the Pilot Grove Road on River Road. Times were good and Dad proceeded to build a new house, barn, hog house and chicken house on the site. So by the time I came along, he had the farm built up to a state-of-the-art diversified operation.

Dad had bought what we called the Jo Daviess 80 from Rinault Ristau, so he had enough grain production to feed his livestock and chickens. The south half of the 80 was prairie grass slough so he made wild hay there, which he sold in town through the winter to folks who had horses, and to some who still kept a cow.

When the county tile came through a large assessment was levied on the 80, almost causing him to lose it. He borrowed money from Grandpa Charley to pay the ditch tax and interest, and eventually worked out of the Hoover Depression. There was quite a celebration at our house when the folks finally paid off the loan to grandpa, the mortgage to Mr. Ristau and the ditch tax. He put tile through the wettest spots and in the 'dirty thirties', broke up the south half of the 80. After the rains came back in 1938, my first year of farming on my own, I sowed canary grass in the slough part and just farmed around it.

The home 80 was in Dad's name and the Jo Daviess 80 was in Mother's name--a good arrangement in case of hard times, which came in cyclical order every few years during the boom and bust days before our government got into the farming business. In the old days, if one got caught on the wrong end of a land boom, he simply lost the land. There was no safety net. There were no government checks. For better or worse, FDR changed all that. Many farm folks feel that farming would have been better off if government had never become involved. They, of course, did not have to battle the farm depressions that wracked the farm business periodically before FDR. The farmers of today are no longer an independent production machine.

When I began farming in 1938, Dad was still in debt after seeing Marie and John through college. When they got jobs and paid back their school debts, he and Mom decided to trade 80s with Neva and me and buy a house in town. They bought a rundown house (the Freer house) on South Moore Street. Neva is an excellent painter and interior decorator, so we helped them get the house up to date and moved them in. They enjoyed more than 20 years of retirement there. We farmed the land on share rent and finally got them out of debt.

After paying the folks a sizeable sum for the 80s trade, we got ourselves on the road, so to speak, and began to pay our debt. Talk about following in my father's footsteps. We both lived most of our lives on a River Road Farm and most of the time in debt too."

Quaday's Quotes (Reprinted with permission from RR Quaday) Faribault County Register Monday March 29, 2004

Dick Salutes His Dad

"I can't believe I have churned out Quotes for so long without giving a word portrait of my Dad. He was the eldest son of Charles and Pauline (Paschke) Quaday born on June 15, 1882, on a farm east of Blue Earth.

He had about the same childhood as all the other farm kids during that era. They worked hard for what they had, which sometimes wasn't a great lot by today's standards. He herded cattle, milked cows, curried horses, and cleaned barns.

His father, Charles, lost his right arm in a horse-powered threshing accident before Dad was old enough to work, which limited him somewhat in doing farm chores like milking cows. He was an excellent hog man with unlimited patience in dealing with the critters. Dad, on the other hand, tended to like taking care of the cattle. Both Charles and Dad liked horses and could get more work done than most farmers, without hurting the horse.

1906 William & Lorena (Levenick) Quaday

Practically all I know about Dad's childhood and youth, I heard from neighbors, Bill Pitcher who lived next door and Benny Hannaman who lived across the Blue Earth River.

Benny lived on the Moses Sailor Homestead farm with only 40 acres of land and a few cows, which gave him a lot of time to visit around the neighborhood. It took very little prodding to get him to tell stories by the hour about neighborhood feuds, dogs that lived in the area, and the old-timers in the square mile surrounding our place.

His favorite story told to us many times concerned the Charles Quaday family--William, Elizabeth, Bertha, Emma, Alice, Fred, Julius and Herman. The boys in the family got an allowance, very meager according to Benny, but when they worked out for neighbors they got to keep the money.

One year it was decided to pool all the money earned in the summer and buy a set of boxing gloves. The first to put them on were Bill and Benny's brother, Emil. He said he never saw anyone so quick as Bill. He had Emil's nose bleeding before he fairly had his dukes up.

Dad was a lightweight, never weighing over 140 pounds but he got so good, no one would take him on with the gloves.

The farm boys in those years worked at home until Thanksgiving in the fall, until the corn was all picked and the fodder hauled. Then the boys got to attend country school, so their schooling was very limited.

Dad went to District 104, three miles north of the Quaday farm. Mother, who was a country school teacher, said Dad probably never progressed beyond the fourth grade level in country school. However, he was an avid reader and thus educated himself to some extent. He must have also had a knack for math because he held the supervisor job on the Town Board, the

1974 Richard & William Quaday

School Board and the Shipping Association, which did all the carrying of livestock on the railroad out of Blue Earth. He was also a steward in Salem Evangelical Church.

He was Chairman of the Creamery Board for many years, including the building of the "new" creamery on North Main Street now used for Day Care and other offices.

Dad never made a lot of money but he could stretch a dollar a long way, thus accumulating a 160-acre farm and a house in town on South Moore Street.

With everything paid for and CDs in the bank, he never applied for Social Security until one day the late Eldon Spencer, who helped him with tax matters, told him, "You are entitled to it and if you don't take it the government will just waste it anyway." So when Dad was about 75 years old he got quite a bit of back pay. As far as I know he never spent a cent, preferring to buy more CDs for his "old age."

The CDs came in very handy in Mother's old age, for nursing care. Due to Dad's frugality, Mother always paid her way to the penny."

Quaday's Quotes (Reprinted with permission from RR Quaday) Faribault County Register Monday June 22, 1992

Dick Follows Father's Footsteps

"I have followed in my Dad's footsteps in many ways throughout my lifetime. We both farmed for a living while raising our families just outside of the Blue Earth City limits. We both were very strict about attendance at church on Sundays unless absence was forced by harvesting, or canning peas or sweet corn. Of course, with a milking cow and other livestock, there was always work to do.

My Father always owned a fairly new automobile and kept it in good shape, as have I. We both hated to wash cars, so they showed that we lived on a mud or gravel road. The River Road was notorious for the highest snow banks in winter and before gravel, terrible mud ruts in summer.

Dad's eyesight never deteriorated much in old age. He only wore glasses to read at age 93, getting his driver's license renewed without glasses or restrictions of any kind. He farmed all of his life without having any broken bones or any serious operations. He had the usual prostate problems associated with old age in men, and kept Dr. Collison, the local chiropractor, in business with back trouble.

With only a fourth grade education, my Father held offices on the Blue Earth Township Board, the Blue Earth Creamery Board, the Evangelical Church Board, the Blue Earth Shipping Association Board, and the District 104 School Board.

With only a high school education and one year of AG School, I have been on the District 104 School Board, the SS Peter and Paul Church Council, The Blue Earth Township Board, the Knights of Columbus State Charities Commission, The KC State Student Loan Board--for which I wrote articles in the state monthly publication *The Knightline*—and was the KC District Deputy for Blue Earth, Albert Lea, Wells and Easton councils. I held all the offices in the local KC council 1836 before being appointed to the district deputy job. I ran the KC Bingo in Blue Earth for three years and was a 4-H leader for more than 20 years. Most of these extra-curricular activities were served without pay or very minimum expense accounts for both Dad and I.

My eyesight has always been my pride and joy, as I only need glasses to read at age 84. This might change since I have a cataract on my left eye.

Dad retired from active farming at age 65 and moved to Blue Earth, living more than 20 years on South Moore Street. He did his own yard work and kept a garden until his first heart attack at age 93. He kept a keen interest in farming all his life, coming to our River Road Farm to help pile brush when we cut wood or haul grain to Frank Brothers Elevator. If nothing else, he would bring lunch out to where we happened to be working.

Grandma's coffee wasn't the greatest, but she was good at baking cookies and cake for farm lunches. Dad was great as a go-fer before we had CB radios. He hauled us between fields or farms to bring home machinery, or to get something we had forgotten.

I only got the chance to be the go-fer, loafer and chauffeur for two years while our youngest son, Mike, farmed the River Road Farm. We had a CB radio and a base station with handles. Mine was "Wool Blind," Mike's was "Lamb Chop," and Neva's was "Jason's Gramma." The CBs were fun and quite useful, saving many trips before better forms of farm communications came along. We had radios in the big combine, two trucks and the plow tractor."

Quaday's Quotes-partial (Reprinted with permission from RR Quaday) Faribault County Register Monday December 6, 2004

Fond Memories of 'Ole Uncle Julius

"I have mentioned my uncle Julius in former columns, but never really put into words my fondest memories about "Old Jule," as all the younger neighbors and friends called him.

He was the biggest and huskiest of all of Dad's brothers.

He had the misfortune to pick up polio while working for Orrin Chestley in Des Moines. The polio left him with a severely crippled arm and leg, but this did not keep him from having a lot of fun. At family gatherings, such as Christmas and Thanksgiving, Jule was the life of the party.

1915 Willie Martin & Julius Samuel Quaday

I can remember Fourth of July picnics at our place, when flies were always a problem. Jule would wait until a cake with thick frosting was uncovered. He would take a piece of cake, and as soon as a few flies lit, he'd tell the kids gathered around, "Boy those flies taste good," and proceed to take a quick bite of cake, knowing full well that the flies would be gone, but giving the little ones the impression that he was eating flies.

Jule never married, but he always had a number of nephews and neighbor kids staying with him. He knew the best way to do everything, and was always willing to have patience enough to teach the youngsters how to make themselves useful.

He was an excellent cook, which was another reason why he was popular with all the teenagers who helped him cut wood or stack oat bundles and hay. Otto Halverson tells me that Jule made the best fried potatoes he ever ate.

I remember one fall when I was asked to help pitch bundles for Jule, when he stack-threshed his oats bundles. This was a first for me, and I wasn't fussy which stack I started on. Harry Woolery and another old neighbor, who had been through the stack threshing routine many times, climbed the wind side of the stacks. This was OK as long as we were pitching down into the thresh machine feeder but turned ugly later, when we got further down on the stack and had to eat the chaff and dirt sifting from the machine. Supper that night was steak, potatoes and gravy, with plenty for our young appetites; a meal to remember, even 60 years later.

Jule was, for his time, an excellent mechanic. Remember, these were Model T Ford days, when everyone knew all about horses, but few could fix a corn binder or figure out why the Model T kicked when cranked. All the Quaday brothers were farmers, and Jule kept the machinery running for the other three--Dad, Fred and Herman.

Uncle August Neuhalfen and uncle Rudolph Baum called him numerous times to figure out why their grain binder would not tie, to put new coils in their cars, or time the gas engines, which were used to pump water in those days. If the windmill squeaked, Jule fixed it. If someone wanted to dehorn cattle, Jule knew just how short to saw them and how to hold down the bleeding. If someone had a bloated cow, Jule was called, as he knew just where to stick the knife to release the gas.

The harvest apples on his tree always tasted the best, most likely because they were the first of the season. His strawberries were always the biggest and tastiest. My Grandfather, Charles Quaday, lived with Jule during the summers, and he was an excellent gardener, with never a weed showing.

When Grandpa went to California every winter, Jule took on a drifter, Jack Gray, who Grandpa never liked or trusted; his gut feeling was later born out. In March of 1941, Jack Gray murdered Uncle Jule, shooting him with a 22 rifle. This ended a most colorful career, and caused a large bare spot in our lives."

Quaday's Quotes (Reprinted with permission from RR Quaday) Faribault County Register Monday April 12, 1993

Catching Uncle Jule's Murderer

"In late March of 1941, I was finishing out the winter term of study at "Cow College" in St Paul. My Mother wrote me a letter telling me of Uncle Jule's suicide and hoping I could get home for the funeral, bringing my sister, Marie, who was in the University of MN, Minneapolis Campus. I went to J.O. Christianson's office and told him I had to go home early for a funeral. It seems that J.O. had heard that before and wasn't going to let me out of the last three days of school until I showed him the letter. We fairly flew home, arriving just in time for the funeral.

Uncle Jule had always been an upbeat sort of guy, even though he had polio in his youth which left him with a handicapped arm and foot. A floater by the name of Jack Gray always rode the rods back to Blue Earth and stayed with Jule after Grandpa went west for the winter. Grandpa Charley didn't like Jack, saying, "He can never look you straight in the eye."

Jule had a 40-acre farm out on the old Elmore road, now owned by Neil Eckles. He really didn't need anyone for what few chores he had but felt sorry for Mr. Gray who had an alcohol problem, as did my uncle.

My cousin, Vernon Neuhalfen, lived across the Blue Earth River on south River Road. Paul Tillia worked for him at the time because Vernon had a lot of livestock to take care of. Vernon and Paul visited Jule's quite often, stopping for a game of cards or just to visit. It was Vernon who Jack called, saying simply, "Old Jule just shot himself."

Bill Mathies of Wells was sheriff at the time, and also managed the Blue Earth baseball team, which Vernon pitched for. Dr. Wilson was the coroner. These two took a statement from Jack Gray and took him at his word. Vernon and Paul, however, did not believe the suicide story. They asked Bill to just let things go for a little while and let them keep an eye on Mr. Gray.

As soon as Jack figured he was home free, he headed for town and the Midget Tavern.

Unnoticed in the back of the Midget, Paul Tillia and two others were keeping an eye on him. When he passed a $20 bill, they knew they had their man because Jule never gave Mr. Gray more than a couple dollars, or at most a five, knowing he would be no good around the farm for a couple of days with a hang-over. Paul and Vernon went to Bill Mathies telling him of the money. The way Jule was positioned, these two knew that Jule could not have shot himself because of his crippled arm. Shortly after being hauled in for questioning, and confronted with the evidence, Mr. Gray confessed to the murder. He said simply, "I thought he had sold hogs, so I thought he would have $300, but he only had $50."

The State Crime Bureau was called in to make sure everything was legal and Jack Gray was on his way to Stillwater for life. In those days if a criminal confessed, that was it. There was no recanting later with a month-long trial a year or so after the crime.

To my knowledge, Mr. Gray is still in prison, although he came up for parole many times. The cold-blooded way he shot the man who had befriended him, for a few dollars, influenced the parole board to keep him incarcerated.

If Vernon and Paul hadn't known the situation so well, Mr. Gray might have been home free. My Dad couldn't believe either, that Jule would shoot himself. Dad noted that Jule had cleaned his seed oats a few days before; hardly the act of a man in deep enough depression to commit suicide.

There were other signs around the farm that showed preparation for spring work.

Sometimes I think the old way of justice was much better. Certainly it was less expensive and time consuming. In today's system the murderer would probably have gone free."

Quaday's Quotes-partial (Reprinted with permission from RR Quaday) Faribault County Register Monday March 23, 1992

Growing up on the Home Place

"My sister, Marie, who was seven-years-old when I was born, was a wonderful friend and babysitter. Now 89 years later, we are still best friends. She put in a lot of time swinging me in the rope swing that hung in the Scotch pine tree in the Tiger Lily patch out in the big yard. Our lawn and garden was well fenced to keep out chickens and farm animals. It had a swinging gate with a weighted chain, so it would shut itself after being opened (a great invention when kids are running in and out all day long).

Marie was the only girl in our family, but she could stand up for her rights, and don't you forget it. When my oldest brother, Carl, who was a chronic tease, dumped her out of the swing once too often, she picked up the swing-board and cracked him over the head with it, drawing blood.

The Scotch pine was a scraggly, ugly tree, with long needles. But it did have a branch sticking out from the trunk, just the right height for a swing. When the rope wore out, Dad put up a single rope swing, with a Model T Ford tire to sit in (an old piece of hay barn rope).

Barn on the Home Place

On rainy days we would play up in the hayloft and swing on the sling ropes which hung down from the carrier track and were about 18-feet long. When the loft was empty we could swing from one 8" X 8" beam to another, a distance of 16-feet; quite a swing for little kids. Missed targets were frequent, as were bumps and bruises. The two big doors where the slings of hay entered the loft from the hay rack were always open unless a storm was imminent; there was an eight-inch beam, which was 18 feet above the ground. Better have good balance!

There was a small door (5' X 5') for pitching hay in and out of the loft about ten feet from the ground level, which we jumped out of a lot. But it was a hard landing on the ground, and shook up one's insides. The first twenty years of my life on the home farm was decidedly different than the later years when it became a working business, and raising a family of our own, with Neva, the mother and housewife. Our children were every bit as venturesome and risk taking as I was, growing up on our River Road Farm."

Quaday's Quotes-partial (Reprinted with permission from RR Quaday) Faribault County Register Monday June 21, 2010

Quaday Remembers Old Tree Swing

"One of the most used items on playgrounds has always been the swing. One of my first experiences on a swing occurred out in our front yard on our River Road Farm.

My older sister, Marie, was delegated to watch me while Mother was busy. Dad had hung a rope swing with a notched board, in our Scotch pine tree. This scraggly tree was a holdover from the previous tenants on the farm. It had one redeeming feature--a limb which grew out parallel to the ground at a height of about 15 feet. I can still feel the sinking sensation in my stomach when we started the downward arc.

When the swing board broke, Dad tied a Model T Ford tire on the rope. This tire had a 30 inch diameter, giving plenty of room for a small child to sit in it comfortably. The one bad feature of this arrangement was the limpness of the tire. They were made to mount on clincher rims and only had three and one-half inches of rubber and bead. If one sat very long in one, the tire started to pinch one's rear end. It was impossible to "pump up" in this swing very high.

When the old Scotch pine gave up and became stove wood, my older brother Carl and Dad rigged a swing in a 100-year old oak tree about 20 feet from the barn. Used hay rope made this swing fairly fool proof and holes were drilled in the swing board, so that once formed the board did not move from side to side. The oak limb came out from the tree a good 20 feet above the ground, so one could "pump up" really high.

This swing served the children for many years until one night we had a neighborhood gathering at our place. Ed Hahn, at that time Wehseners'

62

hired man, and Bill Johnson, who lived where Darwin and Bonnie Oordt now live, decided to show off a bit and see how high they could pump. The two young men were too much for the hay rope, which by then had been out in the weather for a few years. At the highest point in the pump, the rope broke and the two fellows went sailing. They hit on the hard ground of the driveway with only a few skins and bruises.

That swing was never replaced. When we traded farms with Dad and Mother and moved back to the Home Place, our children were still small and still coming. I built a sand box and put up a swing in the oak tree about 20 feet from the house. I made it out of link chain, with the board seat bolted to the chain making it fairly safe. The hanging limb was about 11 feet high, giving the kids a pretty good dropping sensation on the down stroke.

Joan was the first to be able to climb the swing up to the branch, and this became a test of strength from then on for our children. During the dry years, oak wilt killed the swing tree and two adjacent ones had to be cut down also. Fortunately, our children were all grown up before this happened."

Quaday's Quotes (Reprinted with permission from RR Quaday) Faribault County Register Monday October 4, 1993

A Family Thanksgiving Day; Remembering Snow and Ice Storms

"The last 10 years or so, it just doesn't seem as though we have as many howling three-day northwest wind blizzards, as we suffered through when we were little kids walking to School District 104.

In those days we always eagerly awaited the first snowfall; of course we weren't big enough to shovel the stuff yet in grade school. If we would have had a foot of wet snow in those years, our four-buckle overshoes would have been full and wet inside the minute we walked out the door. The half mile to the school house would have taken us all day, and with the rain mixed in, we would have been wet and chilly all day unless our teacher would have let us stand around the pot-bellied stove with the tin shield, to dry off for an hour or so.

I couldn't help but think, while we were getting dumped on, what wonderful snowmen we built, and how the snowballs would sail hard and far. We were not allowed to build forts and have an all-out war in our country school, because if one or two of the first-and-second-graders stopped an icy

63

snowball with their eye, one of the mommas would surely start a protest movement and blame the teacher for letting it happen. Of course, if it happened at home, the momma would probably have told the child, "Only babies cry--go play." A black eye or a lump on the head didn't stop the war for very long.

On our bayou, down east of the farm buildings, many a fall or a bruised rear end happened with the first freeze-up. We had a single buggy axle with the wheels still attached, that we rolled and skidded on the ice. The wheels rotted away after sitting in water for a few summers, leaving the axle stuck straight up in the mud.

It was great fun whirling around the pole on skates, until disaster struck on a Saturday afternoon when my brother, John, and I collided on the way around the pole. I hit the ice hard enough to break off the bottom half of my right front tooth, leaving the nerve hanging out. It hurt! My Mother called our dentist at his home, it being Saturday afternoon. He told her to bring me right in to the office, and he would fix me up. Dad was at a creamery meeting, so there was no other way but for me to walk the two miles to town, with the temperature right at zero and with the nerve hang- ing out in the cold wind.

Dr. Meyer pulled the nerve out and packed the hole with a pain pill, and I walked on home, worrying what Dad would say. Nothing ever interrupted a creamery meeting, as Dad was chairman of the board, and that was the biggest business in town. They were in the process of building the new creamery building, on North Main Street (1930).

I was in high school before Dr. Meyer sawed off the top half of my tooth and put in a peg tooth, so it was not so embarrassing when I smiled. It cost money and that was Great Depression time, so I had to wait a while."

Quaday's Quotes -partial (Reprinted with permission from RR Quaday) Faribault County Register Monday December 6, 2010

Canning & Preserving

Northwest of the farm granary was a large garden space where we raised strawberries, rhubarb, peas, and other goodies too numerous to mention. Of course, along with the pleasant memories, there are also those not so pleasant, like weeds, hot days of hoeing and wet days when work had to be done regardless of the weather.

Besides the woods along the river, our farm had a couple of groves as well as strips along the line-fences, all of which sheltered wild life (rabbits, pheasants and other birds) and had trees and shrubs which yielded delicious fruits (wild gooseberries, grapes, chokecherries, plums, elderberries) and nuts (black walnuts, butternuts) We spent many hours gathering as much as possible of these good things and helping my Mother and Marie process them into jelly, jam, sauce and pies. Dad put the nuts through the corn-sheller to remove the outer husks and then they were spread to dry on newspapers in the attic, until we could find time for the slow task of cracking them and removing the nut meats.

Mom's Canning Carried Distinctive Odors

"The advent of the tomato crop brings to mind the hundreds of quarts of vegetables and fruit that my Mother used to can on a wood burning cook stove on our River Road Farm. Mother never owned a pressure cooker, but with her attention to detail, she had very little spoilage.

One could always tell what was being canned by the distinctive odors emanating from the kitchen; in my estimation the smell of strawberry jam topped them all. There was the slightly acrid smell of beets and string beans, the sweet sickening smell of bread and butter pickles, and the smell of watermelon pickles, my favorite.

She canned many kinds of jellies and jams; tame and wild grape, elderberry, chokecherry, tame and wild plum, and gooseberry. By the time I was old enough to remember canning, Minnesota Valley was canning sweet corn, and she didn't care to run them competition canning her own peas and sweet corn, because Dad owned stock in the company.

Shortly after the folks bought the River Road Farm from Steve Pitcher, Dad planted a 24-tree orchard out on the west side of the road. Only one Wealthy apple tree did not survive, and though replanted several times, it did not ever bear fruit. The orchard was a big item in our entertainment--all the way from the green duchess apples with salt, to strawberry crabs, to Winter's Jewel winter apples, we could eat our fill.

Mother canned applesauce, made apple jelly, dried apples for pies and we wrapped the winter apples and stored them in our attic stairwell, where the temperature was just right. We had northwestern greenings until April if they had not been eaten up by then. The orchard was a great stopping off place for town kids hiking or biking out to the swinging bridge. They could pick up all they wanted from the ground, but if they started knocking good fruit off the trees, Dad would put a stop to it.

After Neva and I moved to the Home Farm, we bought a 16-quart pressure cooker for canning garden produce. Neva's Dad built shelves in the basement for canned goods, and we did our level best to fill them. We sometimes cut and processed green beans and sweet corn until 2:30 am. The pressure cooker took most of the guesswork out of home canning, and Neva lost very little to spoilage.

In 1952, we bought a 22-foot freezer from John Breen. This radically changed the pattern of preserving vegetables and fruits, but most of all the meat saved for family consumption. That freezer only let us down once in 30 years and it took only a minor repair.

Strawberries and apples adapted especially well to freezing and we had plenty of both. One year I picked 30 gallons of strawberries from our patch, and Neva got so sick of processing them that she started giving them away. It didn't take long for me to tell her, "Give them away before I pick' em, not after."

It seemed that I always had time on damp mornings to pick the patch before going on to putting up hay or cultivating corn or beans. I nearly always ended up with a case of hives from eating so many while I picked."

Quaday's Quotes (Reprinted with permission from RR Quaday) Faribault County Register Monday September 20, 1993

When Marie was about 2 years old, Dad and Mother decided to build a new house. My Mother's uncle, Charles Quantz, was hired to do the building and, while later events proved that he was not the best of carpenters, he did manage to put together what, in those times, was considered a very fine house.

The first floor consisted of a bathroom (it even had all the modern facilities), kitchen, pantry connected to both kitchen and dining room by cupboards that opened on both sides, dining room and parlor, between which was a huge sliding door, and a bedroom which Mother also used for a sewing room. A large screened porch extended along the whole side toward the road and along part of the side toward the yard. The second floor had four bedrooms and a sleeping porch, also screened so that we could enjoy it during the hot summer nights. The third floor was a large unfinished room which was used for storing anything that could withstand the bitterly cold temperatures of winter and the oven-like heat of summer.

1942 Marie and Don wedding at Oak Ridge Farm

Sleeping On The Porch Was Cool

"One of my fondest memories of my childhood on River Road Farm was the move about the first of May out to our "sleeping porch." Air conditioning, of course, was but a distant dream for farmhouses in the 20s. Our screened in porch was located on the second story and ran along the whole east side of the house. The floor plan was fairly tight, holding three big beds and two cots. Sleeping out in the fresh air of spring was so exhilarating that one never had a thought of being crowded or deprived of privacy. The screened windows all had cloth curtains with sliders top and bottom so they could be opened in warm weather for maximum air flow, or closed tightly to hold out a summer thunder storm.

The one big drawback to our open air porch was the flat roof. It was covered with layers of black roofing and tarred to prevent leakage. It seemed that my Mother was forever mopping up water after a storm, or putting pans under leaks. It taught me a good lesson on house building--No flat roofs ever in MN.

Oak Ridge Farm Sleeping Porch & 1926 Buick

The old time house builders had the right idea when they made steep roofs and wide eaves, with the least possible dormers and valleys to leak. Dad tarred the roof of our porch every spring because the snow and ice broke the seal.

Everything considered, it was a great place to sleep in spring and summer, and sometimes until Thanksgiving. My brother, John, and I always tried to stick it out, but didn't always make it that long.

The list of benefits was long. Dad was a light sleeper and could hear trouble with the horses, sheep or chickens, almost before it happened. Our house was located on a 40 foot hill, which had a small pond at the bottom. In the spring and early summer it seemed the frogs were doing their special song right under our windows. It was a thrill to look down on bird nests with feeding time every 10 minutes. In late summer and fall the tree toads and cicadas tuned in, punctuated by bird calls, with robins being irritatingly loud at 5 am.

Years later, when Neva and I traded for the Home Farm, our children had the benefit of a few years of peaceful slumber on the "sleeping porch" before the advent of air conditioning. The floor plan had to be redesigned, so we went to bunk beds on the north end. The old farm house raised nine children the second time around. The new owners have closed in the porch with a slanted roof, so their children will have to camp out to experience the joys of open air slumber."

Quaday's Quotes -partial (Reprinted with permission from RR Quaday) Faribault County Register Monday May 13, 1991

Dick Talks About Taking Naps

"From my memories when I was a wee tot, I hated naps. Our farmhouse was surrounded by 100-year old oak trees. Through the summer, I was put down on our screened-in sleeping porch on the second floor. It was a wonderful setting for a nap, with the breeze blowing through.

With the Oak trees came the acorns, and with the acorns, came the squirrels, and our dog, Old Bob, hated squirrels and he would use a loud bark to scare them away.

Try to sleep with all of that ruckus. Mother could never understand why I couldn't nap in such a great environment, since she worked enough to sleep under any circumstances.

On Sunday afternoon, if we didn't have company, my Dad always took a long nap, and immediately after dinner he would pick me up and say, "reech-heardt, nap time." There was no arguing with him. He would lay me down right next to him and put his arm around me so I couldn't get away. I had no choice, so I slept and always felt better after.

By the time I was six years old and going to school, the nap business was over and I was thankful. However, I began to understand why my Dad had been so enthusiastic about this phenomenon after enduring years of hard farm work.

At age 45, I began the regimen of napping for about a half hour in earnest, and I'm sure it saved many hills of corn during cultivating season, and many soybeans plants too. There was no job to compare with the tractor cultivator with the constant stress of precision driving to put the tractor driver into a sound sleep. I would venture to bet good money with any honest farmer that he had during his youth, gone to sleep on the cultivator and dug out some corn or soybeans.

When I retired from farming in 1982, my Naps suddenly went from half an hour to whenever I woke up, and I could really relax.

My Dad, during his retirement years, did a lot of napping in his favorite easy chair, but Mother always felt guilty if someone caught her napping. She would be doing knitting or some other fancy work at her kitchen table, fall asleep, and feel bad for wasting the time. This is the same lady who bought a new kitchen stove at age 92 and expected to wear it out.

Dad, on the other hand, was glad to turn the reins over to me when I turned 18. He had gone through a period of ill health and never did recover his enthusiasm for farming. He liked to take it easy with his small garden and small lawn to mow, taking naps after dinner and coming out to the farm when he felt like it. When something big was going on, he was always available to haul between farms or fields. Having driven horses for most of his life, he never did get to be good at driving motorized vehicles. He hauled corn and beans to Frank's Elevator for me until he was 87 years old. He would drive the truck to the elevator driveway and let Al or Dave pull it in and run the hoist up and down.

I'm going on 87 years, and I guess I could still drive a truck, but have no ambition to do so. I'd rather walk, ride my bike and nap when I feel like it."

Quaday's Quotes (Reprinted with permission from RR Quaday) Faribault County Register Monday July 16, 2007

Dick Recalls July 4th Celebrations

"Different families have widely varying ways of celebrating Independence Day around the country.

When we were kids growing up on our River Road Farm, Dad always bought a huge block of ice at Tressler's on 13th street. Mom would make a custard for ice cream and John and I would take turns on the crank made of wood and cast iron. The freezer was painted green and had a rotating 3/4 gallon tank with a paddle inside, which rotated when we turned the crank. Dad oversaw the adding of salt to the ice chips around the tank. The salt lowered the temperature of the ice far enough so that, with a certain amount of labor on the crank, the custard froze and we had excellent ice cream; honest ice cream, with real cream, not all air. We shared this treat before going to the harness races at the fairgrounds, hence Dad saved the money and hassles of kids begging for ice cream cones.

John and I saved our bottle and gopher money to buy firecrackers and cherry bombs.

When Neva and I were raising our family, Charlie was a firecracker nut and would devise all kinds of equipment to make the lighting of firecrackers and cherry bombs more interesting. We had a four-inch well casing about five feet long, which he used with a cherry bomb and some assorted pieces of junk, effectively making a pipe bomb, which sprayed stuff way up in the air. We had good wooden matches in those days, making lighting firecrackers safer than with the current safety matches.

My way of celebrating the 4th of July was to get up at 6 am and fire my 20-gauge shotgun right below the sleeping porch where our young ones were still sleeping. This started their day with a 'bang'. There was always 'commotion' up on the sleeping porch after the gun went off--some friendly, some not so friendly.

Memories are made of events like this which last a lifetime, for me, and the kids."

Quaday's Quotes -partial (Reprinted with permission from RR Quaday) Faribault County Register Monday July 18, 2005

Dick Recalls Water Sources and Laundry

Our house on the Home Place had a full basement with cement walls and floor, and a huge cistern to catch the rain water so that we could have soft water for baths and laundry. The pipe from a hand-operated pressure pump extended into the cistern so that we could pump soft water into a water heater located beside the kitchen stove. Coils from the heater had been placed in the fire box of the stove, so whenever we had a fire for cooking, we "automatically" had hot water. There was no safety valve on the heater and one of Mother's worries was that on days when she had to have a very hot fire for baking, she might get too much steam generated and the tank would blow. Of course, that never happened even though the sounds of the steam bubbling through the water inside the tank seemed rather threatening at times. We kids frequently got our exercise working the handle of the pressure pump, trying to get the water pressure up to 20 lbs. or more.

"Whenever we have a quiet snowfall without any strong wind, I think back to my childhood days out on River Road Farm when we used the newly fallen snow to replenish the soft water in our indoor cistern. We had gutters all the way around the big house, which ran the rain water into the concrete cistern in the basement. The cistern would usually overflow in early spring and after September rains. With six people to wash clothes for, and six people taking baths, the level was sometimes low by midwinter. We simply opened the basement window above the cistern and scooped the newly fallen snow into the water. If a blizzard had mixed dirt with the snow, we didn't use it.

Cleaning the cistern each spring was a ritual we all hated, but it had to be done to ensure clean clothes for the family.

We had a double action, hand-operated brass pump which forced the soft water into a pressure tank and up into a water heater with coils in the firepot of the kitchen stove. Any time the cook stove was used, we had hot soft water in the sinks and the bath tub. Mother was much more fortunate than most farm wives in her day, in that she had hot soft running water and an electrically operated washing machine. The machine, made by a Dutch company, was named Haag. It had a wooden tub and a wooden agitator which turned back and forth doing a fair job of cleaning clothes. It had a wringer to take out much of the water before the clothes were hung to dry.

She later bought a Maytag--considered at that time the Cadillac of washers. Not used to the wringer on the new machine, she ran her hand into it. Instead of flipping the spring release, Mother became flustered and she ran her hand back out. Her hand was black for about a month, but she never saw a doctor, but simply soaked it in hot water spiked with "Pain Oil," a concoction sold by Raleigh's peddler, Clayton Ankeny.

The Watkins and the Raleigh's man sold a lot of home remedies at our house; salves, bottled tonics for this and that malady, and pills for headaches, etc. Dad would get "sick" headaches, some of which would last for three days, during which he was really incapacitated. The rest of the family would have all the milking and chores to do.

When I remember how much snow it took to raise the cistern a couple of inches, I wonder if it was actually worth the trouble. During the winter, we carried hard water from the well into the house to flush toilets, as we saved soft water for baths and clothes washing. We had drains and a septic tank way back in 1918, and with electricity, we were quite modern.

Transportation on the farms was not that progressive at that time. The Model T Fords gave way to bobsleds in winter. The teams of horses didn't have to be cranked to start, and everyone had two or three teams just standing around doing nothing and needing exercise out on the farms.

When Neva and I moved into the Sailor Place out on River Road, there was no electricity and no drains or running water. Quite a change for both of us. I bought a Maytag washer with a gas engine from George Carr Hardware. I never kept track of how many times I was called home from the field to start that rotten engine, but it was many. World War II was on, so we couldn't dig a new well or put in electricity for two years. When we finally had running water with a stool and tub, it was Heaven, even though the water was hard.

When we bought the Home Farm in 1949, we installed a softener and a gas water heater. A couple of years later, we bought a new side-by-side automatic washer and dryer, eliminating the need for the cistern. We kept it full, though, in case of fire. Dad built it right, with good concrete and re-rod, so it never leaked. I'd hate to be the guy on the jack hammer if it is ever taken out.

After Ted Halverson dug the new well on the Home Place, we had unlimited water; one could turn on every hydrant on the farm and wash clothes without ever running out of water. With the old sand well, if a few grains of sand got into the jet pump, I might as well have started pulling out the pump to clean the jet. In midwinter, that was not fun and games.

Farming certainly did change for the better in my lifetime."

Quaday's Quotes (Reprinted with permission from RR Quaday) Faribault County Register Monday March 10, 2003

River Road

One of the factors in our existence was the road which ran through our farm. It was called the River Road because, instead of being flat and straight, like most of the roads in that area, it followed the course of the river in a winding, hilly path. The road surface was never good no matter what the weather. In the summer when it was dry, the dust was so thick that whenever a vehicle went by, it blew into the house and settled on everything. When it rained, the clay turned into a slippery, rutty morass which pulled our rubbers and overshoes off when we walked to and from school, and caused cars to skid into the ditch or sink down to the axle in the ruts.

In the winter the snow drifted onto the road, which was lower in many places than the surrounding fields. The drifts varied in depth, at times reaching 6 to 8 feet. Then Dad hitched the horses to the sled and we went over, around or through the drifts. If the horses couldn't wallow through, Dad shoveled ahead of them. Sometimes the drifts were hard on one side and soft on the other so that the sled tipped over, and then we had a tangled mess of ropes, harness, etc. After all the work of getting through, the prospects were not too favorable for passage the next time because it usually drifted the path full from one day to the next. After we got the Model T, we managed to go over the top of the drifts during the cold weather. But when it began to thaw in the spring, the track, which had been packed down in the winter, thawed more slowly than the surrounding snow, and the car got hung up when it slid off the high spots.

But in spite of all these difficulties, we scarcely ever missed a day of school. In those days there were no school closings on account of weather. Most of the kids lived in town and those who didn't got there as best they could. Dad and Mother were determined that we should not be at a disadvantage because we lived on a farm.

River Road Was Formidable in 1920

"My personal saga begins Sept 2, 1920, on a farm a mile and one half up the Blue Earth River from the town of Blue Earth.

We lived on the fearsome River Road, which when it rained or snowed, was a formidable obstacle in 1920. It was fit only for a team and buggy or saddle horse in bad weather. The Model T Ford, which was the first car I remember, had high clearance, but still dragged in the ruts or snow banks on our road.

1920 William & Lorena Quaday children: Carl, Marie, John & Richard

Dr. J.A. Broberg and Aunt Addie Willmert had the chore of assisting at my birth. Aunt Addie was Adeline Levenick, who married Gust Willmert. He died fairly young so she became the most popular midwife in the Blue Earth area.

I was the last of four children in our family and I'm told that my oldest brother, Carl, and Aunt Addie couldn't get along, so after two days she packed up and went to town. My sister, Marie, was seven, so she spent many hours baby tending, I am sure. My childhood was pretty uneventful, as most other kids growing up on a farm.

We had a low, red, one-story granary with a walnut tree about 12 feet in back of it. The walnut tree had been deformed when it was small. Charlie Sanders, who then lived on the farm, had thrown some object over the granary. The tree was split so that it grew into a perfect crotch for sitting in and climbing. One limb hung out over the fence just low enough so even small children could learn how to climb the tree, sit in the crotch, climb another limb out over the granary and look out over the yard without being seen.

When our minister, Rev. Tesch, came to call, we would all climb the tree and sit on the granary until he left. He was a nice man, with a rich German accent, which right after the first World War, was not a popular way to talk.

I wish now that my folks had talked more German at home, but Mother was high German and Dad talked low Dutch, so they only talked German when they didn't want us kids to get the drift.

We learned to chew rhubarb, pick gooseberries, pull Morning Glories in the corn fields, eat wild plums and grapes, walk to country school, make elderberry juice, box elder whistles, and rubber guns, all of which are lost arts with today's kids."

Quaday's Quotes-Partial (Reprinted with permission from RR Quaday) Faribault County Register, Monday, April 30, 1990

Birthday Party, Drought And Gravel

"Droughts can happen, even in our land of sky blue water. I can remember well the summer of 1934, when we could walk across the Blue Earth River with our shoes on, stepping on a couple of rocks in what channel there was, nearly all summer.

My brother was selling cars for Howard Essler at the Motor Inn and he had the foresight to hire my brother, John, and me to haul gravel and rocks out of the river bed to gravel our farm driveway. He was single yet, and living at home and he didn't like the inevitable mud on his new cars when it did rain. It was a good investment for him to pay us boys a few bucks to save washing his car every time it rained.

We had a big sorrel and roan team at the time and they pulled well together. We used a lumber wagon with twelve by one inch planks to haul the gravel, and could load a full yard of gravel per load. The planks lay loose on the bolsters and with one of us on each end, we simply tipped the planks over

76

the driveway; no scooping. The polished stones, about egg size, made a good permanent bed for our driveway and they are still there, doing their duty, with some of the finer material on top. We had two fan shovels and we hauled five loads every day when we were not haying or cultivating corn. I think we each earned $25, which was an enormous sum of money during the depths of the Great Depression.

It really wouldn't have made much sense to gravel our driveway before 1934, because River Road wasn't anything but blue mud after a rain, at that time. If there had been a DNR in 1934, they would probably not let us haul gravel out of the Blue Earth River bed, even though the next spring's flood would have replenished the channel with the same material and the same amount of it. A lot of their restrictions, which the DNR foists on the public nowadays, make no sense to me, because nature would replace many of the man made disturbances in a year or two. Of course, the DNR has their job to do, and by and large they do what must be done to preserve the world's ecology and environment."

Quaday's Quotes - partial (Reprinted with permission from RR Quaday) Monday, May 24, 2010

Remembering Brother John

"My brother, John, is two years older than I. There probably aren't many folks who remember him because he graduated from Blue Earth High School at age 16, and hasn't spent much time in our town since. He has had a very interesting life after attending Winona State Teachers College and attaining a teaching degree.

John was born 80 years ago, August 2, 1918, a husky and perfectly normal baby. During his second year, he had a bad fall injuring his spine. As a result of this accident, his left leg grew a half inch shorter than the right. Dad made several trips to St Paul doctors to try to remedy the situation, trying traction along with many other methods. They even tried a built up shoe, to help his spine grow straight. This was Great Depression time, so the folks more or less gave up on doctors for a cure. The hard work and continuous exercise of farm work apparently compensated for the short leg, and he grew up to have a beautiful build.

We did all the things kids did around the farm, finding time to play softball, basketball, skate, and slide on the hills with toboggans and sleds. He

77

showed an inclination for building and fixing at a young age, but it wasn't to really flower until many years had passed. We made our own softball bats from ash poles out of our grove. He traded a bottle lamb for his first bicycle, with many innovations to keep it running.

1945 Captain John Quaday

There was never a day went by that I didn't try to whip him, but hardly ever got it done. The hit and run technique proved the most effective, and most of the time I could outrun him. That, too, changed when he went to Winona State and went out for the five-mile run on the track team. He also lettered on the boxing team, but had to forgo most sports to take a job as night clerk at the Merchant's Hotel, to pay expenses.

He hitched rides home with salesmen and truckers the last two years of college. He passed on to me many of the sports which he learned at Winona, golf, high jumping, and tennis; the coach in him was already taking shape. After graduating from college, he taught at Lynd and Wahpeton, ND.

When World War II began, he enlisted in the Army as a buck private. He had four years of Math in high school, and four in college, so the Army made him a range finder for their big artillery. After a couple months in England, he was assigned to General Patton's armored division where he served for four years until the war ended. At Bastogne, he figured out a way to get caterpillar tracks back on after they ran off from frozen mud, without having to take everything apart.

This got him a nice promotion in the field, and he came out a captain. Our family was just as concerned for his safety as were all other families at war time, and we had a grand celebration when he finally returned home unscathed. He brought home many Nazi decorations, most of which are still in the old attic at the farmhouse.

John held the athletic director's job at Red Wing before moving to the University of ND, as a Physical Education teacher, and golf and swimming coach. Two on his golf team did well in the pro tour later.

1998 John & Stella Quaday

About the time John had four children and a new house in Grand Forks, he decided to go for his Doctorate in Phy Ed at the University of Illinois. This took two years using the GI bill and living in another barracks. He came back to Grand Forks with a Doctor's Degree in Phy Ed and taught there until his retirement.

He and Stella decided to sell out in North Dakota, and move to a Lake Wabana home in the late 70s. After about three months of doing nothing, his building instincts took over, and he began to build a shop in the deep woods surrounding their house. The know-how he learned from our contractor cousin, Roger Quaday, began to come in handy. He sawed down the trees, sawed them into lumber, planed them, and did all the work necessary to finish doors, windows, and paneling. He did all of the septic work, and the electric wiring, the fitting, ceramic tile baths, and the kitchen cupboards. The house is beautiful and everything is professionally perfect.

He began building the shop, which turned into a house in 1978, and is still working on it today. His remark on the time frame, "I'm having so much fun, I don't care if I never get it all done." His basement is full of every machine for building a house and Stella has put up with sawdust for 20 years, but now has a wonderful house for their old age. At age 80, they still dance up a storm every chance they get, so may never get old."

Quaday's Quotes - (Reprinted with permission from RR Quaday) Faribault County Register, Monday, October 5, 1998

Christmas Celebrations

Play Recalls Christmases Past

"The first Christmas Eve program in the old Salem Evangelical Church that I remember was at age five. I recall sitting on Dad's lap and being really interested during the "little kids" portion of the program, but losing interest quickly when the sermon, preached by Reverend Tesch, dragged on a bit longer than my span of attention.

A family tradition developed. After the program, we always had a party as long as our family was all at home or within driving distance of a Model A Ford. Mom would make oyster stew and the children would put on a program. They always learned some songs in school or were involved in a church program which my Mother, who had been a school teacher, dearly loved to hear.

Much later, when our kids grew out of that age, my Dad brought down the house by singing the first song he ever learned for a church program for us in German. This occurred on his 90th birthday."

Quaday's Quotes -Partial (Reprinted with permission from RR Quaday) Faribault County Register, Monday, December 18, 1989

Christmas Along The River Road

"When I was a youngster at home on our River Road Farm, we developed a Christmas tradition. Mother always made oyster stew for supper, after which we all went to the Christmas program at Salem Evangelical Church. After church, we came home and opened presents with of course, candy, popcorn, hot chocolate, coffee, and tea. Tea was my Mother's specialty and she made excellent tea. If there were any children of grade school age or under, they always put on the programs that they had learned in school or church.

During my grade school years the Great Depression was in full swing, so gifts were of necessity not frivolous. The gifts consisted of stockings, mittens, and stocking caps. Dad had a sweet tooth, so in later years, when the children grew up and got jobs, someone always bought him a five pound box of Whitman Chocolates. Mother had baked all kinds of cookies, sweet breads, popped corn, and we would make taffy.

When Mother lived to be over 90, the offspring, all up in their 50s and 60s, tried to take over the party, so Mother would not have so much work getting ready and serving a big crowd, since we all had children. The largest family of course, was our nine, so Neva told Mother she would have Christmas at our house. Everything went fairly well, until the party was nearly over. Neva noticed that Mother was not her usual happy self. We were concerned and asked what the trouble was. She remarked, with tears in her eyes, "Just wait until they put you on the shelf."

The next year, Dad's health was failing, so the tradition stayed in our family home, with a big Christmas beef Stroganoff dinner with all the trimmings, opening all the presents, and attending midnight Mass at SS Peter and Paul Catholic Church."

Quaday's Quotes -partial (Reprinted with permission of RR Quaday) Faribault County Register Monday, December 24, 1990

Flying My Mother To St Luke's

"Early in the fall of 1980, I received a call from my sister, Marie Anderson of Crookston, MN. My Mother, Lorena Quaday, had been living with them for four years, after Dad died. Marie and her husband, Don, both had experienced back operations and as Mother was beginning to require more care, they both thought that it was the opportune time to move her to St Luke's Lutheran Home in Blue Earth.

We discussed ways of getting Mother to Blue Earth and finally I decided to talk to John Patton, then Mayor of our town. He owned a spacious plane and was a licensed pilot for instrument flying. John said he'd be glad to oblige, and a deal was struck. Mother was in her 97th year and although she was still sharp mentally, her balance and her legs were weakening. Thankfully, a room was available at St Luke's so arrangements were made for a checkup at Memorial Hospital and evaluation.

By the time harvest and fall work was done it was near Thanksgiving and the weather was getting brisk. John and I took off for Crookston in bright sunshine, but over St Cloud we flew into a cloud bank and went upstairs the rest of the way. When John came through the clouds, we could see Crookston Airport about a mile away.

Marie brought Mother and her two suitcases out and after taking on fuel and filing a flight plan, John pronounced readiness to fly. I wondered out loud if Mother, who had never flown, would give us a bad time. John did a great job of telling her about his plane and how it would get us home faster and easier than an automobile trip. She didn't exactly like the safety belt, but when told it was the law that did it.

She sat facing me, so she would be going forward on takeoff and all went well, until we entered the cloud bank. She leaned over to me and said in a hushed voice, "I can't see ANYTHING." I told her that as soon as we got above the clouds we would have bright sunshine and when this occurred she exclaimed, "Isn't it beautiful?' She promptly went to sleep until we were over St James.

The next day I took her out to St Luke's and got her settled in her room. She knew several of the attendants and nurses and when they asked her how she liked her plane ride, she replied, "Oh, it was fun but a little scary."

When the attendants would ask her questions to see how sharp she was, occasionally she would answer them in German, which she spoke fluently. They, who did not speak German, would have to check with me to see if she was correct, and it usually was.

Mother found it hard to accept that she could stay in St Luke's without having to cook or do dishes. After all she had purchased a new cook stove at age 92, and expected to wear it out.

One afternoon when I came out to visit, she was nowhere to be found. After about 20 minutes of frantic search, we located her in the kitchen. She told us that relatives from Wisconsin had stopped in and she had to hurry up and prepare supper, so they could get on the road home. The kitchen workers had too much work already, she thought. It was all very real to her, but a check revealed no company from Wisconsin. Right then we were so very glad that we had made the move to bring her home to Blue Earth in Mr. Patton's plane when we did."

Quaday's Quotes (Reprinted with permission from RR Quaday) Faribault County Register Monday December 14, 1992

Neva and I bought the Home Farm in 1949.

1950 River Road Farm Aerial View

On the River Road Farm, I painted all the buildings white, rewired the barn, dug a new well, installed copper water lines with seven hydrants, shingled all the buildings, and built a new corn crib and machine shed. I installed new tile, cleared the land and bought eighteen acres of lower pasture from the Kark family. Later on I built five steel grain bins, with two dryer bins, using my designed wood or gas heaters. I put up a new Quonset steel building measuring thirty feet by eighty feet. I cut the dairy herd down, and had a nine hole golf course in our sheep pasture.

Dick Recalls The Spring Of 1951 (and) The Big Spring Blizzard of 1951

"I was looking at old photos of winters past, when I remembered the winter and spring of 1951. It was a tough winter, but nothing compared to the spring. We had a lot of snow, and it stuck around until spring because of the frozen ground. Out on River Road, the snow banks were over 10 feet high on the week before Easter.

A crew of farmers scooped in front of the county plow, driven by Benny Jahnke, to loosen the firm banks. On Good Friday morning we started out scooping at 8 am with a heavily overcast sky and hints of another snow, which made us nervous. We had been a week snowed in, and the groceries for the family and the feed for the animals was running low. We started at the Pilot Grove blacktop, where Harry Ehrich lived at the time, and cleared it to Ristau's crossroad by 9:30 am.

The wind was coming up as I started for town with a load of corn to be ground up for hog feed at Frank's Elevator. My feeders had been empty for a couple of days and I had emptied the bin, carrying feed for 100 hogs. Neva needed groceries and baby food, so she loaded up the little kids and took off for town.

I drove the loaded grain truck for grinding animal mix at the elevator, and Neva drove the new Buick with the children for groceries. She met me at the elevator so we could caravan home, with me leading in the heavy truck to lay a good track to follow. We hit a white out at the Ristau corner; I made the turn with the truck, but the Straight 8 Buick rode low and Neva got hung up. Arlen Ristau helped us pull the car out and continue our journey home.

 We got through the banks as far as the Sailor Place; there we stopped and put the car in front of the truck, so if Neva got stuck I could give her a nudge to push her through. We made it home by 2:30, and it snowed all night. On Easter Sunday morning the sun was shining and no wind, but it was very cold.

My Mother called about 8 am, saying Dad would meet us at Harry Ehrich's to pick us up for Easter services at SS Peter and Paul Catholic church, followed by a good dinner before taking us back home. We bundled up the little ones, with overshoes for the ones who could walk over the drifts. I carried Mary, our youngest at 2 years, because she couldn't keep up. Mom had a wonderful Easter dinner prepared for us, and we visited until chore time. The trip home wasn't so bad.

We scooped in front of the plow again, two days later. The snow banks were softer this time, and Benny had no trouble clearing the road. We had one of the best groves in the county for blizzard protection, but that year it was blown full, clear over the choke-cherry trees. We had drifts in our yard six feet high, and they were so hard we just carried the milk in and the skim milk out to the hogs.

We were in the middle of lambing and farrowing, so I seldom got much sleep--sometimes not even getting to bed at night. I was only milking 10 cows, but carrying 30 gallons of milk over the snow banks both ways, in addition to the other chores. It sure worked up a good appetite. Fortunately, Neva had always been an excellent cook, so I didn't lose too much weight that winter. Surprisingly, the livestock came through the winter pretty well. I had an oil burner in the farrowing house and heat lamps for the baby pigs, and we had big litters that year. We still used a large straw shed for lambing, and that went well too. But it was a lot of extra work, having to do a lot of checking, day and night, for newborn lambs--sometimes having to take them to the basement to dry off by the furnace.

We thought we were in big business, raising two hundred hogs a year. Now if a farmer doesn't haul over two thousand head to market per year, they are not even in business. The hog factories of today are a far cry from the primitive hog-houses of our day."

Quaday's Quotes-partial (Reprinted with permission from RR Quaday) Faribault County Register Monday March 29, 1993

The Home Place as Remembered by Kay (Quaday) Husfeldt

Oak trees by the hundreds cluttered the hillsides and the flattened valleys. As far as you could see, blankets of rolling green pasture covered the blue black earth. On a particular hillside, as you face the South, nature took care to crowd the Oak trees neatly rowed into groves, forming a natural ridge of Oak. Grandpa Quaday noticed it too. From that time on, his homestead became known as Oak Ridge Farm.

This rich blue black land, populated with Oak trees, has remained in Quaday ancestry for nearly a century. The youngest son of William's brood, Richard by name, tills the soil just as his father before him, taking care all the while to preserve the precious land. About a mile and one-half south of town, the old farm house still stands, four stories tall, castle-like with layers of white wash paint. Despite nature's attempt to rearrange the land, my memories of Oak Ridge Farm remain unchanged.

I remember the old granary, its once white boards weathered to gray, its door hinges frozen to rust, and its cob webbed windows blurred by the morning sun. It was old when I was a child. Every spring the gray mother cat bore her kittens under the sagged foundation, taking care to hoard them just beyond an arm's reach. The granary, an antique hunter's paradise, succumbed long ago, but childhood memories linger still. Usually I looked for a hammer and the rusty coffee can filled with nails; always, I browsed for hours just looking at neat junk, forgetting the hammer and nails. Dad continually cautioned, "The granary is not a playhouse. Find what you need, and be sure you wear your shoes." Rusty floor board nails poked up everywhere, their heads severed years before from stress and exhaustion.

Behind the granary, and next to the old corn crib stood a hand corn grinder. As fast as we could feed it, the wide mouth of the grinder ate the cobs of corn. One kid cranked the handle, while another fed the grinder and caught the swallowed corn in a five gallon pail. Even if Dad didn't need the corn, we ground it anyway, much to the delight of the fat squirrels and birds.

Beyond the hog house, which I usually avoided because of the smell, stood the barn, naturally picturesque, with cob webs triangles both in the corners and under the rafters. When the sheep consumed our hay bale houses, the empty rafters and swing ropes became Tarzan's Jungle. Rain or shine, Mom knew where we liked to play.

The old chicken coop served as the girl's playhouse. The RCA hand cranked Victrola, moaned the "William Tell Overture" fast at first, then slowing to distorted sounds until we cranked it again. I wonder how much money that antique was worth. We used a discarded wall phone to call pretend neighbor friends, mimicking our nine-party-line phone system. Ball and Kerr two-quart jars with glass lids, lined the playhouse walls, neatly arranged on orange crate shelves, each jar filled with blue black mud cooked on our rusty two burner wood stove. On rainy days, our playhouse moved to the attic; our game changed to pretend school room classes. Discarded antique desks from the one room school held the students for attention, while the teacher, usually me, dictated color book assignments.

Below the ridge of Oak trees, on the down side of the south hill, hid our fishing hole. The wind- leaned tree, bearing its roots for benches, hovered over the deepest spot in the Blue Earth River that was on our land. Grandpa Quaday taught us how to set our fishing poles, camouflaged as just another tree root above the brown gurgling water, cautioning us all the while that we were breaking the law. Before school each morning we checked our lines.

One special day stands out in my memory; I remember the sun warmed my blanket, and through the screened in sleeping porch, I heard the songs of the birds greet the day. The clock said 4:30. Quietly I dressed in yesterday's dirty jeans; carefully I tiptoed through the bedroom of my sleeping parents. (That was the major disadvantage of sleeping on the upstairs porch.) Leaving through the door that normally slams, this morning I remembered to latch it without making a sound. Following the usual path to the river, I walked at a brisker than normal pace. I saw my camouflaged pole, but I couldn't see my bobber, which was not the red and white plastic kind but a piece of birch, secured bark side up, tied by Grandpa, using his secret tie knots.

Controlling my rapid heart pounds, I carefully crawled onto the tree root branches, trying to see my fish pole line. Tiny water ripples widened and disappeared, once, twice, and again. Sure enough, I saw my fish line, and the birch bark bobber bouncing on the muddy water. Tugging the line gently, I tested for reaction. Using Grandpa's sure fire method, I played the lure before I jerked one big jerk. Three times this week I almost landed that Catfish; three times his heavy body weight broke my water logged line. Both balancing myself and stepping on a low lying branch that sunk just a little, with one eye on the splash waves of crashing ripples my fish was making his final escape attempt. I freed the line from the tangled tree root under currents.

Photos in the family album historically recorded my catch; he was a beauty. Over the years, nature rearranged the river's bed. As record snowfalls melted, the swollen river swallowed our tree root benches, nature's graveyard forever. Nature filled the deepest hole in the Blue Earth River with the wind-leaned tree, and all that remains are the tree root foundations and my childhood memories.

Further down the river, around the bend, a Blue Earth legend remains, despite nature's call. Just below the barn on the old Sailor Place, a deaf old man, himself a legend, built a swinging bridge. The day I told Mom I didn't swim in the swollen river, I remember using the bridge guide wire for a clothes line, covering my naked body with newspapers while I waited for them to dry in the sun. Running races to cross the bridge tested our balance, as we purposely bounced the boards to dump each other off. Half of the swinging bridge answered nature's call, sagging over the years, to finally rest on the bottom of the river's bed. Even though the DANGER sign replaced the guide wire pulley, my memories of harmless fun remained unchanged.

Oak Ridge Farm will always live as it was. I could lose myself in memory thoughts--the old gray granary, the chicken coop playhouse, the rainy day attic...Despite nature's attempt to change her appearance, Oak Ridge Farm will be that farm in my youth, fondly and forever remembered.

Quaday Clan Skating On The Bayou

"Temperatures hovering around zero triggered one of two things at our River Road Farm back in the 20s and 30s. Either Dad would take us to the woods to cut firewood or if his back was bothering him, turn us loose to skate on the bayou.

I don't remember the City of Blue Earth having a skating pond with paid caretakers until about 1935. A great many town kids would come to our place to skate.

There was a good bayou on the Walter Oelke farm, now owned by Ed Jones just west of town on what is known as the Catholic Church Road. These bayous were surrounded by trees. If the weather got too cold to change skates we sometimes would start a fire with drift wood, which was always plentiful in the early winter.

Our bayou was situated so that a good brisk northwest wind would blow the snow off, putting a nice shine on the ice. In early winter we kept the snow scooped off the main bayou, which formed a semi-circle between the farm and the river."

Quaday's Quotes-partial (Reprinted with permission from RR Quaday) Faribault County Register Monday, December 31, 1990

Remembering Flood Adventures

"The weeks of wet and rainy weather in the first of June brought back memories of other wet years--when the Blue Earth River would come up from a lazy stream to a raging torrent over night, covering all of our pasture land and the six acres of work land across the river from the rendering plant, then owned by Emil Kark. Lake Blue Earth covered several hundred acres, running from our sliding hill, clear past the City of Blue Earth--quite a bit bigger than Imagine Lake where The Flying Goose Campground is now located.

1950s Russell Golay

If the quick flood had happened in March, as it sometimes did, the Quaday kids had a huge ice rink when the weather turned cold and froze the bottom lake land with over two inches of ice. We always tested the thickness of the ice with wooden clubs, washed along the shore by the flood. We could see carp and other fish through the clear thin ice and occasionally a turtle.

When Russell Golay lived on the Sailor Place, he just loved to bring his 12-gauge shotgun over to our pasture when we had a June flood and shoot carp. He would wade around with his overalls rolled up, to where it was about two feet deep, stop a minute, and Kaboom! Usually, the carp surfaced, full of BB's. The Carp came in from the River to feed on angle worms, which were drowned out of the sod, (blue grass), in the pasture.

Russell was stone deaf, a result of working in the coal mines of southern Iowa and Missouri, where a lot of blasting loosened the coal. When he moved up to Minnesota, he brought along several cases of dynamite. He would occasionally go down in the woods and blow up stumps, just for old time's sake back in the mines.

Our younger clan did a lot of roaming along the river bank and curiosity got the better of them. They looked in the cab of his old Chevy pickup, and boy, did they ever get scared when they read dynamite on the boxes inside. When they told us about it, we made it very clear that they had no business snooping in someone else's yard. One never knows for sure what a bunch of kids might do. Russell made good use of the dynamite when he cleared six acres of land of stumps on the hill next to the Clarence Dobson farm. It had never been farmed and man, did it ever raise good corn for a number of years.

In the 1950s, during the Eisenhower Farm Depression, we had to plow up the pasture (which was also our nine hole golf course), to raise corn and soybeans. The cash crop made more money than milking cows and agreed with me much better."

Quaday's Quotes -partial (Reprinted with permission from RR Quaday) Faribault County Register Monday July 5, 2010

Thanksgivings Past and Present

"On our River Road farm, we celebrated Thanksgiving Day quite differently than most folks. We were usually harvesting corn one way or another; picking by hand when I was young and by combine in my later years. During the 1920s, 30s and 40s, we dined on pheasant, as the season was open for three weeks in those days, and there was an over supply of the birds to hunt. Times were hard, so free meat was always welcome, even on farms.

We always had a lot of company during pheasant season after Neva and I were married. Many of her relatives from Staples and Long Prairie came to hunt and bunked at our house. We went fishing in that area of lakes and bunked at their place. One morning for breakfast, she fed 31 hungry kids and hunters.

One year, shortly after we moved into the River house, we had quite a houseful of newly married children come home for Thanksgiving on Wednesday night. During the night it snowed 22 inches. We had our house full, besides Mike's, who was farming by then on the Home Place. On Thanksgiving morning no one went anywhere. People were warned to stay off the highways until they were cleared and the state and county crews didn't have the plows ready to go yet. We had two houses full of worried kids that year.

During my 89 years, we have had just about every kind of weather for Thanksgiving that one could imagine, with no serious accidents either coming home or returning to school, or jobs after the holidays."

Quaday's Quotes -Partial (Reprinted with permission from RR Quaday) Faribault County Register Monday December 7, 2009

Semi-Retirement

In 1982, Michael, the youngest Quaday, decided to take over the operation of the family farm.

Mike Decides to Farm

"I would like to assure any and all of my young readers, that there is life after farming.

At one time, our boys, Jim and Mike, were up at 4 am all winter to feed two yards of lambs--just so they could be on the same wrestling team for the Blue Earth Bucs. They even made plans to farm together, after I retired. (They both liked farms, and the income we earned at that time in the 60s and 70s.)

However, by the time Jim entered medical school at the University of Minnesota, he already saw the writing on the barn for the end of farming as we knew it. I wanted Mike to take over the farming operation so I could ease out slowly, like my Dad did when I started farming back in 1938. He was ready and willing in 1982 when I became eligible for Social Security.

Jim went on to attain his doctor's degree, and two specialist's degrees, while Mike wasted two years and a ton of money fighting the Reagan Depression,

91

which cost our country untold thousands of young farmers.

After Mike and I had our farm sale (a very sad day), Mike went to technical school, in downtown St Paul for two and a half years. He has not had to search for a job since getting his diploma. The economy outside of the farm sector has boomed and still is in pretty good shape, even in spite of thousand worker lay-offs by many big corporations.

Had the boys carried through on their original plans to farm together, they would be mired in the morass the present day farmers are stuck in.

I, for one, am sure farming will get better, as I have been through three nasty farm depressions during my farming career. I also believe that, if one has once farmed on his own, he can do anything he wants to do and make a success of it--after washing the mud and manure off his boots. He will have to adopt a completely different outlook on life, getting away from the attitude of "There's always next year." The farmers of today will have to set their price for produce, before putting a seed in the ground, or setting up a breeding animal program. They will have to pool their productive capacity to set up a profitable enterprise."

Quaday's Quotes - partial (Reprinted with permission from RR Quaday) Faribault County Register Monday September 24, 2001

Quaday's Son Continues To Survive

"The youngest of our three sons is Michael, who was born in the "Baby Boom" generation in 1958. The fact that both Neva and I are the youngest in our respective families, made us sympathize with Mike to some extent, but not to the extent that he was a spoiled brat. He attended kindergarten in Blue Earth School, at which time he emptied the whole system one afternoon by setting off the fire alarm before he could read. He attended the first six grades at SS Peter and Paul Parochial School without making too many waves.

At that time, we watched two school buses go by, sometimes pulling them through the snow banks in front of our place, and then hauling our children to SS Peter and Paul School.

From the start, Mike was destined to be a farmer. He liked livestock and was a very good mechanic early on with machinery. His steers, pigs, and lambs were practically always blue ribbon, and he showed much time and effort fitting for showing at the Faribault County Fair. At that time, the Fair had an auction that was an auction, with blue ribbon stock bringing sizeable margins above market price.

In his Junior year, he went to work for Tafco Equipment Co., on a work study program through the school. He became a top notch welder, a talent he used working for Green Giant, and while working for me on our River Road Farm.

When he went to work for me, the repair bills dropped 50 percent and my machinery never had it so good. We worked together well as a team while he worked for me and later, when he began farming on his own. I worked for him for two years, and there was not one shouting match, which befalls many father-son teams.

The timing of his entry into farming could not have been worse. The Reagan Farm Depression was in full swing in 1982, his first year. He worked hard. He did a good job of farming for two years, at the end of which his $60,000 equity was gone, along with another sizeable wad borrowed from Production Credit Association.

Mike registered at St Paul Vo-Tech in March of 1985. He had attended Waseca Agricultural College for two winters, so had some credits to transfer. After two and one half years of living in a basement room, and studying hard, he graduated. Electronics was his major, with some hydraulics and electrical engineering courses. He repaired computers for Sears for a few months, before going to work for General Motion, an electric motor control company.

It was a new company that didn't get off the ground, and two years later, Mike was hired by a well-known tool company in Courtland, NY. On a visit to the Twin Cities, a friend talked him into interviewing for a job with Fenner International, also a motor control company. They needed him badly, having bought out General Motion, with no one understanding their systems.

Mike has now moved into the engineering division of Comtrex, a spin-off of Fenner Controls Corporation. His official title is technical service representative, whatever that means. Whatever happens, he is a survivor, and loves his job and a steady paycheck, which farming never had."

Quaday's Quotes (Reprinted with permission of RR Quaday) Faribault County Register, Monday, December 26, 1994

The Good Old Days

The Great Depression began with the Wall Street Crash of October, 1929, and rapidly spread throughout the country and the world. The market crash marked the beginning of a decade of high unemployment, poverty, low profits, deflation, plunging farm incomes, and lost opportunities for economic growth and personal advancement. The industries that suffered the most included construction, agriculture, as dust-bowl conditions persisted in the agricultural heartland, shipping, mining, and logging as well as durable goods like automobiles and appliances that could be postponed. The economy reached bottom in the winter of 1932–33; then came four years of very rapid growth until 1937, when the Recession of 1937 brought back 1934 levels of unemployment. The depression caused major political changes in America. Three years into the depression, Herbert Hoover lost the 1932 presidential election to Franklin Delano Roosevelt in a sweeping landslide. Roosevelt's economic recovery plan, the New Deal, instituted unprecedented programs for relief, recovery and reform, and brought about a major realignment of American politics.

The Great Depression in the years from 1931 through 1938, were tough years. Nobody had any money, the banks closed, farms were foreclosed, and farmers bartered their cream and eggs for groceries. Farm land sold for thirty dollars an acre. The harvested corn sold for ten cents a bushel. Farmers burned much of the ear corn for heat. The Quaday family nearly lost the Jo Daviess eighty acres because of the eight hundred dollar County Tile and Ditch Tax.

> "I can remember how, back in my childhood on River Road Farm, every discussion of farm finances invariably ended up in a derogatory mention of "The Ditch Tax." This tax was levied on the 80 acres of land which Dad and Mom purchased from Reinhold and Malvina Ristau, just after World War I. I was never informed as to the exact figure of the tax, but it must have been nearly as much as the purchase price of the land, because it took 20 years to pay it off, and keep the 80. During this time, the folks had a series of second-hand Fords, Model Ts, and later Model As."
>
> *Quaday's Quotes (Reprinted with permission from RR Quaday) Faribault County Register Monday June 28, 1993*

Remembering..."The Good Old Days"

1936 Little Brown Church in the Vale

"In the late 30s my brother Carl and Arlene Pringle, from Lakota, IA, were married at The Little Brown Church in The Vale at Nashua, IA. They stayed at Mom's and Dad's for two months while they remodeled their house on 3rd street. Arlene was a country school teacher, and had a pair of six foot skis to get her to school in winter, when the roads and weather got rough in IA. She decided she would no longer need the skis after giving up teaching to raise a family, and asked me if I wanted them. I enthusiastically said, "Yes." We had a very steep hill right in back of the barn, where we did a lot of downhill sledding and tobogganing--a great place to try out my new skis.

On a fine Sunday afternoon Dad turned the cattle out in the small yard to get some exercise and run in the snow. We had a good sled track down the hill, packed hard underneath, with an inch of new snow. Everything was ideal for skiing. Bear in mind that we had never seen any ski-jumping, because there was no Olympics and no TV. On my first run downhill an 800 pound steer decided to walk across the sled path, just about at the bottom of the sled run. I had a good speed up and there was nothing to do but hit or jump over him. I, in the half second that I had to make up my mind, jumped over him, and fortunately, stayed in the track, way out on the pond at the bottom of the hill. That was my one and only ski-jumping experience.

Later on that winter, we did some skiing behind our Model A Ford which could give one a good ride in the road ditch in second gear. One could take quite a spill going over driveways and uneven snow banks at 30 miles an hour. It didn't work so well after the blizzards banked the snow too high on our River Road. Our homemade toboggan, long enough for four kids, was always a good ride. It had a tin bottom so went pretty fast down the hill, but it had no steering mechanism and everybody bailed out when we headed for a tree or a fence post.

River Road Farm Sledding Hill

During The Great Depression nobody had any money, so we had to do our own things and make our own entertainment, most of the time out-of-doors.

The environment was certainly as healthy as one could ask for and the cheapest entertainment in the world. Usually after Christmas the River Road was blocked for automobile travel, but by then we had the double wagon box on the bobsled, and with a good team of horses we could haul the cream and eggs to town, covered up with our buffalo robe to keep them from freezing. The wood block paving on Main Street and Depot Street worked just fine for horses and bob-sleds. The incoming freight on the railroad was all hauled up to the stores by the W.D. Wilke Dray Line with a team and wagon, or sled.

The river flat west of town (The Pilot Grove Road) in those days was graveled and the north wind always blew the snow off, so the sleds had about a quarter of a mile of bare gravel on which the iron sled runners made the most unearthly squeal--somewhat like the screeching of chalk on a blackboard in school, only many decibels louder. We always held our mittens over our ears until we were back on snow. When the screech stopped, the team would always slow down; they too, were glad when it stopped. The team was tied to a hitching rail in back of Nate Gendler's grocery store where the folks traded eggs for groceries. Dad always saw to it that his team was well blanketed, because he kept them on a steady trot going into town and they were well warmed up. He liked a fast team and we only lived a mile and one half out. Those were "The Good Old Days."

Quaday's Quotes-partial (Reprinted with permission from RR Quaday) Faribault County Register Monday January 21, 2008

Remembering The Worst Years Of Farming

"Every time I hear anyone complain about the weather, I have to think back to the years 1933 through 1935, walking to District 104 School in such a dust storm that one had to walk backward so we could keep our eyes open enough to see the road. We hated to go outside for recess and noon lunch hour with the dirt blowing so hard off the plowed fields. The pastures and hay ground were safe from the wind, and thankfully the small grain areas, seeded down in disked up corn stalks didn't blow.

Our Jo Daviess "80" was particularly vulnerable to high wind, as there were no trees for miles to the west and northwest. It seemed that any wind direction in those years stripped topsoil off any exposed fields. In those days, everyone tried to plow their fields as black as possible to get the soil bed as free of trash as possible. The corn planters of that time had open shoes, which slid along the ground catching any trash in the field. The soil on the "80" was well adapted to raising peas, so we always had 15 or 20 acres of them.

The south 30 acres was still in virgin prairie, Kentucky Blue Grass, Timothy, and Redtop Grass--wonderful horse hay (we still farmed with horses). In 1934, the summer was so dry that the 30 acres of corn was not worth the job of hand picking, so Dad and Carl fenced the 80 with woven and barbed wire. He drove to Omaha and bought four carloads of feeder lambs, which were turned loose on the 80. When the corn stalks and leaves were gone, we fed up the hay stacks. We hauled water from the well at home with a covered tank, with a team and lumber wagon, until it snowed. The lambs ate snow and did wonderfully well. On New Year's Day we drove them home and they were fat, so we drove them to the railroad and shipped them to Chicago.

In the spring of 1935, the dirt on the "80" blew so much that the woven wire fence was covered up and the road ditches were level full. The demand for horse hay disappeared when a great number of horses died from sleeping sickness, so we plowed up most of the low hay ground and planted corn. In the fall, we took the dry cows and young stock over to the "80" until Christmas, again hauling water with free feed. We did this for about 3 more years until the fall of 1938, when the fall was so wet that we didn't get the corn picked until the following spring. I took the top boxes off, as the team couldn't pull any more than that. We reloaded to another trailer out on the road, to haul it home. Much of it was moldy, but the cattle ate it and didn't get sick and the hogs sorted out what they wanted, so nobody got hurt.

When I took over the farm in 1938, I decided that never again would the dirt blow away to Ohio or Wisconsin, so I began to set my plow to leave trash on top so the spring wind would not be a problem. I was ridiculed by some of my neighbors for my awful looking job of plowing, but within a few years the experiment stations had everyone doing the same thing. Now most farmers are going to less till, and no-till, to save soil and moisture, and have adopted conservation practices. I guess I was a few years ahead of my time, but it gratifies me somewhat to have been ahead of the pack on an important issue like soil saving and conservation practices. I still do not feel that the corn-soybean rotation is the best for our soils in this area, but it is easy and makes money, so let's do it for the present.

When one thinks back to 60 and 70 years ago, it's almost impossible to imagine how difficult it was and how much work we did by hand, and the progress farmers have made since horse and buggy days."

Quaday's Quotes -partial (Reprinted with permission from RR Quaday) Faribault County Register Monday September 21, 2009

Surviving During Lean Years On The Farm

"The summer of 1935 was a fairly average one, occurring as it did in the middle of a series of hot dry years. The crops were good but the prices during The Great Depression were disastrous for the farmers. The cream and eggs checks kept life going. We always had food to eat which was more than the unemployed city folks. The eggs were traded for food, the cream check for clothes, gasoline and expenses.

The lack of cash money contributed to the disheartening about the farm debt situations. We could not pay the interest on loans, and taxes on the land.

Our family was no different than most, except the continued pressure to survive injured the health of my Dad to the point where he developed adhesions in his shoulder muscles and a nerve rash around his mouth that would not go away.

1912 William Henry Quaday in California

He had 160 acres all paid for at the start of the Depression in 1931. By 1935 he couldn't pay the interest and taxes out of the farm income. My oldest brother, Carl, was in car sales at the Motor Inn Co. He would take leave during the corn picking time and since he was a fast picker, he made enough to loan Dad the tax money, and also loan money to my sister, Marie, who was then attending Winona State Teachers College.

The biggest problem was Dad's health, because he was discouraged enough to quit farming, which was all he really knew. A family decision was made to borrow $1000 from my grandpa Charley Quaday to pay up the small bills and send Dad to California with him for the winter.

That winter was the toughest of the century with temperatures below zero for 21 consecutive days. I missed one day of school. I had been walking to school most of the time, but we were out of wood for the furnace and had been using a pile of oak stumps which we had pulled up before the freeze-up. I could not get all the chores done, so we made a decision to buy a bobsled of coal. This is the only time I remember buying coal for fuel, but with Dad laid up through the fall we lacked enough wood to get through the tough winter. Dad came home in late March with a good tan and a better outlook on life. He farmed for another 15 years and didn't move to town until 1949. In the meantime I had grown up prematurely and had tough times permanently etched in my memory."

Quaday's Quotes -partial (Reprinted with permission from RR Quaday) Faribault County Register Monday, January 14, 1991

Each winter, we cut down enough trees to furnish our kitchen stove and the furnace with fuel for the coming year. After we had a sufficient number of logs piled up in the yard, the wood sawyers came and in a few hours cut all the logs into stove-length pieces which were then split into small pieces for the kitchen range, or left in chunks for the furnace. In order to have a supply of dry wood for the winter, we loaded it onto the wagon, hauled it to the house and threw it down through one of the basement windows and stacked it neatly next to the furnace.

1935 Blizzard at Oak Ridge Farm

"So far, this winter is shaping up very similar to the winters we old-timers experienced back in the Dust Bowl 30s, during The Great Depression. There was no respite from snow, blizzards and cold weather, which followed faithfully every week. In the winter of 1935-36, the snow wasn't measured in inches, it was feet--but it never stayed on the level long enough to measure. Before it stopped snowing, the northwest wind came up, making white-out conditions which everyone called blizzards in those days. For 21 days straight the temperature never got above zero. Believe me we burned a lot of wood that winter. During the dry summers we took a team of horses and a good log chain out in the woods where the drought had killed about 50 big burr oak trees in 1933-34 and pulled up the stumps."

Quaday's Quotes-partial (Reprinted with permission from RR Quaday) Faribault County Register Monday February 9, 2009

At the time of my childhood years there was only one disease that was under control--smallpox. Everyone was vaccinated for smallpox. But the other childhood diseases we suffered through as a matter of course, including measles, whooping cough, chicken pox, frequent colds, and worst of all was the flu. Nobody went to the hospital unless he or she was on the verge of death. My Mother had many home remedies to ease the discomforts. Some of them, like the mustard plaster and doses of castor oil, were sources of dread and seemed to cause more pain than they cured. Mother also had a good deal of faith in teas of various kinds: clover blossom, elderflower, ginger, pumpkin seed, peppermint, catnip, chamomile, and wintergreen. These we didn't object to--in fact, they tasted very good, especially when sweetened with some of the honey which our bees had gathered. There were four diseases which were especially dreaded and from which several children in our area died: scarlet fever, diphtheria, tetanus and polio. Luckily, we never caught any of these.

Hand Me Downs

"The "Hand me down" sequence of events, out on our River Road Farm during the 20s and 30s when I was a lad out on our mud road and all through country school, was in full force.

I had two older brothers, Carl and John, so by the time I inherited clothes too good to throw away the colors were drab and very probably, Mother had mended a few tears in vital places. Times were hard out on the farm, even before The Great Depression of the 30s. Being the "Caboose" as Dad always introduced me, did have some advantages, but getting a lot of new clothes was not one of them.

The folks, by the time I came along, had been through the mill and understood kids somewhat better than they did on the first three. My sister, Marie, was seven years old when I was born, so she was a built-in baby sitter at home when Mother was occupied with household tasks. When all else failed Mother would take me along, up until the age of four, to Missionary Society meetings which were held in homes at that time.

I can remember having a difficult time going "potty" in a strange bathroom. Of course, Mother, who talked fluent German, used the Kraut version "Tupp," when mentioning such "tings." My childhood also included a two-holer out behind the corn crib. The red paint on the privy had faded but the roof and interior were still in good condition. I read just the other day

1928 William Henry Quaday Family

that the reason the two-holers were always located some distance from the house was fear of germs.

Back to hand-me-downs. The first suit I ever had was ordered from whom else? Sears and Roebuck. I was eight years old and the reason I was blessed with the new suit was because Mother wanted a professional family picture taken before Carl left home. The suit was a tan, two pants, wool suit. One pair of trousers was long which I liked; the other, knickers, which I hated with a passion. Which one do you suppose Mother decided I must wear for the Picture? The despised knickers of course. The photographer could not get a smile out of me to save his soul. To add to the insult, the other boys had a barber haircut in town while Mother cut mine in a "Page Boy" bob, another style I hated. I had a bad day!

Later, when I attended Blue Earth City School, Mother asked around the relation if anyone had a suit which had been outgrown and was still good. Aunt Bertha Neuhalfen found one of Cousin Lloyd's that was in pretty good condition, so after school I went to Aunt Bertha's and changed clothes for the Freshman-Sophomore party, wearing my cousin's suit. It was a good, navy blue, pinstripe and it fit me pretty well. I was not ashamed to go thus to a party, having been brought up to "hold my mouth right," for any and all occasions. I had fun, even though I was too bashful to ask girls to dance. That all came later.

I finally worked my way out of the hand-me-down category by the time of the Junior-Senior Prom in 1936. I bought a new suit, ordered from Mont gomery Ward, for $17.50, paid for with my bicycle shop money. Finally, I could be proud of my clothes and lose some of the country backward feelings that I was plagued with in former times."

Quaday's Quotes -partial (Reprinted with permission from RR Quaday) Faribault County Register Monday July 24, 2000

"During The Great Depression, it was very fortunate for us kids that Mother was an accomplished seamstress. She mended all our overalls and coveralls when the knees and seats wore out, and even sewed dresses for herself and my sister, Marie. She altered patterns and when she was finished, everything fit. The few months that we lived with my folks, we were newly married, and Neva learned a lot about sewing and cooking before we moved over next door to the Sailor Place, where we had no electricity, running water, or sewer system. It was 1943 and Second World War Time, and it was three years before we were able to wire the farm for electricity and dig a new well next to our house and have good water."

Quaday's Quotes (Reprinted with permission from RR Quaday) Faribault County Register Monday December 24, 2007 Partial

Most of our toys and playthings were homemade or else discarded items like old tires which we rolled around the yard trying to see who could keep his going the longest. We also had an old buggy axle with its two wheels still intact. One of us stood on each end, using the hubs inside and outside the wheel to stand on, and controlling the speed and direction of the wheel with our hands. The object was to try to dump the other guy off by suddenly stopping or changing direction. As far as I know that game was an original with us! Discarded bedspreads and blankets were our tents and the ladder was our monkey bar on which we chinned ourselves and did other acrobatic stunts. We made a swing out of a discarded tire and some old rope (sometimes it was too old and let us down with a jolt). On rainy days we put rugs up against the bedroom door and on the floor and bounced marbles off the door trying to see if we could capture the other guy's marble by either hitting it or coming close enough to span the distance with our fingers. We also had a miniature croquet set made out of tinker-toy sticks, clothes-pins, spools and wire, and using marbles as balls. We could set this up on the front room rug and play it by the hour. The one exception to the home-made collection was the red wagon bought at the hardware store. It was regarded partly as a toy but served as a necessity as well for hauling various loads too heavy to carry.

Taken from Overture to Anderson Unfinished Symphony, 1914-1942, written by Marie Anderson.

Christmas During the Depression
Ghosts of Christmas Past

"Our early winter taste of snow and frigid northwest wind reminds me of my boyhood days out on our River Road Farm, and walking the half mile to District 104 School in rough winter weather. Maybe the winters felt colder and more severe to me at that time in life, because I was smaller and younger. The statistics do bear me out on the fact that they were colder. We did always have a least three northwest blizzards every winter. The drifts probably looked higher to me at four feet in height, than they did later in life when I grew up to 6-foot-1. With no snow plows on the road, and no snow blowers invented yet, we did walk through deep snow and high drifts.

Our family had the best winter paradise a person could ask for--we had a 50 foot sliding hill right below the farm buildings and facing the east so it was sheltered from the prevailing winter winds. Twenty rods farther east we had a bayou for ice skating and playing games--which we invented to fit the weather and snow conditions. On milder days when the wind was south, we had a steeper and longer hill out in the 40-acre pasture for sliding, skiing or tobogganing. It didn't take very much snow to make that hill (we called it "The Big Hill") very slippery.

In the depths of the Great Depression, Christmas was mighty slim at our house with a Christmas tree cut from our own arborvitae hedge around the front of our big farmhouse. It was decorated with strings of popcorn, a few ancient bulbs, and several strings of tinsel which was removed carefully, for use the next year. Four or five pieces of ribbon candy and a bright star on the top completed the decoration of the tree. We always strung a couple of well-worn red and green ropes (paper) from corner to corner in our dining room, attached to the central chandelier over the dining table. It was quite festive and economical.

My Mother was really good at knitting, so when times were hard she knit our wool mittens and scarves for Christmas presents. The knit wool stockings were warm, and in combination with the sheepskin moccasins that we wore to country school, kept our feet warm even when sitting still for longer periods of time. The woolen mittens were just fine as long as they were dry, but the minute we got into a snowball fight or played games outside, that got them wet and they were nothing but cold. The knitted wool stockings served two purposes in Depression times, as they were hung up above the register with homemade chocolate fudge, oranges, peanuts in the shell and popcorn--so we always had a present."

Quaday's Quotes - Partial (Reprinted with permission from RR Quaday) Faribault County Register Monday December 28, 2009

Music Always a Big Part Of Family Christmas

"Until I attained the age of twelve I was a boy soprano and could carry a tune. I was used in Christmas programs at the old Evangelical Church. We presented cantatas, plays and Bible story events every year on Christmas Eve on the old stage, with the lectern removed. We were cramped for space but adapted to Holy Land scenery as best we could. The church members took everything and our efforts into consideration and applauded, although somewhat reserved, at the conclusion. Yes, applause was permitted in our Church at that time at Christmas and weddings.

Our family was quite musical, although never professionally inclined. My grandmother, Mary Willmert, played the foot pump organ in the Evangelical Church. My Mother inherited the organ and we had great fun with it while growing up. My sister, Marie, actually could play tunes on it. My siblings all were privileged to take music lessons, but The Great Depression made a casualty out of my miscellaneous lessons. My sister, Marie, could play pretty fair piano and married a concert pianist with a Master's degree in Music Education. My Dad and my Uncle Herman both had clear first tenor voices, but never used them except to sing hymns in church. My brother, Carl, could play piano and accordion but never sang, except after a drink or two of spirits.

When Uncle Herm and Carl got together, Herm played the violin and Carl accompanied him on his accordion, while Marie played the piano. When the rest of us sang along we made a lot of music. I never heard of anyone trying to hire us, but we had a lot of fun, especially around Christmas time.

Before TV, I think families had more good times doing our own thing--playing games, eating popcorn and fudge. We played ping-pong on an extended dining room table, a big one. It would seat 14 adults comfortably. Occasionally, my Mother would invite Frank Willmert, a bachelor farmer and distant relative who lived on South River Road, to Sunday dinner. He loved to sing when Marie played the piano and the family joined in."

Quaday's Quotes -partial (Reprinted with permission from RR Quaday) Faribault County Register Monday December 27, 2010

Politics

The Eighteenth Amendment of the United States Constitution established Prohibition in the United States. The separate Volstead Act set down methods of enforcing the Eighteenth Amendment, and defined which "intoxicating liquors" were prohibited, and which were excluded from prohibition (for example, for medical and religious purposes). The Amendment was ratified on January 16, 1919.

The Eighteenth Amendment was the result of decades of effort by temperance movements and at the time was generally considered a progressive amendment. Many state legislatures had already enacted statewide prohibition prior to the ratification of the Eighteenth Amendment. The amendment and its enabling legislation did not ban the consumption of alcohol, but made it difficult to obtain alcoholic beverages legally.

Demand for liquor continued, and the law resulted in the criminalization of producers, suppliers, transporters and consumers. The police, courts and prisons were overwhelmed with new cases; organized crime increased in power, and corruption expanded among law enforcement officials. The amendment was repealed in 1933 by ratification of the Twenty-first Amendment, the only instance in United States history of repeal of a constitutional amendment.

Remembering The Great Depression and Its Politics

"The December weather makes me think back to The Great Depression of the 30s, when almost every rented farm had new tenants shortly after the first of March. The renter didn't make enough money selling crops off the farm to pay cash rent, and the landlord couldn't sell his share of the crop to live another year until the new crop came in. Some of the renters bought new machinery on credit, and at year's end couldn't make the payments, so it was a time of heavy speculation on farm land, as well as the New York stock markets, and woe unto the guy who bought land on the pyramid plan. He used the equity on one farm to pay down on a second farm, and so on, until he was deeply in debt on all of them.

1925 Frederick G Levenick family

My Grandfather, Fred Levenick, Jr., was one of the plungers who became caught in this trap, and he, like many others, had to go through bankruptcy and start over in WI. He had a large family from his second marriage to Lydia Fenske. His first wife, Mary Willmert, died at age 29 of an inoperable brain tumor leaving a son, Walter, and daughter, Lorena, my Mother. As soon as he was old enough to enlist, Walter joined the Army and went through the First World War in the communications department. From there, after the war was over, it was an easy step into the postal department of the United States landing in Rockford, IL, and finishing his career in the postal department.

Walter had learned to drink alcoholic beverages while in the Army, and was known to relish a drink or two, or three. Mother had several drinking uncles who had the same problem, so she was a strong advocate of alcoholic Prohibition when it became the 18th Amendment and Al Smith, the Mayor of New York City, ran for repeal. Actually, the campaign was fought mainly on this one issue. The country, except for agriculture, was in a great round of prosperity and the stock market was sky high.

Mother wore her Hoover and Curtis lapel button proudly, even to church and Ladies Aid meetings. Dad put his in a dresser and there it stayed. I believe it was still in his wooden jewelry box when he died. I have the box. I must remind myself to look for it someday. It would be quite an antique, as it was never worn. Mother came out ahead on that election, but of course, Mr. Hoover had The Great Depression hung around his neck and was soundly whipped in the 1932 election by Franklin D. Roosevelt. The 18th Amendment was dispatched, forthwith, so President Roosevelt was anything but a hero where Mother was concerned.

The fact that FDR literally dragged the country out from depression never swayed her thinking one bit, even though the farm program, the Agricultural Adjustment Act, allowed Dad and Mom to hang onto the Jo Daviess 80 and forestalled a foreclosure on it. They had the home 80 acres paid for, so could borrow to make the payments on the new 80. They, unlike a great many of their friends, hung on and eventually paid off the mortgage on the whole quarter section. Dad very well knew that the Democratic Administrations of his day were much more understanding of farm problems than the conservative Republicans, so there were never any political arguments in our house. They both knew where the other stood, and that was that.

Dad knew the Levenick history very well, and he was determined to avoid the mistakes his Father-in-law had made, and it made him a little too cautious. Having lived through and survived The Great Depression also made his generation too wary of too much debt, even if it appeared to be a fairly safe bet to succeed. After such a close call in the 30s, he would never again sign a mortgage. I am trying to compare the present day economy to the economy of the 20s, with a hotly contested presidential election in the offing, a war being fought, and billions of dollars to be spent by both political parties to gain control of our government and the power that goes with control.

The difference between the 1928 campaign and the 2008, is the terribly early start and the value of each dollar being spent. One thing that could

109

turn out the same is a New York Mayor singing "Happy days are here, again." Heaven forbid!"

Quaday's Quotes-partial (Reprinted with permission from RR Quaday) Faribault County Register Monday June 20, 2005

The Agricultural Adjustment Act (enacted in 1933) was a United States federal law of the New Deal which restricted agricultural production by paying farmers subsidies not to plant part of their land (that is, to let a portion of their fields lie fallow) and to kill off excess livestock. Its purpose was to reduce crop surplus and therefore effectively raise the value of crops. The money for these subsidies was generated through an exclusive tax on companies which processed farm products. The Act created a new agency, the Agricultural Adjustment Administration, to oversee the distribution of the subsidies. It is considered the first modern U.S. farm bill.

The Agricultural Adjustment Act of 1938 removed the funding of the subsidies by a food processors tax and replaced it with financing from the Federal Government.

Quaday Recalls Fairs Of Yesteryear

"In my childhood days on River Road Farm, the Faribault County Fair was one of the few events I was allowed to "Go along with Dad, all day."

He cared not for carnivals or girly shows, at least not with his youngest son in tow, but when the harness horse races started, Dad was right in the front row, so to speak.

There were usually two days of harness races during the four-day fair, with two and four horse teams entered in pulling contests. The horse events were always rather boring for me at that age, except when the trotters would break stride or the sulkies would run too close together and an upset would occur drawing gasps from the crowd.

It was exciting to see the sulky drivers try to hang onto the reins, which were necessarily short, besides trying to keep from getting run over.

They'd get up, muddy and shouting curses at each other but too busy trying to control their horses to start a fight at that point. Sometimes that happened later down by the horse barn (the old one, which is still there). I'm sure those would have interested Dad, had I not been along. Maybe, in retrospect, that's why Mom sent me along on harness race day. I believe the great trotter, Dan Patch, appeared at the Faribault County Fair, drawing huge crowds.

Dad was not a betting man so that part did not interest him; however, if a fight started he would be in the front row, watching.

1917 Faribault County Fair Grounds

I cannot recall that either of my folks ever exhibited stock or fancy work at the fair.

Mother didn't care for crowds or dust so her visits to the fair were limited to the Floral Hall or, if a renowned lecturer was booked, she was in the front row.

Dad always figured that 4-H clubs were a waste of time and although Mother was in favor of any kind of education, she never insisted that we be allowed to join."

Quaday's Quotes - partial (Reprinted with permission from RR Quaday) Faribault County Register Monday July 27, 1992

The Weather

Think This is Cold? Try 21 Days Below Zero in 1936

"We are having an 'old fashioned winter,' one that reminds me of the winters in the 1920s and the 1930s. Most of them in those days, had feet, not just inches of snow. The parts of those winters that I remember best were the three-day blizzards, with the howling northwest wind blowing enough snow to cut visibility to near zero. When the wind died down, the below zero cold set in and lasted for many days, sometimes weeks.

In January, 1936, we had 21 days when the temperature never got above zero, and one morning we woke up to 31 degrees below zero. I didn't get to school that day. We already had deep snow with drifts filling our dense grove of 90-foot tall Oak trees, and chokecherry trees with undergrowth of gooseberry bushes, filled with drifts.

That allowed the snow to drift across the road and cover our dooryard with drifts 4 and 5 feet high and hard enough to walk over when we were carrying our milk from the barn to the basement and back out to the hogs after separating. No gas-powered engines would start during that month.

Luckily, we had electricity as we were hooked up to the Blue Earth power plant in 1918, when most farmers could only dream about it. We had a three horse electric motor on wheels, which we pulled around the yard to pump water for the livestock, shell corn and grind feed for the milk cows, chickens and hogs. It took two men to drag the heavy motor over the snow banks, but it was too cold to put runners on it. We didn't have an indoor shop at that time.

We did get our mail--except in the worst blizzards--Earl Ryan and Jack McClosky changing off driving the teams and cutter. They drove the light cutter, which belonged to Bill Ryan, Earl's brother, who owned the livery barn on Nicollet Street at the time. Every farmer drove a team and bobsled and had to find their way to town to haul their cream and eggs to town and do their trading. A great deal of business was done on the barter basis in those days, because nobody had any money.

The barber shops suffered because most men let their hair grow until spring. The art of cosmetology had not been popularized yet. The women did their own hair-cutting and styling, with most of them braiding and styling their hair into a bun.

Every church had a hitching rail out back of the church for farmers to tie up and blanket their horses. My Mother inherited a buffalo robe for our bobsled rides to town, and Dad had a coonskin coat and hat with ear lappers and fur mittens for driving the team.

There was a hitching rail back of Eder's Department Store, where the law offices now stand. We usually sold eggs and bought groceries at Nate Gendler's next door. He would pay one cent per dozen more if one bought their groceries there. He paid a penny more for pop bottles that my brother, John, and I picked up along the road and at the city dump across the Blue Earth River.

If Dad bought more than $10 worth of groceries, Nate always gave us each a nickel's worth of the candy of our choice from his glassed-candy case. He also bought wool and hides from butchered animals, weighed up in the big barn on Nicollet that is now owned by Mike and Val Blumenschein, and is dressed up far better than it was in the old days. Sadly, the old Gendler store is now empty. I leaned on many barrels of apples, oranges and grapefruit while waiting for Dad to give us a ride home in the bobsled. There were always many sacks of flour and sugar; the flour in cotton sacks, the sugar in lined burlap bags. The whiskey drinkers, during prohibition times, drank mostly malt for a mix. Malt bottles were one cent higher than pop. When Bill Henderson lived in the Sailor Place, he was the neighborhood bootlegger, so my brother, John, and I had good bottle hunting when we had time. It kept us in spending money for a circus or fourth of July firecrackers."

Quaday's Quotes (Reprinted with permission from RR Quaday) Faribault County Register Monday January 24, 2011

The Flood of 1938

1938 Flood, River Road McCloskey Flats

1938 Flood, Pilot Grove Road West of Swimming Pool

That was the highest water I ever saw in my 65 years of living on River Road. Lake Blue Earth's shore began at our sliding hill and went right past town, with the blacktop flat southwest of town under five feet of water with a mighty strong current. The flood lasted for 10 days and we were out of hog feed. I loaded up our trailer with a triple box with oats and barley mixture and headed for town, and the Farmer's Elevator, after the water had gone down a couple of feet. Dad rode on the trailer to keep me from driving downstream, which is easy to do with a fast current like that. He had done things like this before, telling me to look far ahead at the bridge (the one that was there before the one now being torn out).

There was a crowd on the bridge watching our progress and Norman Hanson was taking pictures. He was always going to give me one--I guess he forgot. We went around the western route home with the hog feed, arriving home at about chore time. Our pasture land was all under water, so we had to feed precious alfalfa hay with some oats and ear corn, long before winter began. While I was hauling manure with our bay team on the oats stubble, the mosquitoes were nearly a half inch thick on the canvas fly nets, which were so crusted with salt and sweat that the mosquitoes couldn't bite them.

114

I didn't get a furrow plowed until late October, and had to wrap the furrow wheel on the tractor with log chains since it was so wet. I couldn't afford manufactured chains, if there were any made yet at that time."

Quaday's Quotes - partial (Reprinted with permission from RR Quaday) Faribault County Register Monday August 30, 2010

Remembering The Blizzards of Past Years

"In years past, the weather warning system was not available to inform people of the forthcoming storm. The loss of life was greater in those years of storms than present day storms. The Armistice Day Blizzard on November 11, 1940, had no warning except the weather pattern itself, which tipped off old-timers born and raised in the area.

That storm happened nearly 70 years ago, but I can remember every detail, perhaps better than it if had happened yesterday. Dad and I had received a shipment of broken mouthed ewes on Saturday morning, November 9, from Omaha. Their two front teeth were missing or broken, so they could no longer graze, but could still raise a lamb if fed a grain supplement. They were tired and weak from the trip, but in good shape otherwise. It rained all night Sunday, then Monday morning at six o'clock (milking time) it was turning to snow and a bit foggy.

Mother woke me up, telling me the furnace was smoking and she didn't want Dad up on the roof when it was slippery. Dad had always been able to climb like a cat, so had no safety rope up on our three-story farmhouse. He put a short ladder on our front porch, raised it up beside the dormer and climbed between the electric wires and dormer, up the side of the house. It was tricky, but I got it done his way and let the old generator down the chimney to clear the creosote and stop the smoke.

After chores and breakfast, we tried to drive the ewes into the straw shed banked with flax straw bales that I had built for shelter. They had never been in a shed and it was dark in there. Many of them had to be helped up, their wool sopping wet and heavy. It took us over an hour to move them 100 feet and into the shelter. Monday morning was cream day, so we loaded up and headed for town.

It was snowing and blowing so hard I couldn't see the road, so turned around at Wehsener's and put the car in the shed. My sister, Marie, brought

115

a guest home from Winona Teachers College and I was going to drive them to Winona that afternoon. It didn't happen! It stormed for three days and roads were not cleared until Thursday--and then were barely passable. When we turned the cows out to water, they sniffed the air and ran back in the barn. I tried to carry hay out of the barn to the ewes, but the wind blew it all away (loose hay). The ewes didn't see feed or water for three days, yet we only lost four, weak as they were. We had a good grove and sheltered yard, but it was still rough on the stock for three days.

The loss of human life, livestock, turkeys, smashed cars and trucks, was almost impossible to calculate. This was well before the advent of computers. The farmers that raised hogs in A-coops on alfalfa pasture had heavy losses, as did the turkey farmers and rangeland ranchers, who had no shelter for their stock. The cattle drifted with the wind until coming to a fence corner, where they were piled up and frozen to death. With no warning system, there was no way to round up stock after the storm struck.

The sod busters who pioneered the Corn Belt and the rangeland back in the 1880s must have been tough individuals indeed, to fight through blizzards, early fall and late spring--sometimes during calving and lambing time. The weather could make or break a farmer or rancher just in the matter of two or three days."

Quaday's Quotes-partial (Reprinted with permission from RR Quaday) Faribault County Register Monday November 24, 2008

Minnesota Lake, MN

In 1865 the early settlers of Minnesota Lake came to hunt, fish, farm the rich soil, and raise their families. The town site, named after the adjacent lake, exists today as a prosperous farming community. The town puts on a celebration known as Festag Days, (Festival of Agriculture) a two-day festival held in July. It includes agriculture and livestock competitions, a carnival, large parade, horse show, tractor pull and a queen coronation.

Festag Parade Was Always Grand

"One Sunday afternoon in early October of 1936, Orval Paschke and I headed for Blue Earth with Dad's Chevy. When we started down Harry

Ehrich's hill we saw a great plume of black smoke coming up northeast of Blue Earth.

We had no particular plans for the time, so we drove east to see what was burning. We got as far as Easton and still hadn't reached the fire. We followed the old nine corner road to Minnesota Lake, where we were informed that the farmers were burning off the grass and weeds in the lake.

During the dust bowl days of the 30s, the lake had been drained and a great share of it was being farmed and pastured. There was very little wind that day, so the black, billowing cloud of smoke rose straight up and could be seen for many miles in all directions. It was my first visit to Minnesota Lake, and the town at that time was not too impressive.

Neva was born and raised in Minnesota Lake, where her Dad, Helmuth (Moot) Fischer was a mechanic for Beske Implement, and later for Putz Brothers Implement. In 1938, the family moved to Blue Earth and Moot was employed by the Faribault County Highway Department. The Fischers were long time residents of the Minnesota Lake area, with Moot's brothers and cousins operating farms near town.

Practically all the businesses in town were agriculture related until Haakon Nordaas established his home-building business. It was no wonder, then, that the yearly city celebration was later named "The Festival of Agriculture, or Festag." Neva and I always took the children to the Festag parade, with Neva's Aunt Lydia Beske, inviting us to view it from her lawn on Main Street.

1924 Festag Day Parade, MN Lake, MN

This was always one of the better parades in our area with many machinery innovations, floats, bands and one time, even Miss America participated. My youngest son, Mike, had been taught to do the "Wolf Whistle" by the older children and I told him, "Now when Miss America comes by, you give a good loud whistle." He did, and at first, she could not believe that much whistle came from such a little kid. But when he blew another one, she turned and gave him a nice smile and a cheery wave.

After World War II, Neva's folks moved back to Minnesota Lake. Moot built a new house, so I got in on quite a bit of finishing, yard work, and landscaping. He went to work for Putz Brothers, which is right next door to the first self-service restaurant in the State.

This establishment was owned and operated by the Penheiters, John and his son, Norbert. Moot and I would come in the back door, pour our coffee, and usually make some kind of sandwich. The refrigerator was always well stocked with several choices. Rolls and doughnuts were always on hand. John, who was getting along in years, did all the potato peeling using his own private stool in the kitchen. When we finished our lunch, we put the money in a bowl on the first shelf.

Norbert, who loved to visit with people, always gave Moot a rough time about some event they shared years back. He always gave our kids a hard time when they came in for ice cream or candy, telling them that he sold goodies to their Mother when she was a little girl.

When we decided to build a new house we dealt with Nordaas, with Tom Wilhelmi contracting the work. We were well satisfied with the whole deal, ending up with a well built house fitting our specification.

Our trips to Minnesota Lake are becoming farther apart these days, but the town holds many pleasant memories for our family."

Quaday's Quotes (Reprinted with permission from RR Quaday) Faribault County Register Monday April 26, 1993

Celebrating the Fourth With Fireworks

"When we were growing up on River Road, we bought firecrackers with our pop and malt money. The six-pack of cherry bombs cost 10 cents and a braided pack of small poppers cost a nickel. Occasionally, when we ran out of money, Dad would give us one more nickel, but that was the end of it. He would always tell us "That's my last nickel" with a straight face. Maybe it actually was his last one.

Times were tough during The Great Depression. The one big splurge I remember was the time Mother packed a picnic lunch and we drove to Clear Lake, IA, in our Model A Ford Tudor. Dad bought ice cream that day; we usually bought a cake of ice and made our own at home.

Years later, when our kids were growing up, times were a little better. We still made our own ice cream with a wooden tub freezer. The ice house on the south end of town was still operating. One cake of ice with lots of salt did the trick, as the children practically fought to turn the handle of the freezer. We made cherry, chocolate, vanilla and lemon. It was good, made with sweet cream and rich, not pumped full of air like bought ice cream. Those were the days."

Quaday's Quotes (Reprinted with permission from RR Quaday) Faribault County Register Monday July 21, 2008

The Sailor Place

In 1855 Moses Sailor came from Iowa looking for the headwaters of the Blue Earth River. He found what he was looking for, and liked it. He built a cabin and stayed there and became the first resident of Faribault County.

> "We kids were always scared to walk by Henderson's on the way to school at 104, because there was a lot of traffic and drunks doing the driving. Years later when Alvin Weber built *The Chicken Shack* in the orchard, the drinking traffic was thicker yet, but we were older and it meant more bottles to sell.
>
> Of course, that all dried up when Franklin D. Roosevelt was elected President in 1932 and the 18th Amendment was repealed. Then all we had to sell were beer bottles. But by then we were older and had other ways to pick up a few bucks. The patterns of life have changed many times through my lifetime, and we had to learn to adapt."

Quaday's Quotes (Reprinted with permission from RR Quaday) Faribault County Register Monday January 24, 2011

"*The Chicken Shack* was a building that was built to resemble a brooder house in the orchard on the Old Sailor Place. There was no alcohol sold in the City of Blue Earth at this time, and Bill Henderson lived on the Sailor Place. He would frequent the local social affairs wearing very high boots that would hold a one-half pint of 'home brew'. Hence the term 'bootlegger'. Word traveled around, and the residents from the city would drive the one-and one-half mile to the Sailor Place to purchase the booze. In the winter months the rear wheel drive cars would get stuck, and a team of horses would have to pull them out of the snow.

Mr. Henderson did not make the brew in a still near The Chicken Shack. The still was located on the Old Elmore Road, southeast of the Rendering Plant. The Quaday potato patch was located across the river from the Rendering Plant in the lower pasture. The bottles of booze were manually carried to the Sailor Place, with a steady stream of groups of two or three people. When the planting and caring of the potato patch was done by the Quaday children, they saw all of this traffic, and it scared them. Grandma Lorena warned them about people who drank and how dangerous they were. All of these events occurred before the repeal of the 18th Amendment by FDR, in 1932. After Alvin Weber was arrested and things settled down, The Chicken Shack was physically moved from the property, never to be seen again."

Conversation with RR Quaday - January 27, 2011, by phone.

In 1942, Neva and I bought the farm just south of the River Road Farm, known as The Sailor Place, paying four thousand five hundred dollars. When we moved in on January first 1943, we had no running water, no sewer, no electricity, no cupboards or closets in the house. We lived there for six years. I was busy making improvements; digging a new well, shingling the house and the barn, installing a new foundation for the barn, painting all the buildings, wiring for electricity, digging the sewer, building the chicken coop and brooder house, building a new machine shed and corn crib, and digging in the tile.

"After I attended "Cow College," I met Neva and we married in 1942. Living with one's in-laws is not the most satisfactory way, so we looked for a farm close to the River Road Home Place.

It happened that Mr. Wesley Morgan owned the Sailor Place next door, where he used to haul garbage out from town to feed his hogs. The rest went into the ravine leading to the river. He agreed to sell me the 80 acres for $60 per acre.

Right then I got my first valuable lesson in real estate. I didn't make out a contract or pay money down. A couple of months went by and I spoke to Mr. Morgan again because it was time to start fall plowing. He said, "Another farmer offered me $65 per acre and he has the money."

I made a quick trip to town, sold my new car to Mr. Howard Essler for the down payment and drew up a contract, but I had to pay the $65 per acre. I went to the old State Bank to borrow the remaining $5000. They turned me down cold unless Dad would sign the mortgage note. All the livestock and machinery was paid for and a good crop was coming in. I went to the bank across the street and they told me the same thing. Mr. Mike Haase was running the Federal Land Bank and sent an appraiser out to the Sailor Place, and assured me it was a sure thing. The appraiser drove by on the road, never even stopping in to look over the situation. There was no crop planted that year due to the death of Mrs. Pete Morgan, which dropped Mr. Morgan into a deep depression. The appraiser mistook the flower of the hour as Canadian Thistles, and refused the loan.

Dad and I went to Elmore to the National Bank, presided over by the late Art Weyer, who had known Dad for many years. He felt that if I was anything like my Dad, I was good for the loan. He needed Dad to co-sign for bank money, but offered me an option of keeping my checking account and buying my insurance through his bank until the $5000 note was paid. The deal was made, and it was a personal loan from his pocket to mine, with a wish of 'good luck'. The interest was 5 percent, and I was a land owner at the age of 22 years. Neva and I moved in 1943, one fourth mile to the Sailor Place."

Quaday's Quotes-partial (Reprinted with permission from RR Quaday) Faribault County Register Monday, February 4, 1991

Sailor Place Abstract

"According to the property abstracts from the safe deposit box at Mid-America Bank, the tract involving the Sailor land showed the first entry was a Patent (Homestead) to Abel Sailor on June 10, 1859, signed by President James Buchanan. Moses Sailor, received a Patent on March 10, 1860, which was not signed by the President. The confusion over who was actually the first settler in our county comes from the next entries. The claims were filed on April 4, 1902, by Moses, and April 12, 1902, by his brother, Abel. The abstracts show a warranty deed acquired by Moses Sailor on March 23, 1889, and a deed for Abel Sailor's 80 acres on April 12, 1889. These deeds were not recorded until 1902, by J.N. Granger, Recorder of The General Land Office. The place of the General Land Office was not noted, but many of the early papers were recorded at an office in Winnebago; there is a strong possibility that was where the early records were kept.

I have always been under the impression that the Abel Sailor 80, where Neva and I started farming in 1943, was the first deeded land in Faribault County. However, we have acquired the south end of Moses Sailor's 80, so I guess we were right either way. The Moses Sailor tract included the spot where Darling's Rendering Plant now stands, on the east side of the Blue Earth River. The Abel Sailor tract lay on both sides of the Blue Earth River. Whoops! I must back up and state that the Moses Sailor land also straddled the river, and we own the portion on the west side. One must have great respect for these settlers who were there first, and settled among the Indians.

A true pioneer looked for several things when selecting a tract of land to

123

homestead--a source of good drinking water, timber for building a house, and material for building fences to contain livestock. Both of the Sailor 80s had a sweet water spring for drinking water, and a good stand of oak trees for building cabins and fences. The Blue Earth River at that time teemed with Walleye and Northern Pike as Carp had not been introduced from Europe as yet, so fishing was also a way of life in the early days. The hill west of the deer and buffalo trail, which later became River Road was a thick oak grove, before being cleared for grain production. The wood was used for cabins, fences, cooking and heating. It was on this hill that I disced up the Indian Stone Axe, now displayed in the Historical Society Museum in Blue Earth. It had lain there undisturbed for possibly hundreds of years. It is the most perfectly formed stone axe I have ever seen, and the work had to be done all by hand. The granite, which has a green cast, is tremendously hard and heavy. A hickory limb was formed and split to provide a handle. Hickory was tough, but warped easily, so was ideal.

When Neva and I moved onto the Sailor Place, there was a good shallow ford across the river with a good gravel bottom, so we could easily drive a team of horses or a tractor across. The river has changed course so that it ran around an island, with the main channel running east under the high wooded hill. One could walk across the shallow part on stepping stones. During one of the summer floods in the late 40s, a great amount of silt was deposited in the loop around the island, with the main channel cutting the island off except during floods. This left a sort of slough full of frogs and crayfish.

A pair of large owls took up residence in one of the tall trees above this area and lived there for many years. On a quiet night one could hear them calling down in the deep woods; a strong hoodoo-woo-woo. They were almost never seen, as they are night birds, but when seen by accident in daytime, their wingspread was a good four feet. The old timers called them Hoot Owls, but I'm not sure that is the correct designation. We also had a family of small Screech or Barn owls, which uttered the awfullest noise through the night, but slept all day up on the hay track or on a ledge in the loft. The owls are very silent flyers, yet have great speed through the air, and rely on a swift swoop to catch their prey. The Sailor Place was an interesting place to live, as we had a tile ditch that emptied on the east side of the road which sang like a waterfall, especially in early spring."

Quaday's Quotes (Reprinted with permission of RR Quaday) Faribault County Register, Monday, October 14, 1996 Partial column

Dick Tells About His Wedding Day In 1942

1908 SS Peter & Paul Church

"January 19, 1942, was as beautiful as any January day could be. There was no snow, the temperature rose to 48 degrees and it was sunny. This was the occasion Neva and I had been waiting for since October, when we became engaged to be married.

I had farmed on my own for three years and had my livestock and machinery paid for and owned a new Chevrolet, all of which I felt qualified us for marriage. A bit later in that year, I began to feel that maybe we should have been a little better qualified.

We lived with my parents for nearly a year until the Sailor Place, which we purchased in August, would be available. During this time we both learned a great deal. Neva learned to cook and sew from my Mother, and I learned that two do not live cheaper than one.

All older couples have some formula for long time, happy married relationships. I may as well tell you ours; maintain love and respect, with respect for each other's feelings being just as important as the love. Never go any place, not even to bed, after a quarrel.

1942 Richard & Neva Quaday Wedding

We were late for some engagements, meetings and parties, and had some pretty late bedtimes, but we never broke our rule. When we were first married, Neva and I agreed that she would run the household and I would run the farming operation.

At retirement time, we encouraged each other to develop hobbies, with Neva finally finding enough time to do her Hardanger and other fancy handiwork, besides belonging to many bridge groups which meet on a regular basis.

I have enjoyed afternoons of poker, besides a weekly Friday night game with friends. We have enjoyed many trips with friends, and just us two. Are we planning a 50 year Golden celebration? Not on your life--I am too emotional to go through all of that attention. We are planning a family get together in the metro area where the children are the thickest."

Quaday's Quotes-partial (Reprinted with permission from RR Quaday) Faribault County Register Monday January 13, 1992

Christmases Glad and Sad Recalled

"Our family was very strict in practicing our religion. We had scripture reading and prayer on our knees on the hardwood floor every morning, no matter what else was going on.

126

In my teens I became somewhat of a rebel and I stayed away from church whenever I had an excuse, and did not think thoughts Ecclesiastic as often as I should have, according to my Mother. I overheard her say to Dad once, "He's right on fool's hill now, but he'll be back."

When I attended "Cow College" in St Paul, I took a "Catholic Tour." Two busloads of young students were bused around the Twin Cities to the Basilica of St Mary's, St Thomas College, St Catherine's College, and the Cathedral in St Paul. I was very impressed by the reverence the Catholic youth showed in their places of worship.

Intrigued, the next year I took instructions and attended Midnight Mass that year with Neva Fischer, who later became Mrs. Quaday. (1942)"

Quaday's Quotes-partial (Reprinted with permission from RR Quaday) Faribault County Register Monday January 13, 1992

Dick Remembers His First Mass At SS Peter and Paul

"I must tell you of my first Roman Catholic Mass, which I attended with Neva a month or two before we were married. I think the first time one shows up in church in a town of this size, he feels that all eyes are on him and they probably are. I had never knelt in church before, and kneeling to say my prayers before Mass reminded me of the hardwood floor in our dining room, where we knelt every morning for prayer after breakfast. They were every bit as hard on the knees.

The choir, singing Mass in Latin, was beautiful and I thought to myself, "at least I understand Latin." I had no prayer book or missal to follow, so had to pay strict attention to what other people did, so I would not be left standing or kneeling alone.

Father Coleman, who was Blue Earth's priest at that time, was great with the incense, I found out later. All of a sudden I smelled smoke and looked around to see if other people were as alarmed as I. We sat next to a wall vent and when the smoke started coming out of the vent, I wanted to shout "fire!" and would probably have emptied the church. The fact that no one else could smell smoke held me in check. We were far back in the church, so I could not see exactly what the priest was doing until we stood up. Being a bit taller than the people in front of us, I could see then where the smoke was coming from. My fears were quieted for the rest of the mass and it eased my mind when Father Coleman said the same prayers, word for word, as our Evangelical minister said in our church."

Quaday's Quotes -partial (Reprinted with permission from RR Quaday) Faribault County Register Monday June 17, 1996

Move To Farm Happened More Than 50 Years Ago

"On January 12, 1943, Neva and I moved from the Quaday Home Farm, on River Road, to the next farm south. This farm, the first deeded land in Faribault County, had always been called The Sailor Place by my parents. Abel Sailor was the first settler to own the 80 acre farm. He settled there because it had everything that a homesteader needed. There was a sweet water spring below the hill where he built his cabin. Half the 80 was covered with dense woods, with the other half easily cleared for farming. The Blue Earth River ran through the middle of the pasture and woodland, for a never ending supply of fresh water for livestock. Most of the river was navigable with a canoe or a flat bottom boat. Rafting was okay, but tough going upstream, because when it was deep enough for rafting there was quite a current.

Abel's son, Perry, farmed the farm for a number of years while raising a large family. During the land boom of the early 20s the farm was sold to Albert Tillia, who needed an outlet for a tile line he wanted, to drain low spots on the 160 acres joining the Sailor 80. It was a tremendous undertaking, because the tile had to be buried 18 feet at one point, before emptying into a ravine by the River Road. All the digging was done by hand by Curt Swift, who lived in the buildings while stringing the tile. According to my Dad, it took the greater part of three years to complete the project. In my lifetime this tile has never gone dry and the cattle preferred to drink there rather than the river.

During the Hoover Farm Depression in the early 30s Albert lost the 80 on a mortgage foreclosure, but he had what he wanted, an outlet to the river which did a fair job of draining his farm. His lowest ground was seeded to pasture, so it just grew better grass in wetter years. The Weinberg Estate in Chicago held the deed to the farm for many years, with different tenants living there two or three years at the most.

The house had been built in two stages, with the kitchen and the attic built first. While Curt Swift lived on the farm, he dug a cyclone cellar northeast

128

of the house. Part of the years I attended School District 104, the house was vacant and we thought it great fun to explore the dugout, which was shored up with oak posts and planks. Pete Morgan built a brand new two-holer over part of the cellar much later.

1943 Charles, Neva & Richard Quaday, Sailor Place

When we moved into the house it still stood fairly straight, even after years of neglect and misuse. It had never been modernized since it was built in the 1880s. Abel Sailor had dug a board well (lined with bricks and lumber), to water livestock during the winter. This became the well used for the house water after the spring fell into disrepair. The main problem with this well was its location, well below both the house and barn. I never had it tested, but I'm sure it was loaded with nitrate. The farm always had the healthiest children in the neighborhood, all through the Swifts, the Kileys, the Childs, the Whitmores, and the Koskoviches. Our kids were no exception and it seemed that we had more health problems with our children after we moved over to the Home Farm, where the well was sanitary and the house had running water, electricity and sewer."

Quaday's Quotes (Reprinted with permission of RR Quaday) Faribault County Register, Monday, March 13, 1995

"That farm kept me busy, winter and summer. The third year, I insulated the house, established electricity, dug a new well, dug a sewer, put in a bathroom, and piped in running water. All this made it a civilized place to live. I painted the house and barn too, which made it look occupied. I had shingled the house and barn the second year, replacing old wood shingles with asphalt. There was a small chicken coop in pretty good shape. I built a new laying house with a time clock and built a new brooder house, which was portable so we could haul it out in the alfalfa field in summer. It was a farm that needed everything when I bought it in 1942 for $65 per acre."

Quaday's Quotes-partial (Reprinted with permission from RR Quaday) Faribault County Register Monday February 9, 2009

"I dug the sewer system myself, and plumbed water into the sink and newly designed bathroom; even a bathtub. I could write a book about the Sailor Place, although we only lived there for six years. When we moved there the only water supply was a board well situated lower than the barn and hog house. I hired Charley Bassett, the local well driller, to dig a well up on the hill beside the house. He hit good water about 60 feet down, but it was a sand vein and very hard, so he went to 90 feet and hit a good sand vein, much softer. That was a good fit as we had no softener. We had a Maytag motor on our first second-hand washing machine, purchased from George Carr Hardware, which was almost impossible to start. So when Neva wanted to wash clothes she would have to come to the field to get me to start the blamed thing up. We also had a Maytag motor on the pump-jack on the old well for watering livestock. If it got wet it wouldn't start either, so I'd run it for an hour or so with the tractor pulley to dry it out; it always worked. Milo Miller and Oliver Kohlmeyer wired the farm when wire became available and what a blessing! I've always had a soft spot for The Electric Service Company ever since."

Quaday's Quotes - partial (Reprinted with permission from RR Quaday) Faribault County Register Monday December 24, 2007

Sailor Place Barn

"While thinking of things that age well I must mention the barn on the Sailor Place. It was built by Abel Sailor, I think during the late 1870s, and still sits squarely on the foundation I put under it in 1943. Prior to that time it sat on several boulders, strategically placed around the outside and under the middle. The hand hewn oak stringers under the plank floor are just as sturdy and twice as hard as when put in. It was built to accommodate four horses, eight milk cows, and some young cattle. An oats bin in the northwest corner and a full loft with two hay chutes, made it very serviceable for a small farm. A hay track in the loft was an added convenience that not too many barns had at that time.

130

1943 Quaday Family & Sailor Place Barn

A double wide door on a sliding track was original equipment, but I replaced it with a single wide door for loading livestock. We were about through with horse farming by the time we lived there. I only milked eight cows by hand when we lived there, but later we had hundreds of feeding lambs in the yard and around 20 steers, which used a sheltering straw shed made out of oak poles. I replaced the cedar shingles with new asphalt the second year we lived there. I hope the present owners keep a good roof on the barn, as it is truly of antique heritage."

Quaday's Quotes -partial (Reprinted with permission from RR Quaday) Faribault County Register Monday December 20, 1999

First Spring At the Sailor Place

"When the sun begins to warm things up in late March and early April, I think back to the first spring living at the Sailor Place on River Road. The house, built in the 1880s, had very little for a young, city-bred housewife to cheer about. We had no indoor plumbing and no electricity. When the wind blew strong from the southwest, the kitchen or living room linoleum would rise an inch or two from the floor. The two story section of the house rested on huge rocks--a rabbit could escape our dog by running under the house on one side and heading out the other. There was a square trap door right in the middle of the room, where rumor had it that Perry Sailor hid his sugar, molasses and apple sauce during World War I, for fear it would be confiscated.

The two-holer, perched on the brow of the 60-foot hill at the back of the house, was a stark contrast to the house. We purchased the farm from Wesley Morgan, a bachelor, who had only owned the house for two years. His brother, Pete, and his family lived with him. Just prior to moving to the farm Pete's wife took sick and died, leaving Pete with several young daughters to raise. They didn't live in the house long enough to get a good start fixing things up before World War II was on, making home repairs hard to find. The brothers did prevail upon the rationing board for lumber to build the brand new two-holer. Pete was a jack-of-all-trades and did an exceptional job of carpentry.

1943 First Corn Crop, Sailor Place

In 1942, around 10 percent of farm houses had indoor plumbing or electricity, and even if they did, an outdoor biffy was left over from days gone by. My folks had one in back of the corn crib for the children to use while playing--keeping them from tracking up Mom's floor. That one was supplied with Sears Roebuck or Montgomery Ward catalogues, used as toilet paper. With such sanitary facilities, is it any wonder the country school teachers called the urchins "little stinkers" in those days? The first thing I did upon moving into the Sailor Place was install a toilet paper holder, and stock it for use. We then had the most modern and the best looking two-holer in the neighborhood. It was two years before I got around to painting it white to match the house.

In late afternoon, with the sun shining on the un-insulated building, the temperature was always 10 or 15 degrees warmer than outside and fairly comfortable while doing one's duty. It was a time to stop and think ahead to spring planting and plan our next project. I really don't know why the biffy was always constructed with two holes--except that the family might be large or a young child might be afraid to go out alone at night.

Spring and early summer are pleasurably recalled, I suppose, because at that time of year there were no flies, no mosquitoes and no malicious odor, as the pit was still frozen solid and didn't thaw out until mid-June."

Quaday's Quotes -partial (Reprinted with permission from RR Quaday) Faribault County Register Monday March 24, 2003

Thanksgiving The Second Year on The Sailor Place

"The second year we lived on the Sailor Place we had a wonderful fall, finishing all the field work before Thanksgiving. The day that year was clear and cold, after a snapping cold night. It was one of the rare years when the Blue Earth River froze over hard enough to carry one safely.   Neva and I walked for a mile or two on the river in the afternoon, and as it was a full moon we took another walk at night and it was just beautiful, especially when we were young and in love.

1944 Richard & Neva Quaday

Some years, it had snowed by Thanksgiving, and the ground and river were frozen. We always turned the cattle out into the corn field after picking, to save on the winter hay as long as possible, and it was customary to take my shotgun along when bringing in the cattle to pick off a rooster pheasant. There were so many pheasants in those days, that they almost made a nuisance of themselves. No one ever dreamed of them getting scarce.

As with many farm pleasures it was good while it lasted, and changing methods of farming plus an overflow of fox, coon, and other varmints, has made the sighting of a pheasant a rarity."

Quaday's Quotes -partial (Reprinted with permission from RR Quaday) Faribault County Register Monday November 25, 1996

Expected Women's Work

"In my Mother's days on the farm, she was expected to harness up and drive a team of horses when help in that department was needed. She also could milk cows, in case Dad was really sick or laid up with a bad back. She changed and washed diapers for the very youngest, packed school lunches for the school-age kids, and got breakfast for everybody before 7:30 am. By then, it was time to see to it that the scholars were properly dressed and didn't forget their lunch and overshoes, if needed. There was no bus and no school lunch in those days. She had it better than most farm wives; she had electricity, running water and sewer, and lived in a new house just a mile and a half from town. She was very satisfied with her lot in life and seldom complained, as her married life was so much better than her childhood with a step-mother.

In our generation, Neva was a city girl who had to live with her mother-in-law for a year before we purchased our first 80 acres. This period of time was not easy, yet she looked at it as a learning experience and used it to the fullest. Moving from a new house with all the amenities of life to one that was 90 years old without electricity, running water, or sewer, was indeed a shocking experience, especially with three youngsters to raise almost immediately.

There were only a few times when she was pressed into service to drive a team of horses and it scared her half to death, but to her eternal credit she did it when called upon. The time of parochial school busing had not yet come, so we sometimes pulled two school buses out of the drifts in front of our place, then hauled our kids into SS Peter and Paul's School in town. The school did have noon lunch with excellent cooks and a new dining room.

When our children were all in school, Neva took on the Green Giant for summer employment, along with a big garden to make ends meet. The canteen job was better than the huskers and led to a job in Ray's Bakery. The 6:30 to 1:00 hours fit her better also. She was hired to run the goods and notions department in J.C. Penney's basement, where she worked for 10 years, and was running three departments when she needed back surgery. The back trouble put an end to many activities which she formerly enjoyed, such as dancing, golf, and bowling. Picking up an unmarked battery in the freight department crushed two discs, which had to be removed. Her interests turned to cross-stitch, Hardanger, and bridge for entertainment. She loves to cook and bake cookies and I like to eat, so we still get along well. She writes many letters to our nine children, so we get quite a lot of mail."

Quaday's Quotes-partial (Reprinted with permission from RR Quaday) Faribault County Register, Monday February 15, 1999

Christmas With Neva In the 40s

"In the early 40s, when Neva and I lived on the Sailor Place, we had many good things to look forward to at Christmas time. My folks still lived next door on the home farm out on River Road, and Mother always insisted on having the family home on Christmas Eve for supper, with a gift exchange later in the evening.

She went to great lengths to buy the best oysters for stew, which the Quaday side of the family thoroughly enjoyed. With Neva and our children, it was a different matter. They did the stew, but couldn't down the oysters except one to be polite. She realized Neva and the kids didn't relish oysters, so she made a delicious hot dish for them.

On Christmas Day it became a tradition to load up the kids and some food, drive to Minnesota Lake, and have another feast, with a gift exchange in the afternoon on the Fischer side of our family. With Joan's birthday on December 26, and Kay's birthday on December 27, things didn't always go as planned. On those two years we felt doubly blessed, with the girls' birthdays coming so close to that of Our Lord Jesus.

Schedules were changed to fit the occasion, sometimes earlier, sometimes later, but celebrate we did to the best of our abilities.

Times were hard during the Second World War with price controls on all farm produce, so many of the gifts were homemade. I rebuilt and painted kiddy cars, trikes, tractors, and bikes, so the children always had some shiny toy without much cost.

Neva's aunt, Lydia Beske, made it a tradition to have many of the Fischer family as guests for a New Year goose dinner at her home on Main Street in Minnesota Lake. In that way we had a chance to meet her cousins, aunts, and uncles, many of whom lived on farms in the area or in surrounding towns. Aunt Lydia was a wonderful cook, using many of the old German recipes, and her own private coffee cake recipe was a well guarded secret.

Unfortunately the recipe died with her, so all we have is the memory. On one memorable Christmas, tradition was upset by unclear planning. Neva's folks and her sister, Gloria, and our family met just south of the Pink School House. Luckily, we took the same road. It was decided to return to Minnesota Lake, as that was the closest, and clean the ice box for dinner. Actually, it was great fun and nobody got indigestion that Christmas dinner.

1950s Dick Quaday Chopping Firewood

On one very memorable Christmas night, Neva and I walked for miles on the River, which was high that year and froze up smooth as glass. The full moon made it light as day and the zero temperature dispelled worries about thin ice. We were young, healthy, and in love, so miles meant nothing to us. Gloria had stayed at our place, so no worries about our young children. When we got home, we played three-handed clubs for a few hours. We stayed

136

up late during those years, to bank fires in the heartrola and the cook stove, so it didn't get too cold for the little ones.

We burned wood in both heating elements, which I cut from our own woods. All it cost was hard work, for which I was willing and able. In fact, I really enjoyed myself getting out in the woods all by myself and making wood. We had a multitude of good, hardwood trees on the farm, and I had good looks at the wild life along the Blue Earth River.

Quaday's Quotes (Reprinted with permission from RR Quaday) Faribault County Register Monday December 18, 2000

"My Dad, who was raised in the woods in his early years, was perfectly in rhythm at all times on a two-man saw. When John and I were learning the art, he would say, "Quit riding the saw"--meaning that we were trying to push our end of the saw instead of just pulling our own handle. I stayed home longer than John so I got to learn the proper rhythm, and even learned to operate our one-man saw, which only had one handle. On the Sailor Place--where Neva and I lived for six years--I sawed all our wood for a cook stove and a parlor furnace with our one-man saw for two years. The farm had 30 acres of timber and there were always dead trees to work up."

Quaday's Quotes -partial (Reprinted with permission from RR Quaday) Faribault County Register Monday, January 14, 1991

Animals on the Family Farm

In many ways, life on the family farm revolved around the animals. Field crops were vital for income and stability, but it was the animals that provided food, cash flow, transportation and brute strength for working the farm. Our River Road Farm was home for horses, cows, sheep, hogs, chickens, dogs and cats over the years. The wise farmer gave his animals the best possible care, knowing that the family was dependent on this food chain.

Chores were done morning and night, every day, without fail. Cows were milked, fences were maintained, sick animals were doctored with home remedies or veterinarian care, and all were fed and watered on a regular schedule, most often before the people sat down to eat. Children learned responsibility early by filling the water tanks, collecting eggs and feeding the smaller animals. Even the dogs and cats had jobs, herding, guarding and keeping the vermin in check. There were no pets on the family farm, but every animal had its own personality, character quirks and value.

For example there was a horse named Mike.

> "My uncle Fred Quaday was about to quit farming, and he had a branded bronco named Mike to sell. Dad (William Quaday) bought him and like all broncos, he was hard to catch out in the pasture. He could run like a deer until caught or run in the barn; then he turned into the laziest nag in five counties.
>
> He had one attribute which distinguished him from all others. He was broke to ride and was that rarest of all broncos, a natural pacer. He was a dream to ride because his gait was continuously smooth, as he moved two feet on the same side at once.
>
> He was stone deaf, so on hunting trips you could rest the gun between his ears, fire, and he'd never turn a hair. I rode him in the 1936 Armistice Day Parade for the Fairmont football game. The firecrackers that were shot off didn't bother him one bit.
>
> One time we were hunting jack rabbits along the line fences. When we changed from one side of the fence to the other, Mike fell through the snow banks with front feet on one side of the barbed wire, back feet on the other.
>
> With most horses that is a predicament, with the animal thrashing about

until he is wire cut pretty bad. Not Mike. He had so much savvy that he just lay there quietly until I shot the two top barbs in two with my .22 rifle. He knew that when I pulled on his bridle all was okay and he struggled up and continued the hunt."

Quaday's Quotes-Partial (Reprinted with permission from RR Quaday) Faribault County Register Monday, May 7, 1990

Dick Rides Horse In Homecoming Parade

"The fall of 1936 was dry and, for the most part, warm. At that time the big fall event of the sports season was the Armistice Day football game with Fairmont. I believe it was also the Homecoming Game that year, with each class encouraged to furnish a float for the pre-game parade downtown main street to the football field.

At that time, the field was located where the skating and hockey rink is now. It was considered one of the finest in the state. It was a true Depression Baby, with land cost near zero and W.P.A. labor teamed with high school volunteer kids leveling and sodding the field. I remember getting excused from school a couple of days to help spike the plank seats, ranked up the hillside, together.

Our football team that year was solid but not spectacular. Coach Baldy Hayes could be counted on to have a team which knew well the fundamentals of the game. Francis Brady, a junior, was our heaviest lineman at about 245 pounds, with Wayne Rorman, at six-foot-two, our tallest member. "Gus" Cherland was captain and quarterback. Their work ethics were good, and "Gus," later Reverend Cherland, saw to it that his boys trained pretty well.

The senior class was composed of true Depression Kids used to making do without spending any money. Consequently, when we held the class meeting to decide on a float, the financial outlay was a deciding feature.

Thus occurred the one and only time I ever appeared in a football uniform, with spiked shoes, pads, helmet and all, in the classic Blue Earth maroon and gold colors.

Most of our class was more interested in their scholastic standing and saving money for college than they were in sports, even though the coming of Baldy Hays in 1934 had rekindled much school spirit.

Anyway, it was decided to employ our "parade horse," Mike, as the motivation, with myself decked in full uniform astride the equine wonder.

I believe I have mentioned before that Mike, in spite of being a branded bronco, was also a natural pacer. For those of you who do not understand horse language, this means the horse moves both feet on the same side at the same time, making the smoothest possible gait for the rider.

After Coach Hayes had issued me a uniform the struggle began. (I had never worn one, let alone seeing one assembled piece by piece.) Fortunately, one of the players came to my aid, saving me the embarrassment of appearing in public with something wrong.

Someone in the class made two placards with B. E. printed on, with the theme being that of a workhorse team prevailing on the football field. This was before saddle clubs became popular in our area, so the sight of a real live horse in the parade caused the kids on the route to try to scare the horse, and give me a "good" ride by whistling and shouting at the horse. That part didn't worry me because, of course, I knew that old Mike was stone deaf.

As long as no one threw a rock or a stick, I felt things would go as planned. Needless to say, we didn't take first prize. The junior class, which had always

1937 Parade, Richard on Old Mike

been more sports-minded, used the Carr Hardware pickup to assemble a beautiful float with much crepe paper and streamers in school colors. Our float, I'm sure, attracted more attention among the younger children just because it was alive.

Much later, I made an appearance in a school basketball uniform at the School of Agriculture in St Paul, but that's another story."

Quaday's Quotes (Reprinted with permission from RR Quaday) Faribault County Register Monday December 9, 1991

141

Farming With Horses

The introduction of tractors revolutionized the agriculture industry in the late nineteenth century, but the majority of family farms continued to use horse power until the Depression years.

"In my younger years horses were very necessary around our farm. Dad carried four horses on our 160 acres of Blue Earth Township, and 80 acres of Jo Daviess Township. He hated big, clumsy horses, so he had one small bay driving team for buggy and surrey use. They were sure-footed animals which could get around in the winter drifts which piled in on the River Road, sometimes telephone pole high. I have pictures to prove this.

The other team was a larger pair of sorrels. The Ryans, the Sailors, and the Gieselharts were all in the horse business in varying degrees. The trick was to build a matched team which could pull together.

Dad traded for a buckskin bronco in the early 1930s from the Gypsies. She was named Bird which fit her to a tee. She drove just fine until she was hitched to a hay rack or a dump rake. Both vehicles made her nervous and she ran away with the dump rake, and kicked the front boards out of Dad's hayrack. Dad still kept her around until she kicked him at currying time, then she was gone.

About this time Dad bought an extra horse from the Gieselharts. His name was Tony. He was a race track horse and he always remembered that. He wanted to race other horses until he was 20 years old. He was the kids' riding horse and cow horse, besides doubling for draft when others had sore shoulders.

One day in August, my brother John was driving Tony and a bay named Baldy on the threshing run hauling bundles. John always had to haul the biggest loads on the run.

It was a 90 degree day and they were threshing at Frank Willmert's. On the second load of the afternoon, Tony dropped dead of a heart attack or old age. One minute he was racing another load up to the machine, the next he was a corpse. Many tears were shed over Tony."

Quaday's Quotes-Partial (Reprinted with RR Quaday permission) Faribault County Register Monday, May 7, 1990

Dick Recalls His Horse Tony

"I had the most vivid dream about Tony, a riding and working horse we owned back in the early 1930s. Tony was a white gelding, matched up with Baldy, a bay gelding. They weighed about 1100 pounds each and pulled perfectly together. They had never been overloaded or misused, so believed they could pull anything we asked them to. The best thing about Tony, in my young estimation, was that he, in his youth, had been on the race track circuit. Consequently he always wanted to race when I was riding him around other horses.

By the time we owned Tony, he was at nearly age 20, and just perfect for a kid who probably couldn't have handled him in his prime. There was a saddle hanging in the barn, left from when my oldest brother Carl owned a pony, Prince, which he rode to high school years earlier. It was a western style with a horn for roping, but very light construction.

Having Tony as my constant friend and companion took the loneliness out of herding cattle. He saved Dad a lot of corn. We herded the milk cows and young stock out in the stubble field after threshing the small grain. The old milk cows knew the succulent corn was much better tasting than the pigeon grass and weeds of the pasture.

The Fred Paschke family lived a mile south of our River Road Farm, and the boys had an old gray mare named Rosy, which they rode all over the neighborhood when she was not needed herding cattle. She was swaybacked, and didn't look like she could run a lick; she was Tony's age or more. We almost always gave in to Tony's thirst for racing, and when we were going towards Paschke's place Rosy would win. Poor Tony had the handicap of a saddle and quite a bit more weight to carry. If no other horses were around, Tony would go twice as fast going toward home as he would just going somewhere. Tony's mate, Baldy, was a branded bronco and very young when we traded for him. He had never been ridden, but saw how much fun Tony had with us kids. We used to ride the horses out to water and one day I climbed on Baldy, because my brother, John, had grabbed Tony before I got there. Baldy shivered twice and turned around and looked to see what he had, but turned back around and headed for the water tank, happy to be a part of the fun.

John was 14 and old enough to run a bundle team on the threshing run.

He preferred the small team over our larger sorrel team, because the mare pranced all the time and was hard to hold for any period of time.

I will never forget the day they were threshing over at Frank Willmert's place; it was a hot August afternoon. I had just brought the cattle in on foot and was not in a good mood, because the cows would run in seven different directions without a horse to herd them. Mother came running out, telling me to harness up the big team, hook them to a buggy, and go to Willmert's. I had to stand on a five-gallon pail to get the harness up on the big sorrels, but got them hooked up on the buggy, heading for Willmert's.

When I got there, John drove them out of the driveway to the field, where Baldy was standing patiently waiting for Tony to get up and get going. Tony had died from heart failure, and lay in the driveway, stretched out as far as he could be, trying to make it to the thresh machine. He had never given up; death just overtook him under full power and dropped him right in the harness. I asked John why he didn't unhook Tony and he said, "He's your horse." I looked up at the huge load of bundles that John had stacked and told him, "You do it, you killed him." I still cry 65 years later remembering us two boys unhooking our friend Tony for the last time. We rolled the wagon back and hooked up the sorrels on the bundle wagon. I rode Baldy home and John pulled the buggy home behind the rack that night.

Life for me had changed forever with the death of Tony.

1951 Richard Quaday in Montana

I could not bring myself to ride another horse until 35 years had elapsed, and I was offered a horse to ride up in Montana."

Quaday's Quotes (Reprinted with permission from RR Quaday) Faribault County Register Monday August 17, 1998

Of course, horses were used in the fields for everything from planting to plowing.

"I was introduced to the art of corn cultivation at a very early age. We had a team of elderly gray geldings, named Tom and Joe, who knew much more about cultivating corn than I did, fortunately. A one row John Deere cultivator, with both hand and foot steering was my first corn machine. By steering, I mean the two gangs were movable from side to side, so one could cultivate wire checked corn crosswise without digging out too much corn. Weather permitting, we always cultivated our corn three times, twice lengthwise and once crosswise. Using horsepower in the hot summer sun was much different than planting when the weather wasn't so hot. The teams of horses we used for cultivation were about 1150 pounds each, which was small as work horses went. They didn't tromp on so much corn, and turned around at the end much faster than larger horses. They also required more rest, which we always tried to arrange in the shade of a plum tree, if possible. Wild plum trees grew on many of the fence lines, with elderberry bushes, and wild grape vines growing up in the chokecherry trees. 2,4,5-T and 2,4-D had not yet come into vogue."

CORN TALK. Quaday's Qorn. Monthly newsletter for corn producers who are members of Minnesota Corn Growers Association Vol 14, No. 5 June, 1994

Corn planting with horses was an art that required precision and hard work. Stakes and wire were used to lay out straight rows and operate the planter.

"In the 1920s and early 1930s, when I was growing up on our River Road Farm southwest of Blue Earth, my thoughts always turned to horsepower about the middle of March. If some of the horses showed signs of old age or other infirmities, they were either doctored up or traded off. Their hooves were trimmed, the winter coats of thick hair and sometimes manure patches were curried off, and their manes and tails were trimmed and thinned. After having very little care all winter, some of the younger horses objected strenuously when curried for the first time. We had one sorrel mare that everyone was afraid to clean up the first time in the spring. She wasn't mean, but she involuntarily kicked the curry comb sometimes, sending it flying across the barn.

The harnesses had to be cleaned and oiled, with the worn pieces replaced. Dad was pretty fussy about the harnesses and the collars, seeing to it that every collar fit perfectly. He was also careful about the neck yokes, eveners, and draw pins. His perfectly matched team of mares, which he called his "Driving Team," could get us to town in eight minutes if allowed to do a steady trot. The mile and one half to Blue Earth had five frost boils (every clay hill), so the teams were slowed to a walk in these places. (Usually these spots were soupy until early June.) I remember one instance, when the family started for church in our surrey on a beautiful May morning. We had just crossed the bridge on the way into Blue Earth and were half way through the last frost boil, when the evener bolt broke. The bays kept right on going, pulling Dad over the dashboard and out into the clay ooze. Dad was not one to cuss or swear, but he looked pretty unhappy after picking himself up on the far side of the muck. He borrowed a bolt from old man Kilman and pulled us through. He missed church that day.

The bays were our corn planting team, as they were light and fast, capable of planting twenty acres per day. One had to be moving right along pulling the stakes and stretching the wire on each end of the field. We owned a John Deere two row planter with our next door neighbors, the Wehseners. The partnership worked well, as one farmer would be working up the ground while the other planted. Our young farmers today would throw up their hands in horror at the thought of jumping off the planter at each end of the field to pull up and reset the stakes, which held the notched wire. A good team and a careful farmer could have what we called a "perfect check," if he never broke the wire, and the stakes held."

Quaday's Qorn. Monthly newsletter for corn producers who are members of the Minnesota Corn Growers Association Vol 14, No 4, April, 1994

Transportation Meant Horses, Not Cars

"In my youth out on River Road Farm, at every gathering of farm folk, whether composed of relatives, neighbors or some of each, I can remember the men gathering in one room or under a shade tree, with the conversation inevitably turning to the sources of power used at that period of time.

In horse and buggy times, stories would be told about how smart one farmer's team of mules were, and how well another's four horse hitch of Belgians pulled together on a sulky, or gang plow.

Nearly every farmer kept what was known as a "driving team," and the farther one lived from town the more likely he was to have a light, fast team, usually as well matched as possible for show times when driving to church, weddings and funerals.

The small towns of the farm belt were located close enough together so that grain, lumber, and various other freight could be hauled to and from the railroads, which at that time had a network covering the small grain elevators and depots.

The county seat towns, such as Blue Earth and Albert Lea, had rails going in both directions; for instance, the Chicago and Northwestern tracked one way and the Milwaukee Road, the other.

There were many small rail companies hauling freight and passengers; all of which had been given right of way by the government in order to develop smooth, all-weather roads which would be maintained at the owner's expense. As these rail companies grew and prospered, they were taxed on equipment they owned.

In Blue Earth, the next busiest street after Main was Sixth, or Depot Street, as it was known at that time. I believe that outside of the business section, Depot Street was the only one paved with wood blocks.

The freight was hauled with horses and some loads were very heavy. With our heavy rainfall, the street would be heavily rutted and probably impassible in spring when the frost came out. The wood block paving was much better than dirt or gravel but they, too, developed "frost boils" which would have to be dug and re-laid by hand.

The dray line business was one of the better paid in Blue Earth at that time with the Wilke family doing the greatest share of the hauling.

Occasionally, a farmer's team unaccustomed to the steam engine trains, would get spooked when excess steam was let out by a "pop off" valve on the engine, and a run-away would result.

The railroad stockyard was one of the busiest places in town, with hundreds of head of cattle and hogs being shipped to Chicago. Bill Schandel, John Domes, Adolph Roske, and Holmes Pedelty were some of the larger buyers and shippers that I remember."

Quaday's Quotes (Reprinted with permission from RR Quaday) Faribault County Register Monday May 18, 1992

The End of Horse Farming

In the Blue Earth area, it wasn't machines that pushed the horses out of the fields, but an equine encephalitis plague that wiped out the horse population in the Corn Belt.

> "I have spent most of my adult life within sniffing distance of the Blue Earth Rendering Plant, which was built around 1928-1930. Our River Road Farm was directly across the Blue Earth River from the facility, which was originally a partnership, known as Kark and Witte, I believe. Among the youngsters attending District 104 school, it was known as the "Stink factory."

Actually, our farm was situated so that we had very little odor problems, and as farms went in those days it didn't over-power odors created by the feed lots and dairy barns.

The first trucks used for transporting dead animals to the plant were cut-down sedans of the heavier makes of cars. These were equipped with a box and hand cranked windlass, and a slide for loading horses and cattle. As with most business, the operation became touch-and-go during the Great Depression, and was nearly out of business when the "Sleeping Sickness" epidemic of 1934-1936 wiped out the horse population of the Corn Belt.

This was the end of horse farming as we knew it, although some farmers had purchased tractors for the heavier farm work, such as plowing with a mold-board plow which required four or six horse hitches. We lost two horses to the equine encephalitis plague.

This did not move Dad to buy a tractor. He bought two more horses from Harry Gieselhart, had them vaccinated for encephalitis, and continued horse farming after vaccinating the ones we had. It was up to me, when I began farming in 1938, to buy the first tractor on the farm. The sleeping sickness proved to be a one-time plague, thankfully, but the damage had been done, hurrying by many years the demise of horse farming. The rendering plant had a hard time keeping up with the call for dead horses to be picked up. The large carcasses were a bonanza for the business, and Emil

Kark never looked back. He enlarged the plant, raising the capacity many fold.

At that time it was perfectly legal to dump raw sewage into the Blue Earth River and solid wastes on the city dump, which was positioned just down the hill from the plant.

Quaday's Quotes -partial (Reprinted with permission from RR Quaday) Faribault County Register Monday July 19, 1999

Horses Continued to be a Part of River Road Farm

"For the first time in history, none of our children own a horse. Mary sold her horse, Jesse, and purchased a mule (Jenny), which she says is twice as smart and sure footed as her big horse.

Our River Road Farm was a four-horse farm up until 1938, when I took over as a young man. I had the distinction of bringing the first tractor into service on that land. It was a wonderful chunk of progress, as far as I was concerned. Cleaning the horse barn and currying and harnessing the brutes, besides walking behind a drag all day in the dust, had already gotten old for me by age 18. I did keep one team of horses to plant corn and haul hay and grain bundles until 1952.

I would not allow my children to have a horse because I was sure one of them would get kicked, or have a run-away.

Mary, who especially loved horses, would go to "Dutch's" pasture where he had riding horses, and would allow kids to ride under his supervision. He took a liking to Mary and "rented" her a horse they called Sputnik, against my wishes. When Sputnik arrived at our farm, I wouldn't let any of our kids ride him until I checked him out. He was a well mannered mutt who didn't cause trouble, except when he reached over the fence and ate off the first two rows of corn along the pasture."

Quaday's Quotes-partial (Reprinted with permission from RR Quaday) Faribault County Register Monday October 2, 2006

Dogs
Dogs on the William & Richard Quaday Farms

A good farm dog was companion, guardian, herder, hunter and field hand. Breeding was not as important as intelligence and adaptability.

"The first dog I remember was a gray collie with a white collar and white feet, named "Old Bob." From infancy on up, old Bob put up with me-- through the stage when I had to hang on to his long fur to stand up, until he was old and had gray around his head. Old Bob knew too well that I was too young to understand that it hurt when I pulled his hair or his ears. He was taller than me and was anti-squirrel--he just barked at them. With all the Oak and Walnut trees on Oak Ridge Farm, the squirrels knew just how high they had to go in the trees to irritate Old Bob. Bob was a tough dog, protected the farm animals, and didn't chase cars, but his eyesight failed and he was hit by a car.

A small, tan, long haired shepherd dog named Jerry lived and worked for us for many years after Bob died. Dad had her spayed and she was an excellent farm dog--understanding just exactly how to nip at the cows' heels without getting kicked and how to round up sheep and pen hogs. She was deathly scared of thunder and equated firecrackers with thunder. When about the 3rd of July came, Jerry knew what was coming. She would hide under the granary for three days until all the shooting was over. One time my brother, John, threw a firecracker under the granary and she stayed an extra two days.

When I was 11 years old, Oliver Wendt drove into our yard and when he opened the car door a tan and white puppy jumped out. He was not full grown yet and still had the confidence of a puppy. We had no dog and we had livestock, so we named him "Butch" and proceeded to train him in the ways of the farm. Butch was the smartest dog I've ever known.

He would play with the children, and be ready in an instant when I said, "Let's go get 'em Butch." He instinctively knew everything a farm dog had to know, and could hunt pheasants better than any Labrador without a bit of training. Butch and I would go across the road to our grove with massive oak trees, gooseberry bushes and chokecherry trees, full of pheasants. I had my Winchester .22 rifle. When the bird fell, Butch would put his front paws on it until help arrived.

We couldn't fake him out when it came to playing fetch. At threshing time, we played a mean trick on him by throwing a stick up in the straw pile un-

der the blower. He'd poke around right there until he found it, and would come out spitting chaff and rubbing his eyes with his paws. He could actually climb trees; squirrels didn't have a chance unless they were higher than 10 or 11 feet in the Oak trees.

In 1943, when we moved to the Sailor Place, a mongrel puppy came to our place in the spring looking for a home. She looked like she wanted to stay, so we fed her and she adopted us. We named her "Lizzie." She was different from the start. She had a different way of bringing the milk cows across the river to the barn. After a few trips across the

Richard Quaday & Butch

swinging bridge to let her know what was to be done, she would swim the river, disappear for a few minutes, then start up a furious barking campaign and head for the ford in the river. The old cows knew it was milking time and would follow her down the hill and across the river.

We bought a purebred collie female from Kenny Kohlmeyer; a beautiful dog. She stayed over at my Dad's place because he still milked cows.

We, of course, named her Lassie and she was a wonderful guardian for our first three children. When Dad drove over to our farm, she would cut across to our place through the woods--taking the same route when he went home. One day he didn't turn into his driveway as usual, and drove on toward town. She expected him to turn in, and he ran over her. Oh! Did the tears flow over that!

When we sold the cows and started to feed lambs, we had a series of black

151

1954 Charles Quaday & Lassie

and tan English Shepherd dogs. These were natural sheep dogs and very useful and necessary in the handling of a flock. They were always named "Suzy" after the first one we received from Oliver Wendt, who was nearly perfect. The second one we had made a better Christian out of me. I had a tendency to get irritated and holler and cuss when things didn't go quite right. The minute I started to mouth off, Suzy would head for the house and it took a lot of persuasion to get her back to work. We never had very good luck with purebred dogs; they were hard to train and they chased cars which shortened their lives considerably."

Quaday's Quotes-partial (Reprinted with permission from RR Quaday) Faribault CountyRegister Monday June 3, 1991 (and) Monday, January 25, 2010 –Partial

Livestock
Livestock Operations

Family farms depended on diversity to make ends meet. Animals provided food for the family but were also sources of revenue. Farmers maintained a herd of milking cows, and raised or bought yearling calves or sheep, and shipped them to the stockyards for sale to the meat packing companies.

"Often, when I drive or walk past the creamery building on North Main Street, I think back to the days when it was one of the largest businesses in the Blue Earth area.

Almost every farmer kept a few milk cows, because they could convert tremendous amounts of roughage into a saleable product. Most farmers separated the cream (butterfat), then hauled the cream to the creamery, where it was churned into butter. They fed the skim milk to hogs. At that time, most farmers were diversified, meaning that they had cattle, hogs, chickens, and sometimes sheep. This way of life used all the labor, right down to some of the smaller children, whose job it was to feed the chickens and gather the eggs. It seemed that the age of 10 was a sort of dividing point; the boys learned to milk cows and drive a team of horses shortly after this age.

At a class of 1942 reunion, Blanche (Northwick) Wells, who was the secretary at the Blue Earth Creamery for a number of years, asked me if I still remembered my number. The reply, "yup, No. 33."

1932 Blue Earth Creamery

You see, each patron was designated a number, which was painted on the cream cans, and if one bought butter or hauled buttermilk it was charged to that number. Cream checks were issued once a month and were eagerly awaited, not only by the farmer but by the town business men, who could expect to be paid any bills accumulated during the month.

Most creameries were organized as co-ops, which meant that the farmers owned the facility, and the creamery board hired a manager to churn the butter, weigh the cream, and test the butterfat. The job of butter maker was a prestigious one, as one had to have quite a bit of education to qualify.

When the Schwen Ice Cream and Candy Company went into the business across the street, they bought a certain amount of whole milk to manufac-

153

ture their ice cream and Eskimo Pies. If a farmer sold cream there, he could receive his check right away or be paid monthly.

I milked eight or ten cows for the first ten years we farmed, sort of living from cream check to cream check. As soon as possible I sold out of the dairy business and started into the business of live-stock feeding. The regulations for dairying were becoming more strict each year and it cost too much for the farmer to upgrade his facilities, with bulk tanks and cooling systems.

Any farmers who decided to stay in dairying bought milking machines, and milked more cows to help pay for the expensive equipment. My back really decided the issue for me, as I could squat down beside a cow, but getting up with big buckets of milk was another matter. I began to feel that the only way to make money with cows was to buy them cheap and sell them high. We were afraid that we'd miss the cream check a great deal, but it didn't work out that way. My Dad was quite disappointed when I sold the cows, because he had been Creamery Board Chairman for many years, when the "New" creamery was built.

I continued to haul buttermilk for my hogs for many years after selling the cows. We expanded the hog and sheep business to cover the loss of the cream check, and it all worked out very well. I still feel that whatever the price of milk or butter, it is not enough for the producer."

Quaday's Quotes (Reprinted with permission from RR Quaday) Faribault County Register Monday February 1, 1993

Our Farming Operation Changed Over The Years

"Having been raised on a farm with a sheep flock, I have always had an interest in the production and marketing of the woolly creatures.

In the 1940s we farmed on a conservation basis, rotating row crops, which allowed me to maintain 100 ewes, 12 milk cows, and 20 brood sows, besides the chicken flock which varied according to conditions. Conditions were determined by how many Neva and the kids could take care of.

As the family grew, we were forced by economic circumstances to change our pattern of farming. We sold the cows, increased the brood sows herd, and kept the ewe flock the same.

1948 Pasture Golf

I started buying feeding lambs in the fall to raise the volume of business and use the child labor available. The ewes kept the 40 acre pasture mowed so well that I laid out a nine-hole golf course for free entertainment.

Again, economic conditions forced a change. We plowed up the pasture, raised more corn and went to alfalfa hay to get more volume of business. It was then we started buying more feeders and sold out the ewe flock. When we started really feeding lambs, there were 35 feeders in the business in the county. I always hauled my own lambs in whenever possible because it was a bit harder to face me the next day if I had been cheated on a deal."

Quaday's Quotes- partial (Reprinted with permission from RR Quaday) Faribault County Register Monday, November 27, 1989

Feeding Cattle

Investing in young livestock to feed up to market weight has always been a gamble. Luck plays a big role in whether the farmer makes a profit or goes broke. There are no set rules to follow and disastrous weather, illness, or economic turns can really turn a farmer's hair gray. The successful farmer is hard-working, savvy, intuitive, inventive and extremely adaptable--able to see and take advantage of opportunity when the best laid plans have gone awry.

"When I started going to Montana on buying trips, Steve Boyce's Ranch which I made my headquarters, was stocked with excellent Herford cattle. Steve kept close contact with the Montana Experiment Station, located about five miles up Clear Creek Canyon from his ranch. When I told him that our kids were all in 4-H and showing steers, he couldn't wait. He was very anxious to have some of his cattle in the fair show.

1959 Joan Quaday 4-H Steer Project

I took the oldest three kids along out to the ranch, where they had their pick of hundreds of steers to show at our fair. When we wrote him that his steers had all made a Blue Ribbon Beef, he was proud as could be. His stock looked just as good to a judge in Minnesota, as it did to him out on the range.

In spite of my interest in cattle feeding, there were times when I felt that I'd lose money at it, so I'd feed lambs instead. My rule for buying feeding cattle was this; when the best cattle feeders I knew lost money at it for three years in a row, I would feed cattle that year, and it most always worked. When

Lester Arends sponsored a fat steer show I showed several Blue Ribbon steers, but the fast turnover and quicker paychecks provided by the lamb business won me over. I was never interested in showing fat lambs at the fair, because I was always sold out by April 1 to be ready for field work."

Quaday's Quotes (Reprinted with permission from RR Quaday) Faribault County Register Monday July 25, 1994

Sheep
Raising and Feeding Sheep

According to a *Special Report on the History and Present Condition of the Sheep Industry of the United States* published by the US Department of Agriculture in 1892, "The climatic conditions of Minnesota are favorable for the sheep industry." The report went on to state that "The adaptability of Minnesota for the sheep industry and the favor with which it is regarded by the farmers and breeders is clearly manifest by the steady development of the industry since sheep were first introduced into the State."

And the conclusion of the report's authors stated "From the present condition of the sheep industry there is every reason to believe that sheep will from this time become more and more the favorite class of stock for the enterprising and general farmer of the State."

"I remember one particular time during the Christmas of 1934 when Dad shipped 1,000 fat lambs to Chicago. We trailed them to the stockyard over some pretty big snow banks on River Road and north on Rice Street. The Pilot Grove Road and Rice Street had been plowed and the banks on each side made it easy to keep the lambs together. The flock stretched out over three blocks.

We brought them from the Jo Daviess 80 and after two days rest went on to Blue Earth, from the home farm. The corn crop on the 80 was too retarded from the drought to make it worth picking by hand but the lambs did a good, cheap job of harvesting.

We hauled water to them at the 80 with a team and tank wagon until it snowed. Then the lambs got their moisture by eating snow. The lamb deal, which started in Omaha, turned out to be the one profitable effort that year."

Quaday's Quotes (Reprinted with permission from RR Quaday) Faribault County Register Monday May 18, 1992

1948 Sailor Place Feeder Lambs

"In 1950, we took our first trip west to Montana, Dakotas, Idaho, Washington, Oregon, California, Nevada, Utah, Wyoming, Colorado, and Nebraska. We stopped in Havre, Montana to see Steve Boyce at his Ranch.

We ended up staying for three days, and we bought two carloads of his feeder lambs, which came back to Minnesota on the Great Northern Railroad. We drove the sheep to the Sailor Place on the River Road. My Dad drove the truck ahead and would park in the side driveways, to block the sheep from turning off the road.

Our neighbors at that time on the Old Sailor Place, were Russell and his wife Unna May Golay. They had a dog named Jackie, that was a major pain; he was not a sheep dog and since Russell was deaf, he didn't hear the dog barking at the sheep--but he did hear me cussing his damn dog.

158

The shipment of lambs was full of spear grass, which if left spears its way into the skin of the sheep. It cost me a lot of money to shear and keep the sheep healthy. Mostly, it taught me to examine the lambs before I ship them, next time. I continued buying lambs and cattle this way for 18 years. I worked with several ranchers, including Steve Boyce, Mitch, Tony, and Concepcion Bengochea."

2011 Letter, Typed pages from RR Quaday 01-12-2011

Boyce Ranch Definitely A Working Ranch

"We're at Boyce Ranch, Bear Paw Mountain Country. This is definitely a working ranch, with a big ranch house, a bunk house for the hands, and wonder of wonders, running water.

Steve Boyce had piped a spring up the mountain which never went dry, even in three-year droughts, down to the main house and put a shower room in the basement. He also had a varied number and assortment of ranch hands, which mostly were drifters off the Great Northern, or striking miners from Butte.

On the way to the upper ranch, we drove through two ponds which actually were beaver damns on Clear Creek. Steve said he blew them out about twice a year, but they always put them back.

The log cabin on the upper ranch was a very typical movie set with a corral, a stream of clear water running by and ringed by high mountains covered with conifers. The furniture consisted of three beds, one cast iron wood stove, a gun rack, chairs in various states of repair, and a wash stand with a small cupboard for dishes and cooking utensils. The ceiling was so low that long legged Gloria sat on one of the beds and put her foot prints on it.

The foreman of the ranch was a dour Scotsman named Bob Sterling, who, when he had a stiff neck, put the liniment on the inside in the form of 85 proof whiskey, straight. A day or two after we left, old Bob was heard to say of Gloria, "She could put her shoes under his bed any time." But it never came to pass. This is still one of the most wildly beautiful scenes that I remember.

After supper that night Steve said, "I'm going to show you the sunset around the mountain." We all climbed into the pickup and bounced five

1962 Boyce Ranch in MT; Steve and Mavis Boyce, Bob Sterling, Sadie Boyce

miles up around the mountain, to a bench land high above a valley, which stretched 75 miles to the sweet grass hills.

It was combining time in the valley, and one could see dozens of combines threshing wheat, each trailing dust for about 80 rods. At dusk, there was very little wind and the scene was so colorful, every would-be artist should see it. We stayed there until, one by one the lights came on, on the combines.

Steve was one cattle rancher who could fraternize with Indians, sheep ranchers, and drifters, talk everyone's language, and come away friends with all. He realized very soon after buying the home ranch, that one high section of range was especially adapted for raising sheep. Needing to have a bit of his ranch pay, he started a flock of sheep. Years later he said they lived on steer money, but the sheep paid off the mortgage.

At the time we visited in 1950, the ranchers all had herders who lived in covered wagons out in the mountains through the summer with the sheep, and trailed them into a sheltered area a little closer to civilization for winter. A great number of these herders were of Basque decent and had been herders in the Pyrenees Mountains in what is now Spain. The Basques are fiercely independent people who once had their own nation, and still cling to their language and customs. I became acquainted with many of them in the 18 years I went west buying lambs and calves.

These sheep wagons had no refrigeration, so food had to be hauled out to them periodically. Usually the hardest job was finding the sheep camp in about 5,000 acres of mountain. The herder had a horse, two dogs which talked his language, and usually a bellwether, which is a tame, educated, two or three year old castrated male (sheep).

This wether knew all the best pastures, having been there before, and he made the herder's job much easier by leading the other sheep where he, the herder, wanted them.

This system all changed when the conservation department came out with a coyote poison called 1080. The poison was laced into a piece of raw meat, the mother coyote would eat the meat, go back to the den, regurgitate the meat for the pups and the whole family would be gone.

Ranchers started fencing their sheep pastures and firing herders. The herders than started buying into the sheep business and some were very successful.

If I'm boring my public, just write Rich at the paper or better yet, call me to complain. The story is running on and on, so I'd understand."

Quaday's Quotes (Reprinted with permission from RR Quaday) Faribault County Register Monday June 11, 1990

Buck Was Ahead Of His Time

"The moment Steve Boyce of Montana, and I shook hands, we were friends. There was chemistry between us then and for years to come.

I guess no two men could ever be much more different, he being about five-foot-six, and I at six-foot-one. Steve weighed in at about 275 pounds, I barely weighed 165. I was a practicing Roman Catholic, Steve didn't set much store in ministers and churches, although he lived by a rather strict code of ethics which a good many church people would do well to follow.

1962 Steve & Sadie Boyce

Steve had the short, powerful legs of the classic cowboy, with a short, thick body, which, in spite of the height-weight ratio, did not carry much fat. He continually gave Neva and I a rough time about being fish-eaters for the first few years we were acquainted, but much later, after he found he could not get us riled that way, admitted that most of his long standing friends were Catholic.

One of his near neighbors (only 12 miles) and an old friend, was not only Catholic, but a Fourth Degree Knight of Columbus, named Lars Golay. Steve and I and one of the boys went over to Golay's to see about combining some wheat once, and ran smack into a lot of excitement.

Lars was a cattle man who also raised some wheat on summer-fallow ground, but the trouble was with his sheep flock. One of the bucks had broken out of the buck pasture the night before and, horror of horrors, had gotten into the ewe flock months early.

The flock was pasturing out in an open wheat field which had been combined, with the summer-fallow strip between each 80 acres. With no fences or corrals in sight, the only thing to do was to compress the flock as much as possible, with the dogs keeping the flock running in a tremendous circle.

Lars had two hired hands and, of course, us three to pick out the buck in the midst of 1,500 ewes and lambs. John Boyce and I were by far the youngest and most agile of the men, so we were commissioned to get into the flock and tackle the buck (western bucks weigh about 250-300 pounds).

We worked our way into the packed mass, located the buck and hit him front and rear. Now you'd think a buck sheep, being out all night the first night from captivity, would be worn out, or at least slowed down some, but believe me he was no pushover for the two of us. John had his head and I held onto one hind leg until the others could work their way through the tightly packed flock to help.

Next year, we again went over to the Golay's, this time to visit, and I asked Lars how many lambs resulted from the night of freedom, and he said about 75. The lambs from this fracas were born in February, while it is still bitterly cold up in The Bear Paws. At that time, most sheep men had lambing time come in May, hoping for warm weather or at least a Chinook, which is a down draft wind from the Rocky Mountains that warms from its own friction, and melts and evaporates the snow all at once.

Steve told me about a winter in Havre, when snow piled up on Main Street to a thickness of 18 inches, packed into practically ice. A Chinook came down in the night, and with all the gutters frozen shut, the water ran into every store on Main Street.

Many present day sheep men arrange their lambing pattern for March-April, so the feeders will be heavier in the fall at shipping time, but they must have lambing pens and shed room enough to protect the lambs from heavy snows or frigid blasts, which can occur in a frighteningly short time in The Bear Paws."

Quaday's Quotes (Reprinted with permission from RR Quaday) Faribault County Register Monday June 18, 1990

"In 1958, I left on Sunday for a sheep buying trip to Havre, Montana. Steve, his brother, Earl, and Corrigan also wanted to buy ewe lambs. I was looking for wethers (castrated bucks). We stopped at every watering hole in every small town. I tried very hard to miss a few rounds of drinks because I was driving, but on the way out the bartender would put drinks on the house, and we would start all over again. I put bids in for the sheep on two ranches, which is a lot of miles and time traveling. On Wednesday night

1952 Richard Quaday at Boyce Sheep Ranch

I returned back to the Havre Hotel at ten. I had not eaten supper, and I called Neva after I had already called the ranchers to raise my bids and buy four carloads of lambs. I got her out of bed at midnight, MN time, with my news. She stayed awake for the rest of the night. The call was three days late, but it was one of the best buying deals I had ever made. I bought good lambs, with the price likely to be higher in the spring. I thought I knew everything about sheep buying, but traveling with Steve's bunch I learned more in one trip than I had in thirty-five years raising sheep at home."

2011 Letter Typed pages from RR Quaday - 01-12-2011

"In South St Paul, when Steve was shipping in his livestock from Havre, MT, Charley Govern, who was an old Billings Commission man, was employed at South St Paul Stock Yards. Unknown to Steve, Charley would get a couple of Iowa and MN buyers to climb up and look at the pens of stock for about fifteen minutes. I would climb up onto the gate and holler, "Charley, if this guy don't take 'em, I want 'em. The farmer/buyer couldn't wait to raise the price and write the check to Steve. It worked every time, and made Steve a lot of money. He found out about our selling efforts many years later, when his sons told him the story.

I helped introduce corn silage to Montana, and hauled seed out to Milk River Valley, which helped buy machinery for planting and chopping on the irrigated lower ranch, which turned out to be very successful."

2011 Letter Typed pages from RR Quaday - 01-12-2011

Dick Not Sheepish About Lamb Business

"In the course of many years of lamb feeding, one fact stands out in my memory. No two years are ever the same. Either the method of buying changes, one goes for different sizes, or the conditions on which they reach one's lot vary.

The first year I bought Steve Boyce's lambs from Havre, Montana, they were a picture book lot. They weighed 80 pounds average, and I doubt there was 10 pounds variance among them. Feeders were high that year with feed plentiful and cheap. One can take a six or seven cent drop in market price under such circumstances and still make money with light death loss.

This was my first experience with Montana lambs and I figured to make the connection, get the experience, and establish myself as a lamb feeder even though it might cost a few dollars. We only lost two lambs out of a rail car full, about 285 head. Normal death loss runs from 5-8 percent.

1947 Oak Ridge Farm Feeder Lambs

I sold the first half to Wilson and Company of Albert Lea. Two days later "Doty" Donovan, the sheep superintendent, called. "Luckily for me," he said, "they had bought the lambs on the hoof for a set price, so there was no recourse."

They had a great number of "needles," a common name for spear grass. In wet years out west this grass grows two or three feet high, and the seed sticks in the wool when the sheep walks through the grass. This seed is shaped like a barley beard, with all spines going one way. The only way to keep them from penetrating the flesh is to shear the lamb. Once into the meat, the needles cause infections which have to be cut out of the carcass.

This knowledge came in handy on future buying trips. Malley Johnson, an old timer and sheep feeder from Guckeen told me, "don't believe anybody when you're talking about needles. Get right in the corral and check 'em."

Several times through the years, I bought loads of lambs full of needles. We always sheared these, but one needed a dry place for a few weeks for the short wool allowed colds and pneumonia to develop. A two or three day cold rain could hit fresh shorn lambs pretty hard.

When I first fed lambs, the common saying among most sheep men and the general public was, "a sick sheep is a dead sheep," and it wasn't too far off the truth. After running into this problem and that, I developed a system which though not completely fool-proof, did cut my death loss to about 2 percent.

The one big exception was a package of 850 bought at South St Paul. In the early 1960s, there was a gentleman more or less running the sheep business in the St Paul yards who everyone called "Friday." He came from the Little Falls area, and what he didn't know about sheep and lambs you could stick in your right eyeball.

His proper Polish name was Ed Pawlenty and we still exchange Christmas cards. Anyway, Friday sent me four semis of lambs about October 1. By October 15, I noticed a few cases of sore mouth, nothing to be alarmed about.

Within hours every lamb in the lot had it. The late Dr. Paul Eder was the veterinary doing my work at the time, and he pronounced the malady to be Texas sore mouth, a virus which goes in the front and comes out the back causing lesions all the way through.

We traced it back to a man who had bought some Texas lambs and when the problem showed up, he loaded those that didn't look bad up and sold them as natives. The stock yards at St Paul at that time was a loose sort of co-operative, and I couldn't find anyone to sue. When that happens one makes the best of a bad deal and goes on. I lost 240 lambs out of the 850.

It had been a hail year, and the 60 acres of corn right across the road was hit hard, making many gooseneck stalks and dropped ears left in the field.

I had 40 bred gilts to glean the corn through the fall and winter. After getting their fill of corn, I had 10 burned lamb carcasses ready for them at home. They ate bones and all. I bought no protein, mineral or supplement that winter for them. In March, they farrowed over 10 live pigs per litter. All were big and healthy.

The virus that went through the lambs cost us about a month of growth and condition. During the month in the spring when I would have normally been sold out, the price advanced about 11 cents a pound.

So what could have been a real disaster turned into a profitable feeding year when all was said and done. Good luck always figured strongly in my farm-ing operation."

Quaday's Quotes (Reprinted with permission from RR Quaday) Faribault County Register Monday February 3, 1992

A Quick 1959 Montana Buying Trip

"In the middle of September in 1959, we had our work pretty well finished up for a week or so, and I wanted to take Charlie along out to Montana to help drive. We had the third crop of alfalfa in the barn and our fall pigs wouldn't farrow for about 10 days, so it was a chance to get him acquainted with my ranch connections in and around the Bear Paw Mountains south of Havre, MT. He was a good FFA member and an A student, so I figured the experience would fit right in with Ramsey Johnson's livestock program--and Charlie could easily catch up with his schoolwork. He was 16-years-old and had been driving for a couple of years on a farm permit, hauling the younger kids to SS Peter and Paul's Parochial School, and Kay and Joan to Blue Earth High School.

Neva said she would run the farm for one week, but no longer. So we didn't have any time to waste. We drove the 975 miles to Steve and Sadie Boyce's ranch, starting at 5 am and made it up the ranch driveway at 6 pm, after gaining an hour due to mountain time. We stopped only for gas and lunch. I drove 90-100 miles an hour between towns; there was no speed limit in North Dakota or Montana at that time. I held Charlie at 70 mph. I don't know how fast he went while I was sleeping, because he had learned to have a heavy foot like me.

It was Saturday and one of Steve's daughters, aged 16, was visiting at the ranch. The ranch boys kept her busy, not giving Charlie much time to get acquainted. On Sunday, Steve had to show us his Herefords on all three of his ranches, which killed the day for us. Steve was in his glory, as he was justly proud of his stock--both cattle and sheep. He had a voice like a bullhorn and when he called, the old cows always came running with their frisky calves trailing right along. On Monday, we visited three cattle ranches in his neighborhood but didn't do any buying, as I felt the asking price was too high. On Tuesday, Steve hadn't looked his flock of sheep over for some time, so he wanted to bring them down to the corral for me to check for speargrass.

This was a routine thing for me, having bought a bunch one year before being wised up about that problem. In a wet year a variety of grass in the high plains and low mountains grows tall enough to deposit sharp pointed needles into the sheep wool. The spears have tough hairs, which keep working the needles into the wool until they cause festers in the skin. The lambs have to be sheared, which is risky in the fall, as they need shelter for a couple of weeks. Shearing is a lot of work and costs money, so one must buy them a bit cheaper.

Steve's were clear that year but we couldn't agree on a price, and I thought the other ranchers we talked to were asking too much for their lambs, so I turned my attention to calves. I was equipped to feed either calves or lambs with a good barn, straw shed and with a good grove as a wind break. The ranchers had all sold out the year before for a good price and were in no hurry to sell, so by late Friday I had given up on finding any bargains out west that year. On Saturday morning we took off for home, right after a big ranch breakfast at 6 am, with Charlie driving. He knew the way into town and by the time we had gone the 27 miles to Havre, I was fast asleep. I had worked hard trying to make a deal somehow, and was somewhat disappointed at the outcome. I had made offers on some lambs on two ranches, but I hadn't made any firm deals.

Charlie couldn't figure out how to get onto Hwy No. 2 going east, so he stopped and asked a local policeman how to get there. At about that time I woke up, completely startled, seeing a cop in the window and thinking the worst. I needn't have because he was a good fellow, giving us directions to our road. They don't like to be tough on buyers from Minnesota or points east. Charlie took off and the first thing he did was run through a stop sign with the cop right behind us. He was laughing as he waved us on toward home. We made good time coming home, watching our speed carefully after entering Minnesota.

About ten days later, one of the ranchers called asking me for two-bits a hundred more and I was happy to close the deal. On Oct 1, Steve went to the railroad scale and weighed them, seeing to it that they were properly loaded with dry corral overnight penning. He sometimes would drive over two hundred miles to do this favor and would never accept a cent for doing it. He was PCA Chairman for Hill, Blaine, and Chautou counties, so he used me to get on borrower's ranches as a buyer, so he could check on the job of ranching they were doing, without being a snoop. Smart man."

Quaday's Quotes (Reprinted with permission from RR Quaday) Faribault County Register Monday September 20, 2010

Dick And His Dad Travel To Montana

"The year that my Dad, Bill Quaday, turned 85, I persuaded him to go to Montana with me on a feeder buying trip for a week or so. He liked to travel and had never been to MT. We packed a tarp and some blankets so we could stop and sleep anytime we felt like it. Charlie was going to be in charge of farrowing 25 sows while we were going be away, so I had everything ready for him, which put back our departing time until noon that day.

We were around Wolf Point when we no longer could stay awake and the temperature was 80 degrees, so we pulled out the packed sleeping supplies. It seemed we had been asleep for an hour when I jumped awake with a cold rain in my face. The wind had changed and the temperature had dropped about 30 degrees when it started to rain. We hurried into the car, turned on the heater, and drove about 50 miles before our teeth stopped chattering. By then it was 4:30 am. We loafed around Steve Boyce's ranch that day because Steve spent the day at the Upper Ranch.

The next morning we started to travel to look at lambs, starting at Bud Corrigan's Ranch. Bud and his brother were ready with some saddle horses because they planned to move the flock home from a distant pasture, so our help was welcomed and I got a good look at the lambs.

All went well until we happened onto a lamb lying upside down and kicking like mad. The native MT folks said, "rattlesnake." Just then I heard a commotion behind me and my Dad had picked up a David-sized rock, bashed the snake's head and had his knife out to cut off the rattles. He prized those 3-inch rattles until his dying day, re-telling the story many times.

After an hour or so of haggling over price, we all went into Chinook for a drink. I had qualms about Dad's behavior in a saloon, because he never drank alcohol. I wasted my worry; he ordered orange pop like he always does, and when it was his turn to buy he brought out a $20 bill. Steve protested, but Dad insisted. Dad was about half the size of Steve, but he was a very big man to me that day.

On the way home I took a short cut through SD to see a big lamb feeding operation at Columbia. We were again driving at night and hit a detour; stopped to ask if the road was open. The lady assured us that people had driven on it all day, but it might be a bit muddy. We drove 23 miles in the dark following the deep muddy ruts left by the earlier travelers, never getting out of low gear. The next day we visited with the owner of the lamb operation, then came on home where everyone was glad to see us, especially my Mother who worried that "Will" would be too old for the trip. He actually stood it better than I did."

Quaday's Quotes partial (Reprinted with permission from RR Quaday) Faribault County Register Monday October, 4 1991

Raising sheep could be tough when the weather got rough.

"In my book, the St Patrick's Day storm of 1965 was the most severe this part of the country has ever known. That storm also started with rain which froze onto overhead wires as the temperature dived, freezing extra tons of weight on trees and power poles.

The rain turned to snow and toward evening, the wind switched to the northwest, getting strong enough to snap power poles like match sticks.

I only had about 400 feeding lambs left in two lots. The lot around the corn bins was exposed to heavy drifting in the storm so we moved all the lambs into the yard back of the barn. We had a six-foot high board fence around this lot for wind protection, but the drifts inside the lot piled up to 10 and 12 feet.

We had to shovel out the fence to keep the lambs from running all over the neighborhood. This did not get all done for several days, and I can still remember Jim and Mike running over to where I was feeding hay, all excited.

"We heard something," they exclaimed. "It sounded like lambs where we were scooping out the fence."

1965 Blizzard, Jim & Mike Quaday

Sure enough, when I beat the scoop shovel on the drifts I heard a lamb blat! When we dug down along the fence, there was not one but three lambs that had laid down along the fence and were drifted over.

It was a good thing they were sheep because no other farm animal could have stayed alive that long. They were none the worse for wear, although they wasted no time heading for the feed bunk.

A sheep, you know, if trapped in an impossible situation will just take it easy, not get excited, and wait for something good to happen, while cattle or hogs would struggle to the death trying to free themselves, thus using up all their energy right way.

Sometimes we should be so smart."

Quaday's Quotes (Reprinted with permission from RR Quaday) Faribault County Register Monday November 11, 1991

More Snow and Old Time Chores

"I can remember winters back in the 1960s and 1970s when we had heavy snow pack and blizzards, and we were feeding four or five yards of lambs. Jim and Mike were going to Blue Earth High School and were on the varsity wrestling team. They wanted to compete on the same team, even though they knew that I really needed them at home for feeding chores. They volunteered to get up early enough to feed two yards of lambs before breakfast, if I had the pickup truck loaded the night before. If it snowed through the night and the feed bunks had to be scooped out, they had to work a little faster. One morning it was so cold that Jim broke off the shift lever on the pick-up, trying to get it into gear. That caused a catastrophe, because I had to do all the feeding that day with the tractor and spreader.

I did practically all the veterinary work in those years, and I made it a point to see every lamb every day--which made the chores nearly twice as long. We had a severe blizzard during that time in mid-January, with two of the yards drifted in with four-foot drifts which turned as hard as ice. We simply chopped the feed bunks out, lifted them up on top of the drifts, and fed off the tractor and spreader until we could sell some fat lambs. The soup from the top of the drifts ran down into my orchard. I had four apple trees planted in a lower fenced-in area. The soup was so rich that it killed three of the apple trees. The fattest lambs were in that lot, making it a lucky accident, before the banks all melted.

The boys didn't have to worry about cutting weight that winter; they worked it off. If the wrestling meet was out of town, they didn't have to feed the next morning. I'm sure they were sometimes pretty tired before the meets started. Years later, at family gatherings and after a few beers, Jim would start telling stories about how they worked hard out on our River

Road farm. He would say, "One thing Dad taught us was how to work."

I guess that came from way back, because my Dad taught us all the advantages of hard work. One of his favorite sayings was, "Hard work never hurt anybody." All his life he was a small man doing a big man's work. Near the end of his farming career he endured a lot of pain and made a lot of visits to his old friend, Dr. E.E. Collison the blind chiropractor, and to an osteopath in Winnebago to keep his back and shoulders working properly. The grain and stock farming in those days involved much more hand work and back work, than the present day farmers endure.

I started farming in 1938, when practically all work with livestock was done with a fork, a scoop shovel and a five gallon pail--or worse yet--a bushel basket (much heavier)."

Quaday's Quotes -Partial (Reprinted with permission from RR Quaday) Faribault County Register Monday February 22, 2010

South St Paul Stockyard

According to a *Special Report on the History and Present Condition of the Sheep Industry of the United States* published by the US Department of Agriculture in 1892, "There are three stockyard companies in the vicinity of St Paul and Minneapolis, which are designated as follows: The Union, Twin City, and the Minnesota Transfer. Officials of these stockyards give the amount of sheep handled in each yard for the year 1891 as follows: Union, 89,423; Twin City, 00,550; Minnesota Transfer, 20,895."

"While these live-stock markets are yet in their infancy, their growth has been vigorous and substantial. With the rapid yet substantial development of the live-stock interests of the Northwest, the "twin cities" seem likely to have one of the leading live-stock markets of this country. The establishment of large packing houses indicates what may be expected. The farmers of Minnesota are peculiarly fortunate in having a home market of such magnitude both for wool and mutton, as well as all classes of live-stock. Dealers as well as manufacturers handle considerable wool at Minneapolis, and there are located here branch wool houses from Eastern markets."

The Quaday family shipped many animals through the South St Paul stockyards.

"Another farm connected subject, I see that South St Paul is closing the stockyards in mid-April. This is really the bitter end to a hundred-year-old institution; one in which I have written and received a great many checks involving at least a million dollars, or more. During the 40s, and through the 70s, I sold fat lambs and cattle there, and also bought feeder stock, lambs and calves from commission companies. I bought feeder calves from an old Montanan named Charley Govern, who ran the South St Paul Commission Co. He at one time handled most of the Montana cow and calf shipments and my rancher friend, Steve Boyce, always sold through him. He was from Billings, Montana, originally. Steve brought in fifteen carloads of cattle and five carloads of sheep every fall, around the first of November. He delayed his shipping date because the sheep were dipped until the first of November. After that the dipping process stopped. It was hard on the lambs especially, causing much pneumonia and shipping fever. The dipping process was a complete inundation of the lamb in a tank filled with water and carbolic acid. If some of this mixture got into the animal's lungs, pneumonia followed. The dipping was mandated on account of scabies, which caused the wool to fall out and lesions on the skin of the animal.

On November 2, 1935, there were 38,000 sheep processed through the commission companies each day, and many millions of dollars changed hands in The Exchange Building on Concord Street. I understand that The Exchange Building has been designated a historic site. If not, it should be. Once a deal was made with the Commission Company it didn't take very long, hardly over an hour, before the seller could pick up his check and head home to do chores. Of course, if he bought more feeding stock he might stay overnight, party a bit, and see to it that his purchase was properly loaded for the trip back to his farm, where the cycle would start all over again.

The Stock Yards at South St Paul were in business for over one hundred years (started up in 1888, full name Union Stock Yard) and soon had an odor all its own. The South St Paul athletic teams are still "The Packers."

Quaday's Quotes - Partial (Reprinted with permission from RR Quaday) Faribault County Register Monday April 14, 2008

Chickens

Chickens were an integral part of the farm scene. They provided a regular source of meat and the eggs were often traded or sold for much needed cash during the depression years. Many farmers survived the lean times on weekly milk and egg checks in town.

"Raising chickens was a secondary operation, where my Mother always had setting hens in the basement of our farmhouse, her favorite breed being the Rhode Island Reds. These were a dual purpose chicken for egg production and meat."

Quaday's Quotes-partial (Reprinted with permission from RR Quaday) Faribault County Register Monday July 29, 1991

"West of the barn and south of the garage was the chicken coop consisting of an enclosed room with roosts and boxes where the hens laid their eggs, and a screened sun room where the chickens could get the necessary fresh air and sunshine on cold rainy days. One of the chores assigned to my brothers and me, was to gather the eggs--a task which required quite a bit of courage at times. Some of the hens didn't want us to take the eggs out of the nests and pecked at us when we put our hands anywhere near them. We also had one rooster that delighted in flying at us and pecking our legs. One time John was supposed to get the eggs and when he hadn't come back after about half an hour, I was sent to find out what had happened to him. I found him on top of the roost in the chicken coop throwing eggs at the rooster who wouldn't let him come down."

Overture to Anderson Unfinished Symphony, 1914-1942, Written by Marie Anderson

Mixing Motorcycles With Hatching Hens Results In One Mad Mother

"When I reminisce about things as they were through the 20s and 30s while I was growing up on our River Road Farm, I have to feel that farm animals are really not all that much different from us humans.

For every 100 hens we had four roosters--the reason was the fact most farm wives raised their own chicks from fertilized eggs hatched out by setting hens or "clucks" as they were called.

Survival of the chicken flocks was downright hazardous, from the varmints that lived in the woods.

In the spring of 1934, my brother, John, got the motorcycle craze. He had very little or no money to gratify his wants. He scrounged around until he found a cycle, which was considered junk and hadn't been ridden for many years. It was red under a thick coat of grease and dust, and I believe it was manufactured before 1918. The spark from the plugs came from a magneto which had to be timed perfectly on the power stroke to make the motor run. The magneto on this cycle was burned out and provided no spark.

Gust Ristau was the electrician of the neighborhood and John prevailed upon him to rewind the Bosch mag. John had worked on the cycle in the basement of the old farm house, and the time to install and time the magneto coincided with Mother's hatching period for little chicks.

The cluck hens hatched the eggs in segregated boxes and were let off every day, twice for feed and water. On the night Gust came over to get the motorcycle running all was quiet in the chicken department, with the clucks settled for the night.

Without an instruction book, timing of the engine was by guess and by gosh. There was no clutch, so one had to either push it to start, or jack up the back wheel and turn the whole drive train. Choosing the later of the options, they turned on the gas and turned the back wheel. The engine was at full throttle and there was no muffler, so you can imagine when it started on the second turn, the roar it produced in the basement. The cycle jumped up and down on the jack, forcing two of us to hold it down, while John turned off the gas. The basement was full of black smoke and the cluck hens were jumping off their nests in fright.

By the time we had the presence of mind to turn off the gas, everything in the basement was in an uproar. Mother came down the stairs to a scent of smoke, chicken feathers flying around, raising dust and the din of an unmuffled motorcycle. To put it mildly she was plenty mad at us, but eased off a bit when she saw Gust Ristau in the middle of the fracas.

Needless to say, that was the last chance for the basement cycle mechanics. They were banished to one of the outside sheds."

Quaday's Quotes -partial (Reprinted with permission from RR Quaday) Faribault County Register Monday September 19, 1994

"When Neva and I raised chickens on the Home Farm and slept on the sleeping porch, the night time sounds amplify and wake you from a sound sleep. One night I woke from a sound sleep after hearing a strange sound, and remembered I had not shut the south brooder house door. Putting on my shoes and walking outside in my shorts, I walked across the yard. I heard a car coming down the River Road so I started to run from view, and I stumbled and fell down on the gravel driveway. I lost one shoe and it came down and landed on my head while I was laying there. After the car passed, I saw four young raccoons with their momma run out of the brooder house door and climb up into the big Oak tree. I immediately shut the brooder house door and ran to the house to get Neva, a flashlight, and a gun. Neva held the flashlight and the younger raccoons opened their eyes as she shined the light on them. I was able to shoot all four of them, having to reload each time since I was using a single shot twenty gauge gun. This all happened at 2:30 am. I proceeded to tell the story at our 500 Card Club game to Rollo Greimann. He said, "I wondered what you were doing out in the yard in your shorts at two-thirty in the morning."

2011 Letter Typed pages from RR Quaday - 01-12-2011

The weather really affected the operation of the farm in our early days of farming. Rough winter storms put people and animals at risk.

Blizzards and Cold Weather Cause Livestock Problem

"Thankfully, we don't get a foot of snow this early in the fall every year. It does happen though, and the weatherman always chalks it up as "The Snowstorm of the Century." I can only remember three such phenomena in my 90 years. One was the Armistice Day blizzard of 1940, which I have written about in this column several times in the past.

In 1946, on Nov 6, I was plowing with my 10-20 McCormick-Deering tractor on the Sailor Place, with my shirtsleeves rolled up and the old tractor running on a boil. The temperature was above 80 degrees, and our pullets were still on range in the brooder house across the road from the farm buildings. I had been thinking about moving them to the main chicken house for a couple of nights, but with near perfect weather I had kept putting it off.

We woke the next morning to a 7-inch snowfall and a 30 miles per hour northwest wind; in other words, a blizzard. After the milking and feeding chores were done, I cranked up the pickup and hunted up our two chicken crates and some gunny sacks, in preparation for moving our pullets across the road. The first thing I did was to get the pickup stuck, so the heavy work would have to be done by hand. The chickens were beginning to pile up in the corner of the brooder house to stay warm, so it had to be done in a hurry. The kids were too young to help, so it fell on Neva to keep them

177

from smothering while I filled the gunny sacks and carried them across the road to their permanent winter shelter.

I had never realized that half-breed leghorns could be so heavy. I was in my prime at age 26, yet I was completely pooped out by the time they were all safely moved. We only lost 4 chickens, but they didn't begin to lay eggs for nearly a month from the trauma of being moved in daylight, in such a manner.

Our next door neighbors, Arvis and Jean Meyers, were not so lucky. They had 20 bred gilts still pastured on alfalfa, housed in a small shed across the road from the barn and other buildings. Arvis tried his best for over an hour to drive them home, but when the blizzard hit them, they turned around and ran into the shed. They piled up in a corner and smothered six of them, worth about $100 each. Practically all the turkey farmers lost all the birds still out in the fields; they smothered from ice build-up on the nostrils.

The Halloween Blizzard in 1991 happened after we had moved into Blue Earth, and I thanked the Lord all night that we were all through farming; I would have been loaded with either 2000 feeding lambs or 150 head of feeder cattle and perhaps 200 head of fall pigs, to take care of. We had freezing rain all night; building up an inch of ice on trees and wiring before it began to snow. My arbor vitae between the house and driveway got so heavy with ice that the tops bent over, touching the driveway. I had some boards in the garage and propped them up, or they would have snapped off. Many branches broke down from the weight. October that year had been warm and dry, so many of the song birds were still here. The ice killed millions of them, smothering them if they didn't have buildings for shelter. All we had left were English Sparrows, and very few of them.

Our 2000 feeder lambs would have been a disaster for us, because we didn't have that much building shelter and an inch of ice would have frozen them all to the ground; that's a lot of lamb to chop loose and lift up.

We went through some mighty tough blizzards, some years, when we were farming and feeding a lot of stock, but our thick grove of oak trees, choke cherries and gooseberry bushes stopped most of the northwest wind and the snow piled up quite deep in the grove before drifting up into the farm yard. The River Road was always drifted in after every blizzard, from our farm to the blacktop. In horse and buggy days, we just drove a team of horses and a bob-sled, with two boxes high for wind protection, over the snow banks into Blue Earth to go to school, church, creamery or grocery store. River Road was all ice from December 1 until spring, making it necessary to shoe the horses. A slip on the ice with a team on a trot could very well be the end of that horse's career.

When the Model T Fords came on the market, we could usually make it to town with a set of chains, if the drifts didn't get too deep and if we could get the T started in winter. The first ones had to be cranked by hand, or jacked up so we could turn the engine by turning the rear wheel. The Model A Fords were a great improvement, as one could use an electric starter and help with the crank on super cold mornings. If that didn't work, there was the ever ready team of horses to pull it. We called it, "Giving it a ride." The "Olden Days" were not always peaches and cream, believe me."

Quaday's Quotes (Reprinted with permission from RR Quaday) Faribault County Register Monday November 29, 2010

Hunting
Dicks Buck Fever Doesn't Last Long

"In the early 50s, the Conservation Department decided that enough deer had migrated to southern Minnesota to have a buck season for one weekend in November.

A great many residents of our area made a yearly pilgrimage to northern Minnesota to hunt deer in the forests and swamps where deer are plentiful. No one even imagined how many deer had Faribault County, except the local farmers who started seeing more deer each year in their corn fields.

A great many arguments occurred about how many deer there were actually living in the area. I had never gone up north hunting, because I was hardly ever through picking corn and usually had fall plowing to finish. We also had a yard full of young livestock to tend, most of which required extra care while getting it weaned to eating feed.

I had been seeing deer all summer and because there had been no open season here, they seemed almost tame, unlike the deer up north. My neighbor, Ralph Ficken, had gone up to Tofte nearly every fall deer hunting, but as he had corn to pick yet, he decided to hunt here.

179

By the time I had made up my mind to try a day of hunting in our neighborhood and had purchased a deer tag, there were only three 20 gauge slugs left in John Breen's hardware store. I bought these three thinking, "I'll have to shoot better at deer than I ever have at pheasants."

The season started at daybreak on Saturday, but by the time I had all the chores done and everything ready for the hunt, it was after lunch. I walked alone through some woods and elderberry thickets on what was known as the Benson Place for about an hour.

At about the time I had decided that there were no deer out there, I headed for my car parked up on the road. Just as I was coming up to the creek, three deer jumped out of the brush on the other side of the creek.

I had heard of buck fever where a person is completely unable to move, let alone cock and shoot a gun at a moving target. I have to admit the buck fever lasted for the first two lucky deer, but the third one to jump out got it in the neck.

Ralph had told me, "When he shifts into high gear, aim for the head and you'll get him in the neck." It worked perfectly. The gorgeous buck col-

1952 Richard Quaday Deer

lapsed like a wet sack, got up and ran like nothing had happened for about 20 rods, and staggered to a stop. He was dead when I caught up.

I was about a third of a mile from my car. The way to the car lay across the creek, across a plowed field, and up a hill to the road. He was too heavy to drag with one hand, so I took my single shot 20 gauge shotgun apart and after sticking the barrel and stock through my belt, could use both hands. Lifting him onto the car fender was another struggle.

Driving by Ficken's place, I got the idea of hanging him up for dressing on Ralph's wagon hoist where we let him hang overnight. The next day I hauled him into town for Cort Viesselman to cut up and wrap for the freezer. He weighed 235 pounds gutted. Neva doesn't care for venison so we gave Ralph and Dorothy half of the meat.

So, having gone deer hunting once and shooting one shell, my deer hunting ceased on a successful note. I love to see deer around, anywhere except on my car windshield.

Quaday's Quotes (Reprinted with permission from RR Quaday) Faribault County Register Monday October 28, 1991

Farm Equipment

Steam Power
Steam Engines and Threshing Machines

In 1786, Scotsman Andrew Meikle invented a threshing machine. The early machines were powered by horse or later by steam engines. Many of them were stationary. The threshing machine did four different tasks. It removed grain, separated the grain from the cob or husk, cleaned the grain, and then gathered it or stacked it. The threshing machine was never widely purchased by small farmers. They were very large and often too expensive for the average farmer. Often they were used in custom operation going from farm to farm. Later these threshing machines were combined with reapers and became known as combines.

> "When I was a youngster growing up on our River Road Farm, the highlight of the farm year to children was threshing time. The excitement of all the big machinery, the teams of horses hitched to the bundle wagons, and the elevator running the grain into the bin, all contributed to the organized chaos. By the time I was old enough to haul bundles and pitch them into the threshing machine at 13, the gas tractors had more or less replaced the steam engine here in the Corn Belt.
>
> There were three of these monsters still operating within a few miles of Blue Earth in the 1930s. The Tillia Brothers, who lived across the field from us, owned two--one of which they bought out in North Dakota for parts to keep the other one running. They hired it out to run the McCloskey pea viner, which was over by threshing time.

1944 Woods Brothers Threshing Machine

The main trouble with steam engines was the amount of help it took to keep them operating. They generated so much horsepower that it ran a big separator (usually a 42 inch or bigger) which required 12 bundle teams to keep it running. Earnest Ziegler had a steamer, as did Archie Swingdorf near Guckeen, and Roy Spencer, who used his to run the saw mill in town. The Preschers, out toward Delavan had a threshing run. The steam engines required a prodigious supply of water hauled to the steamer by a tank wagon, usually made of cedar wood, with a hand pump. The tanker had to be in pretty good shape, because it was usually hot and running the pump was hard work.

The steam engines were also used for plowing on the bigger fields, road grading and silo filling. The big problem when plowing was the turning radius of the behemoths. The going joke was "It takes five acres just to turn around on the ends." In 1934, when the River Road was first graded and graveled, Earnest Ziegler's steamer furnished the power on the grader. The biggest gravel trucks carried a maximum of three yards so with the gravel coming from Kiester, the project used up most of the summer. My Dad was on the Blue Earth Township Board and did the gravel checking, so John and I did the farming that summer."

Quaday's Quotes-partial (Reprinted with permission from RR Quaday) Faribault County Register, Monday October 27, 2008

Dick Recalls The Days of Threshing Grains

"The threshing of grain on our River Road farm was always an event featuring flurried activity by all family members, including those too young to be of much use in the threshing operation labor. In the best years of O.J. Wendt's run, we had 10 bundle teams, two grain haulers, the machine operator, and a tractor man.

The tractor man was always our favorite when we were just little kids hanging around, watching the grownups work. He seemed to have more time to talk to us and answer the thousand and one questions we'd ask. His was a clean job until someone plugged the machine by pitching too fast or too many bundles at once. Then tempers got real short real fast, as that made lots of unnecessary, hard and dirty work to get things on the move again.

Bob Ankeny Sr. told me the other day that being a tractor man was one

1944 1020 McCormick Tractor

of his first jobs on O.J. Wendt's run. He had to help clean up around the machine every night and every time it was moved to another farm. This was very important, mostly to blow out all the mustard seed and other early maturing weeds that could be carried from farm to farm. (Canadian Thistles were the worst.)

At age 10, I had my first paying job with the crew watching grain wagons. This was usually a fairly clean job, because the farmers did not want a lot of chaff and dirt blowing into the grain after paying good money to have it blown out. I made 50 cents a day. However, the eating was always spectacular in our run, with mostly good sound, German cooks and no restrictions on the volume consumed.

After a year or so of that, I was put on the blower tender's job. That was usually a dirty job especially if the wind changed during the day, and always when the straw stack was being topped out, requiring constant attention by the tender.

With 10 small grain jobs, our run could go for as long as three weeks if we had a rain or two. At that time, nearly everyone had a few acres of flax for a cash crop. Flax brought a good price before soybeans came into vogue because linseed oil, a basic ingredient of paint, was high priced compared to the wheat, oats, and barley. Oats were a must on all farms because most of the draft work was done by horses and mules, who thrived best on oats and grass hay, with the straw being used for bedding.

We always hated to thresh barley because the crop nearly always had rust, which itched when the thresh machine blew it into the air. The bundles of barley were hard to build a good load with as they were slippery on the head end, and if care was not taken a whole side or end of a load could slide out.

1944 Dick Quaday Pitching Threshing Bundles

At age 13, I was allowed to pitch bundles, the premium job on the run. We finished up at our farm and moved on to Fred Paschke's place. Dad was busy unloading grain after stacking straw, one of the dirtiest jobs one could ever imagine. I'm sure, in retrospect, that he didn't relish the idea of going to pitch bundles without first washing the dirt and chaff off. At any rate, once I had loaded a few bundles and gotten them up to and through the machine, I got to haul bundles until I started farming on my own at age 18.

I was only farming 80 acres the first year, so I had about 20 acres of oats and no flax. O. J. had a 32-inch Huber separator by then, so the run didn't take so long. Everyone kept track of their bundle team time; we had a meeting after the run was over and I was paid 25 cents an hour for helping the larger farmers thresh their grain. Therefore, it didn't set very well with me two years later when I was farming 240 acres, with 100 acres of oats and flax, that overtime was figured at $1.25 an hour and I had to pay. This prompted my Uncle Herman Quaday and I to go into partnership, with me furnishing the tractor and he furnishing the thresh machine. But that's another story."

Quaday's Quotes (Reprinted with permission from RR Quaday) Faribault County Register Monday September 16, 1991

Equipment Manufacturers

Before the organization of the International Harvester Co., there were a number of independent companies manufacturing grain binders, mowers, rakes and other farm machinery. Here they are as remembered by J. F. Percival in the article "History of the Grain Binder", in the Farm Collector Magazine, September/October 1955 issue: McCormick Co., Deering Co., Jones (Plano) Co., Walter Wood Co., Milwaukee Co., Osborn Co., Minnesota bu (Minnesota State Prison), Acme Harvester Co. All of the above were absorbed by the I. H. C. (International Harvester Company) except Minnesota and Acme. The I. H. C. continued manufacturing the McCormick and the Deering machines, also the Champion for some years. They finally dropped the Champion and then consolidated the McCormick and Deering, and that has grown into the present I. H. C. McCormick Deering line of machines. The John Deere Company started making grain binders about 1910 and later on added other farm machines to their line. Originally John Deere manufactured only plows, discs, harrows and wagons.

Tractors and Plows

1930s Lug Wheel Tractor

Early tractors utilized wide metal tires, especially in the rear of the machine to disperse the weight. Front wheels often had ridges to help them steer in the dirt. Problems with traction pushed engineers to come to another form of wheels. A continuous belt with slats were fitted to the front and back wheels. Fordson was one of the first mass produced tractors, starting in 1916. Plowing speed was 2.8 mph weighing over a ton. It ran on kerosene and could plow 8 acres on one tank of fuel.

In 1932, Allis-Chalmers began to use pneumatic tires from Firestone Tire and Rubber Company. The tires had a much better grip in the soils and had many advantages over the metal tires, including their weight. Today most of the tires used are wide and grooved for best results.

I owned fifteen tractors: a Farmall F-12, two Farmall Bs, one 10 to 20 McCormick Deering, one Farmall H, three Allis-Chalmers WDs, one John Deere B, an International 460, an Allis-Chalmers I-90, two Allis-Chalmers D-17s, an Allis Chalmers 7000, and an Allis Chalmers 7045.

> "The Christmas I remember best, in my early years, was the year I had a real factory-made toy, at age six or seven. My uncle Rudolph Baum worked for D.D. Murphy during the 1920s, selling Ford Model Ts and Fordson tractors. When Rudolph's father, an old gentleman with a long beard, died, Rudolph decided to go into farming on the family farm southeast of Elmore. He made a deal with Murphys for a new Fordson tractor, getting a cast iron miniature replica of the tractor--at that time painted gray with bright red lug-type wheels. There were no rubber tired tractors in 1926. My Dad knew about the deal, as he spent quite a lot of time in their garage at that time.
>
> He asked Uncle Rudolph how much he wanted for the model tractor, just making conversation. I was always the apple of Mr. Baum's eye, and when he learned who was getting the tractor, he said, "Nothing." Dad might have had an inkling way back then, who would someday be operating the home farm, and having a tractor in those sparse times was quite an incentive. I played in the house with it, making a lot of noise on the hardwood floors and driving my Mother crazy, I'm sure. When spring came I had to hurry up to get it into the mud out in the yard.
>
> One day I was playing with it and Mom called me to the house. I left the tractor in the driveway and when I came back brother Carl had run over it with a load of wood, breaking the axel. I shed many tears, but he said "That

will help you remember to take care of your machinery." Good lesson, but hard for a six-year old to take."

Quaday's Quotes - Partial (Reprinted with permission from RR Quaday) Faribault County Register Monday December 28, 2009

The problem of plowing the plains was solved by a blacksmith from Vermont named John Deere. Deere moved to Grand Detour, Illinois, in 1836. He invented a blade which was self polishing and combined the share and moldboard into a one piece plow. Deere moved his factory to Moline, Illinois, and began manufacturing in 1847. The blade was an amazing hit and began the John Deere company. Today plows are pulled by large tractors and can do large tracts of land in a single day.

Dick And Neva Buy Their First Farm

"The first money I ever borrowed was a $900 note to my Dad. It was a demand note for a half interest in 10 milk cows, 10 brood sows, 30 ewes, 3 horses and 150 laying hens. He had not bought any new machinery for a number of years since he wanted to get out of farming.

1938 Farmall F-12 Marie Quaday

The first thing I did in the fall of 1938 when I was sure of a crop, was to go to Sid Johnson Implement and buy a tractor. It was an F-12 Farmall with a two row cultivator. It had Monkey Ward knobby tires on the rear and a single rubber tire in the front. I then bought a single bottom 18" John

189

Deere plow from the D. D. Murphy Co. To pay for these I borrowed $700 from Harry Pfeiffer, Sr. at eight percent interest.

By the end of 1939 I had the tractor and livestock notes paid."

Quaday's Quotes-partial (Reprinted with permission from RR Quaday) Faribault County Register Monday, February 4, 1991

Tractors Changed With The Times

"Since the age of horse farming rolled into history at about the time I started "rolling my own" on the River Road Farm, tractors and horsepower have been main topics of conversation among farmers everywhere. The ease of manipulation, the power output and the traction of each make and model, have resulted in endless arguments among neighbors, relatives and friends who were involved in farming.

1938 Farmall F-12 Dick's First Tractor

The first tractor I owned was an F-12 Farmall, with Montgomery Ward knobby rear tires and a single wheel in front. It came with a two row mounted corn cultivator (soybeans were not here yet), equipped with a hydraulic power lift. I purchased it from Sid Johnson Implement, located at that time on North Main street, where the Callaghan Apartments and the Loren Lein Insurance now stand. I paid $625 for the complete outfit. It was a heavy machine for the amount of power it produced but still, in my eyes, a great improvement over animal horse power. I can't help but amuse myself thinking what the animal rights people would have done to stir up trouble with farmers, who absolutely had to depend on horses to get their farming done. That, however, was another age when people had enough to do just doing their job, and happy to get by without making waves.

Through the years I have owned Farmall (Made by International Harvester), John Deere, and Allis-Chalmers tractors, with horse power ranging from about 20 up to around 200. At first, when farming just my farm along with Dad's, the F-12 was sufficient. We farmed an 80 in Jo Daviess Township, two-and-one half miles away, so I soon traded for one with a higher road gear.

1947 Farmall Dick Quaday, Charles, Kay & Joan

191

When live power came in, I changed to an Allis-WD, which would pull two 16-inch plow bottoms. When we expanded the acreage by renting more land, I bought a D-17 Allis, which did a good job of pulling three 16-inch plows. The machinery companies, realizing that farms were inevitably growing larger, kept coming out with newer, higher powered tractors costing infinitely more money. At that time moldboard plowing, which turned the soil completely over, was the only way to go. The blacker the soil showed after plowing, the better the job of plowing.

1950 Charles Quaday Allis-Chalmers Tractor

I was one of the first to abandon the black plowing during the 50s. I found that if I set the coulters a certain way, much trash was left on top, which kept the soil from washing away or blowing off. Most of my neighbors gave me snide remarks about my messy job of plowing, but watched it closely nevertheless.

As we added rented farms to our farming operation, we bought larger and heavier tractors, and rather than change the wheel width to adapt the tractor, we simply bought more tractors which we used for specific purposes. Time became so important, that it was not feasible to waste one's energy and time revamping tractors to adapt. When we booked our sale, we had a five-plow tractor (7045 Allis), a 706 International for planting and cultivating, a 1-70 Allis with hydraulic leader, and a D-17 Allis for choring and hauling wood. In a bind, the 706 International could pull a four bottom plow.

1979 Charles Quaday Allis-Chalmers 7000 Tractor

It was a real treat believe me, to have a cab tractor for late plowing after 30 years of frostbite and northwest wind. It was a pleasure also, to have nearly 600 horsepower standing ready to serve at a moment's notice. Our last new tractor cost $28,000, or thereabout."

Quaday's Quotes (Reprinted with permission from RR Quaday) Faribault County Register Monday October 26, 1992

193

Corn Pickers

In 1850 Edmund Quincy invented the corn picker and the commercial corn and wheat belts began to form, initiating what has become our current form of industrial agriculture.

> "When we began to raise hybrid corn, the volume of product increased so drastically that a mechanical corn picker became a necessity. I bought a mounted Belle City one row picker for my steel wheeled 10-20 McCormick tractor. On frosty mornings and dry afternoons, the rollers were so slick that they would not drag the stocks through to snap off the corn. That picker nearly cost me an arm one frosty morning when I rode on the fender, driving with one hand and pulling the stocks back with my other hand. My butt slipped on the fender, dropping my hand into the rollers. My leather glove went on through, but when I looked down my hand had stayed behind. This scare prompted me to weld ridges on the snapping rolls. This caused some shelling on damp days, but stopped the plugging.
>
> During the 2nd World War, I bought a John Deere one row picker with a wagon hitch. Then, for the first time, I could do the whole operation by myself, since I had picked up an old elevator that was on sale. There was no new machinery built during the war years, so someone had to quit farming and sell out their machinery in order to make used machinery available. It was quite a relief when new machinery finally became available again. The forced buying vacation had helped accumulate money enough to make new purchases."
>
> *CORN TALK, Monthly newsletter for corn producers who are Members of Minnesota Corn Growers Association, Vol. 14, No. 8*

Combines

The first combine was invented by Hiran Moore in 1838. It took several decades before the combine came into wide use. Early combines were driven by as many as 16 or more horses. Later they were pulled by steam engine, and then combined into a single machine by George Stockton Berry. Berry took the straw and used it for fuel to heat the boiler. The header (or cutter) was over forty feet. This machine could cut and thresh over one hundred acres in a day. The cost of the machine was also cheaper than the horse drawn reapers and stationary threshers. The cost of the reaper and thresher was about $3 an acre, while the combine was between $1.50 and $1.75.

The modern combine has many luxuries. Most are now equipped with a full stereo system, comfortable seat, and full air conditioning. The inside of the cab is slightly pressurized so that the air pushes out of the cab, which does not allow dust and dirt to come in.

1946 Allis-Chalmers Combine

"My first combine was an Allis Chalmers straight through machine, with a three-foot cylinder and three-foot header controlled with a large lever. This machine took only one 40-inch row of soybeans, thus was able to shave the lowest of beans without scraping much dirt. With only one row to watch one could avoid any rocks which would raise hob with any combine. The first year I had the 3-footer, I combined 40 acres of my own then did 60 acres for Gust Ristau and finished up with 30 acres for Lester Arends out on the Tressler land north of town. I believe the combine fee was $3 per acre at that time. Gas was cheap and with very few combines around, the operators were in great demand. I might add that this little combine was an excellent clover huller. The wind could be fine tuned to save every seed and still blow the dust and hulls out with the stems. Later and larger models of combines had so much capacity that it was almost impossible to hold the seed and still clean it as well.

1949 60 Inch Allis-Chalmers Combine

The first year I pulled the little combine with an H-Farmall tractor, and got along fairly well. The H was a two-plow tractor and had enough power, but did not have live power take-off. In heavy grain we had a lot of plugging trouble so I traded for a W-D Allis Chalmers tractor with live power, which means that one could stop the forward speed of the tractor and still run the power take-off at full speed and when the slug went through the combine, pull the hand clutch into action and proceed without shifting gears. Later on, all self-propelled combines came out with a hydro-static drive somewhat

196

on the same principle.

Yields of 15 to 30 bushels per acre were typical of that era. What seems so simple today was really a wonderful invention back about 1950. My 8-row Gleaner would have swallowed the little three-footer and never even stopped to burp if they appeared in the same field today."

Quaday's Quotes (Reprinted with permission from RR Quaday) Faribault County Register Monday October 7, 1991

My first combine was a one-row Allis-Chalmers. Gradually I increased the size of the combines to a two-row John Deere, and then an eight-row Gleaner Allis-Chalmers.

Automobiles

While not strictly farm equipment, the automobile had a tremendous influence on the modernization of the family farm. Not only did it allow more frequent trips to town for necessities, it also vastly increased the farmers' opportunities for social interaction. But it was the pickup truck that became the new workhorse for farm operations, pressed into service for hauling everything from animals to groceries.

The first factory-assembled pickup was based on the Ford Model T car, with a modified rear body. It debuted in 1925 and sold for US$281. Henry Ford billed it as the "Ford Model T Runabout with Pickup Body." The 34,000 built that first year featured a cargo box, adjustable tailgate, four stake pockets and heavy-duty rear springs. In 1928, the Model A replaced the Model T, introducing the first closed-cab pickup. It sported innovations like a safety glass windshield, roll-up side windows and three-speed transmission. It was powered by a four-cylinder L-head engine capable of 40 horsepower. In 1932, the 65 horsepower Ford flathead V8 engine was offered as an option in the truck. By 1936, Ford had already produced 3 million trucks and led the industry in sales.[1]

One day, a most memorable event occurred. Dad came home with a shiny new car--a Model T Ford. It had a top which could be raised or lowered and side-curtains with isinglass windows which buckled onto the top and side supports. It had a horn which said ah-ooo-ah and a crank which, if the spark lever wasn't set exactly right, might reverse its direction and break the cranker's arm. And it needed a shelter, so another building was added to the farm complex--a garage.

[1] "The History of Ford Pickups: The Model T Years 1925–1927." PickupTrucks.com. http://www.pickuptrucks.com/html/history/ford_segment1.html. Retrieved 2009-06-04

Dick Recalls Cars His Dad Drove

"My Dad was born in 1887, when our country was still strictly horse and buggy, with a surrey (two-seat buggy) for driving the family to church and special occasions.

When he was about 35 years of age, Dad bought his first automobile--a 1919 Model T Ford touring car with side curtains for cold weather. The car had been used for two years before he bought it. The engine had to be cranked to start and the spark for the engine came from a magneto and was magnified by a coil system. It was pretty much a summer car as it cranked hard in cold weather and the gasoline in those days was not very high in octane.

Most farm people simply drove their Model Ts into the shed or corn crib, jacked up the wheels and let it sit until spring. A good driving team of horses on the bob-sled was less work and more dependable than the Ford. Dad was still young enough to adapt fairly well from horse power to Ford power, and changing mechanism from reins to foot pedals. The Model Ts had three foot pedals--low, reverse and brake. Each pedal controlled a spring-loaded band lined with a fiber coat. When the driver pushed the pedal, it tightened the band on the desired drum, activating the gear or brake.

The planetary drive had a larger drum and band, which was activated by an emergency brake located on the left side, so when the desired speed was attained one simply shoved the emergency brake forward and he was in high (road) gear. I can recall grinding the half mile of mud road from the Pilot Grove Road to our place in low gear, all the way. There were quite a few accidents in those days, with some of the old timers switching from horse to auto hollering "whoa," while pulling on the steering wheel wanting the machine to stop. It didn't.

When gear shift cars came into vogue in the middle 20s, Dad had a bad habit which developed after an accident he had on 169 south of Vernon Center. An old farmer driving a Model T Ford went through a stop sign right in front of Dad and John, coming back from the Twin Cities. The re-sulting crash nearly killed the old farmer and wrecked the 1928 Durant Dad was driving. The guy sued but lost, as he was driving without lights on--besides not stopping for the highway. After that episode, Dad always rode

198

the clutch which wears them out fairly fast. It was a blessing when Chevrolet came out with an automatic drive. He didn't trade cars very often, even though his number one son was a car salesman.

He pulled pea vine wagons, sweet corn wagons, and grain trailers with his 1930 Model A Ford. The first thing Dad did with every new car was add a trailer hitch, installed by his good friend and blacksmith, Emil Henke. These were always sturdy enough and pulled from the right places so that no accident happened, unless the pin fell out and broke. He pulled thousands of trailer loads of grain to town, until I started to farm more acres and bought trucks to haul grain and livestock to market. He still drove loads of grain to Frank's Elevator at age 87. Al and Dave took good care of him, running the hoists, emptying the trucks and seeing him on his way.

The 1955 Chevy was his last car and he drove it for nearly 20 years. The automatic choke in it malfunctioned one day on our Jo Daviess 80, starting the carburetor on fire. I had to scoop dirt on it by hand to put it out, but the car survived several more years until he turned his keys in at age 93."

William Quaday's 1955 Chevy

Quaday's Quotes -partial (Reprinted with permission from RR Quaday) Faribault County Register Monday November 17, 2003

Quaday Remembers Trips To New Ulm Park

"The first enclosed auto my parents owned was a used 1924 Model T Ford with winter sides, which were panels on either side with sliding glass windows to open up in the summer. The summers in Minnesota were fully as hot then as they are presently.

This was the auto we drove to a family reunion in New Ulm in 1925. The previous owner had tampered with the rear end and differential, installing a "three to one" gear--this meant that it would go about one and a half the speed of a regulation Model T. One must recall that all roads in our area at that time were graveled (or mud) to fully appreciate the scary rides the family had in that car, especially when my brother, Carl, got behind the wheel. He was still in his teens and enjoyed speed in any form.

My Mother's aunts, Lydia and Minnie Willmert, were very family minded and masterminded these reunions. Minnie had married Ed Oehler and lived on a farm near Buffalo Lake, MN. Lydia married George Kirchner and lived in Wells. Uncle George had a business and owned a farm southeast of Blue Earth. He had died, and Aunt Lydia lived with the Earl Boettcher family in Wells. Our next door neighbor, Julia Wehsener, was a Willmert girl and they decided to attend the reunion also. Walt had a brand new 1925 Chevrolet sedan. The Boettchers drove a new 1925 Dodge sedan.

We were to meet part way over and form a convoy so if anything went wrong one would have help. Outside of a children's pit stop at a rural school to use the facilities, things went well until our Model T, which Carl had been pushing pretty hard to maintain close to 60 miles per hour, started to heat. Carl and Dad carried water from a river up the hill to cool it (it was July).

New Ulm Herrman Heights Statue

We could see the Herrman Heights Statue when we entered New Ulm, but getting up to the Park Road took a bit of looking. This is a grand park for children and we had a great time running up the hills and climbing up in the statue. Everyone brought food, and I've never seen a small man eat as much as Uncle Ed Oehler. Everyone was giving Aunt Minnie a bad time for not feeding him at home. Dad drove on the way home and we didn't make near as good time. Believe me it was quite a thrill going 60 on a gravel road with only 30 x 3 1/2 inch tires between you and the road."

Quaday's Quotes (Reprinted with permission from RR Quaday) Faribault County Register Monday June 28, 1993

200

Giant Days Brings Family Memories

"Mentioning German reminds me of a Willmert family picnic, held back in Model T Ford touring car days at Herrman Heights, The German Park up on the high hill above New Ulm.

We were all sitting down for the usual feast of German cooking. An elderly, white-haired gentleman, with a long white handlebar mustache (or moustache as some old Germans spelled it) stopped, leaned on his cane, and told us we had to all be Germans because, he said, "We don't allow any Norwegians in our park--Germans only." He gave a big belly laugh and moved on to inform all the other picnickers. He talked pretty loud, perhaps because he was deaf. I heard him say at another table, "Ah! Baked beans, wienerschnitzel and sauerkraut, good German food." After dinner we youngsters were more or less turned loose to run around up and down the hill, and climb the Herrman the German statue. It is a formidable statue, some 60 or 70 feet tall, with Herrman in full battle gear--with a great view of the city of New Ulm down in the Minnesota River valley.

I can remember my brother, Carl, who was a smart-aleck teenager at the time, ribbing Ed Oehler, my Aunt Minnie Willmert's husband who farmed near Buffalo Lake, about eating so much that it made him poor just to carry it around. Ed was not a large man, but a prodigious eater--downing three or four well-filled plates of food if it was to his liking. Ed and Minnie were in love in their younger days, but for one reason or another, they broke up and Ed married another girl. Three years later she died leaving Ed a bachelor farmer. After a short grieving period, Minnie took the train to Buffalo Lake, walked out to his farm, and when he came in from the field she had a wonderful dinner ready for him. They reconciled and were married a few months later, and raised two girls.

A trip to New Ulm does not sound like a big deal in 2009, but in 1925 on gravel roads, 60 miles was quite a trip, especially driving a 1924 Model T Ford touring car. I'm sure Carl, who did the driving when we were on a trip, had checked the gasoline tank but he might have missed the radiator. Anyway, our Model T began to boil a few miles short of New Ulm. Luckily, we were above a small creek (possibly the Cottonwood) when the boil began. We checked and had no vessel to carry water. Dad was wearing a felt hat, which was the style at the time, so he slid down to the water's edge and filled his hat and carried it up to the car. It took three trips to fill the radia-

201

tor. Earl Boettcher, who ran a grocery store in Wells, drove his new Dodge Sedan and recognized us and stopped to see the fun. He was married to Anna Kischner, the daughter of our Mother's Aunt Lydia (Willmert). Yes, there were a lot of Willmerts around the country in the early days.

1920s Frederick G. Levenick Harness Shop

My Mother's mother, Mary Willmert, was married to Fred Levenick, Jr., a prominent Blue Earth businessman who owned several farms, in addition to the Brush Creek Cheese Factory and a harness shop on North Main Street. Walter and my Mother were born to that marriage. Everything went bad for Grandpa Fred in 1908-09, when Mary died of an inoperative brain tumor and the land boom ended. He lost all of his businesses, as well as the farms--one at Ledyard, Iowa, and two at Barnesville.

He married Lydia Fenske, and this marriage produced six boys and one daughter. They moved to Wisconsin and ran a mom-and-pop grocery store and meat market in Madison. Grandpa Fred came to visit Blue Earth several times that I remember. He had gotten blood poisoning in one leg, and had a wooden replacement. I can still hear the squeak of that leg when he knelt on our hardwood floor for morning prayers after breakfast. He lived into his high 80s, and Lydia outlived him by about 10 years. Times were tough then, too."

Quaday's Quotes (Reprinted with permission RR Quaday) Faribault County Register Monday July 27, 2009

A Litany of Well-Loved and Well-Worn Cars

"Since I was 14 years old, I have had a love affair with the horseless carriage. Since my oldest brother, Carl, was a car salesman, he could have had an influence on the way I regarded autos. The first car I owned was a 1924 Model T Ford touring car with the top torn off--a genuine "Tin Lizzie." I purchased it for $5. It was the tail end of a trade-down with brother Carl, of course. My brother, John, and I practiced driving out in the pasture on the River Road Home Farm many times when I was 10 years old. We drove the old Ford down on our bayou in the winter on the ice and skidded around on the ice until I skidded into a frozen hump of dirt and broke one back wheel off. In this condition, it was useless to me so I traded it to Bob Bassett for a Winchester .22 repeating rifle. He found a wheel in the junk yard and drove it until the license wore off. Since this was The Great Depression, and no one had any money to spend on things, we bartered. Dad didn't really want me to get too interested in the car business, so he always let me drive his until I graduated from high school.

After one experience with a 1929 Erskine Sedan, I owned a series of 1929 Chevrolets and Fords for a few months at a time. When tires blew or the batteries died I simply traded them off for something that would run.

I was 19 years old when I bought my first new car, a 1939 Chevrolet four passenger coupe. Mr. Harry Pfeiffer loaned me the money on monthly payments at eight percent interest. After about a year of car payments, I tired of it. I traded it down for a Model A Ford Pickup, 1931, which turned out to be very handy on the farm. The best part was no eight percent monthly payments.

By the time I reached the age of 21, I'd owned over 50 different cars and pickups, but hadn't owned a truck yet. The next year I went to Frank Nitz's

1929 Richard Quaday Chevy Coupe

farm sale and bought a 1937 Chevrolet one and one half ton truck. It had all new Montgomery Ward tires and I remember Herb Schwen telling me to buy it because the tires were worth more than I paid for the truck. I used this truck for two years to haul peas and corn for Green Giant. With the war on, the price of trucks got so high I traded it for $200 more than I paid for it, in cash--plus a 1927 Master Buick Sedan. It was cut down for use as a pickup by Mr. Frank Siebert."

Quaday's Quotes-partial (Reprinted with permission from RR Quaday) Faribault County Register Monday April 29, 1991

Brother Carl -And Cars - Machinery

"Neva and I have been attending a great many funerals lately; four last week and my oldest brother Carl's, on Monday this week. Carl's funeral was held at the First Presbyterian Church in Mankato. He spent most of his adult life in Mankato, where he owned Quaday Motor Sales for over thirty years, in two different locations; first on North Main Street, and later on North Third Avenue. He catered to the working class of people, mainly handling pickups and cars to drive to work. They were usually sold 'as is', but if something wrong showed up within a reasonable period of time, he fixed them to the customer's satisfaction. Most of his customers were repeat buyers, some buying four or five cars through the years.

I would have to jog my memory back quite heavily to remember all the cars, pickups and kids' cars that I've bought from him. If he didn't happen to have just what we needed, he knew where he could find one that would fit our needs. When he sold for D. D. Murphy (Ford), and later for Howard Essler (Chevrolet), he always saw to it Dad had a good, late model car to drive, many times a demonstrator which he could sell much cheaper. Even in The Great Depression, the very toughest of times, Dad had a fairly new Ford or Chevy to drive my sister, Marie, and later my brother, John, to Teachers College in Winona.

1956 Richard Quaday Buick

When I had made enough money from my bicycle shop, I formulated a deal with Carl when he worked for the Motor Inn Company. He had worked for North Iowa farmers, picking corn by hand for several years (after Dad's was done), so he sold many cars in that area.

A lot of these Iowa cars were traded in with tobacco juice and hog manure all over the inside, and rich Iowa clay and mud covering the outside. I would buy them for fifty or sixty dollars, "as is," take them home and clean them up, paint them if necessary, fix what needed it, replace tires or battery and tune them up to start in winter. After I had all the ills cured, and a set of new seat covers on, I'd drive them a while and trade them in for another, or sell them to my friends, and start on another one. Carl saw to it that I was well paid for my work, quite often over $100.

In between farm work for Dad and going to school, I always had a few hours to ding with these cars and I loved it. I had owned over 50 cars before I was 21 years old. Of course, it all became a thing of the past when Neva and I got married and began raising a family and went into serious farming. That training, and learning how to deal when I was a kid at home, saved me a lot of money in later years dealing for trucks, cars and farm machinery. I could fix almost any simple car, pickup, or farm machine, well enough to get the job done so I didn't have to buy new. Carl trained his boys to fix and drive almost any breed of automobile, pickup or truck, so they are all associated with the auto industry in one way or another. Frank runs a repair shop at his home. Leon is an over-the-road trucker with his own truck. Duane is a parts man in a franchise dealer in Mankato."

Quaday's Quotes-partial (Reprinted with permission from RR Quaday) Faribault County Register Monday January 21, 2008

Oldsmobile Had Unstable Character

"Have you ever noticed that some automobiles have distinct personality traits?

Such a car was my 1936 Oldsmobile, which was my transportation through the greater share of the Second World War and the period after the war,

Roger and Gloria Woitas, 1936 Oldsmobile

while America was tooling up for peace time endeavors. This two-door, six-cylinder, Oldsmobile was a sorry sight when first we met.

Rob Smith had purchased a nearly new Olds Sedan, so the old one was relegated to the corn crib alley, a roosting place for sparrows, gathering dust, and rusting away. The clutch was worn out, but held good enough to drive it home to the Sailor Place. There were no mechanics just waiting to fix one's car at that time, so it became a do-it-yourself project.

I had never changed a clutch, so it was also a learning process. I had painted a couple of cars and many bicycles, so knew how to proceed with the redecoration. We lived on a gravel road so I chose a gray color, which wouldn't show the dust so much. Mr. Smith had told me, "Now don't do any speeding with this car; it has original pistons and they are getting worn a little." The Olds had 120,000 miles on the odometer when I bought it. With gas rationing, and a 50 mile speed limit, that was the least of my worries.

I soon found out that this Olds had a cantankerous habit of vapor lock, every month or so. Just about the time one forgot about it, the darn thing would do it again. With vapor lock, no matter what one does otherwise, if one does not remove the gas cap and blow into the filter, the car will not run.

During the war, Benny Kaus at Minnesota Lake, had a direct connection with an egg pool, in Chicago. We had a laying flock of hens, who outdid themselves in 1944. Neva and I would wash up and candle the eggs, load up the Olds with 30 dozen cases of eggs, and haul them to Benny's. We made an even $60 over Blue Earth prices, every trip.

With the end of the war the speed limit was lifted, but we still had to remember the limitations of our car. One Sunday, we had gone to Minnesota Lake to visit Neva's sister, Gloria, when it became clear that we were in for a rain storm. I had little chickens out across the road, with the brooder house right out in the wind. I got a little excited driving home and drove a little too fast, and noticed that we were trailing a plume of white smoke. Sure enough, I had blown a piston. I had never changed a piston before but like the clutch, it became a do-it-yourself affair. The flanges between the rings broke, because of the piston slap. Altogether, I replaced three pistons before selling the Olds in 1947.

When my brother, John, came home from the Army, we drove up to Canada on a fishing trip. I cautioned John not to drive over 50 miles per hour, but on the way up near Ely, he passed a car and sure enough blew a piston. There was nothing to do but keep driving. Would you believe we drove that car the rest of the way up and all the way home, without scoring the cylinder walls?

One night in June after the war, Ralph and Dorothy Ficken went along with Neva and I to a dance at The Terp, in Austin. In those days it was still customary to dress up in a suit and tie to attend a dance. It rained six inches while we were at the dance, and the Olds wouldn't start. It rained so hard, that the pockets of my suit filled with water. A man pushed us to a station, and we spent a half hour drying out. After all that it was still no go, so I took off the gas cap, releasing the vapor lock. While we were at the station, a manhole cover in front of the garage blew up about four feet in the air, creating a three foot fountain. We got home just in time to change clothes and milk the cows. It was 49 years before we owned another Olds."

Quaday's Quotes (Reprinted with permission from RR Quaday) Faribault County Register Monday May 10, 1993

Crop Farming

Since the early days when wheat dominated and then began to give way to dairy in the 1880s, Minnesota farmers have moved into many more areas of production. From massive fields of corn, soybeans, and sugar beets, to efficiently run hog, cattle, and turkey farms, Minnesota farmers have always produced plenty of food. In 2008, Minnesota was the sixth-largest agricultural producer in the nation, and today, hundreds of farm families, often recent immigrants to Minnesota, are returning to local markets for their harvest in the form of community-supported agriculture and farmers' markets.

Early family farms in southern Minnesota usually combined livestock and cash crops. Most common crops were corn, oats, some flax, alfalfa and later, soybeans.

> "After the threshing was done in the late summer it was time to haul the piles of accumulated manure from the barns out onto the fields. It was loaded onto the manure spreader which scattered it over the grain stubble fields and then it was plowed under using a single-share plow pulled by a team of horses. By the time that was done it was probably going into October and the corn was ready to be husked. This was done by hand and the husked corn was tossed into a wagon pulled by a team of horses.
>
> In the spring, as soon as the ground had thawed, the corn stalks were disked down into the soil and those fields were sowed with grain, thus rotating the crops each year. The grain fields, which had been plowed in the fall, were dragged and then planted to corn. Every few years clover and alfalfa were sowed on selected fields in order to replenish the nitrogen in the soil. This may not have been as efficient a way as using the modern commercial fertilizers but in the long run it was much better for the soil. Weeds were controlled in the corn fields by going through the rows several times with the horse-drawn cultivator."
>
> *2011 Letter. Typed pages from RR Quaday. 01-12-2011*

Crop Viewing; A Learned Tradition

> "Crop viewing season is upon us. It is great fun for old gaffers like me to get in the station wagon and drive around the county, looking over the crops

that the neighbors, relatives, or old friends are raising. Kyle MacArthur and I have been trying for two years now to get together on a sunny afternoon and view the county crops. It is a technique that must be passed down over many years from one old farmer to another, much as Indian folk lore is transmitted from one generation to the next. Our Editor, a sidewalk and pavement child, has not the slightest idea of the intricacies of crop viewing. I learned the proper way to view crops from watching an old neighbor, Fred Paschke, who lived just south of our River Road Farm. Walter Oelke, who farmed just west of town, was another excellent crop viewer.

One must never travel over 10 miles an hour, except between farms or past open pasture stretches of little interest. Of course, if the pastures are full of dairy or beef cattle, one must slow down to five miles an hour for a real close look at the condition of the livestock. The viewer must always stay right in the middle of the road, especially on narrow township roads, so he does not run off the road. To do a perfect job of crop or livestock viewing one must be oblivious to everything else, such as speeders trying to get by, or tractors pulling heavy equipment, hurrying to get to their field.

The crop viewer must be sure to take a county plat book, up to date, so that he can find each farm and check out the ownership, while cruising slowly down the road. You know, the title changes come so fast that even the courthouse has a hard time keeping up. The small farm of 80 to 160 acres is a thing of the past, with small family farms being bought up or taken over by operators of one to five thousand acres. The U.S. Department of Agriculture has, for the last 80 years, told farmers to grow or die. By and large, this has happened, with the percentage favoring the die folks. Thousands of good farm houses were abandoned, vandalized, or burned up, besides the ones bulldozed and buried. Most of the fine groves have been erased, one way or another, making wide open spaces much like the Indians used to roam.

With the coming of GMO corn, and Roundup Ready soybeans, the monster machinery of the present day is only seen briefly during planting and harvesting times. The fields of 40 to 50 acres which used to slow down the crop viewer, have turned into 500 or 1000 acres, so the old gaffers can actually raise a bit of dust now between farms. Having raised sweet corn for Green Giant for 44 consecutive years, I am always interested in viewing sweet corn fields, sometimes with a purpose of buying a couple tubs full for freezing when the time comes. The corn picked right out of the field by hand makes a much higher quality frozen product, as one can select the ears right at their prime.

Crop tour, from page 13

Just a few miles east, from Easton to Wells, the soybeans again were somewhat shorter, and some fields had less than 50 pods per plant.

Plus, the corn was not quite as tall or filled out to the end of the cob.

"That doesn't mean that it isn't going to be a heckuva corn harvest here, too," Quaday says. "Just not quite as big as other areas."

By Wells there were miles of corn fields where the ears just stood out for row after row.

The corn fell off a little moving from Wells south to Kiester, but not by much.

"For being on the tops of hills, the corn looks mighty good," Quaday says. "The tops of the hills in this area don't always look as good as the sides of the hills, but this year they do – because they got adequate moisture."

West of Kiester, toward Bricelyn, the beans were big and tall, while the corn was not quite as tall as other parts of the county. The same tendencies were noted near Bricelyn.

"There really isn't a bad set of fields anywhere in the county," Quaday says. "Frost, Elmore and Blue Earth, too, all have some great looking fields of both corn and beans. I don't see how this is not going to be a very successful harvest season, if the weather cooperates."

Quaday thinks the harvest will get underway a little earlier this year, and that could mean an easier time as far as weather and equipment troubles for farmers.

"If I was a little younger I would be right out there," the 90-year-old says. "I predict an excellent harvest and a big yield. We should see some happy farmers this fall."

Dick Quaday makes a close examination of a Faribault County corn field, at right. At left, Quaday counts the number of bean pods on one soybean plant. He was able to consistently find plants with 50-60 pods. Although there was some damage due to aphids, overall the crop appears to be in good shape throughout the county, and Quaday expects a large yield.

Staff photos by Chuck Hunt

2010 Dick Quaday Crop Tour

I must admit that there was a time, when we farmed more land in the later years and we were always in a big hurry, that old gaffer crop viewers were not popular with me getting from farm to farm. The pace of farming had to speed up, when one had livestock to care for and more acres to cover. Actually, the best period of time for old crop viewers was during the horse and buggy days of my early youth. The horses would only travel so fast, giving one ample time to check the mustard in the oats, and the thistles in the young corn fields. A person didn't have to pay much attention to the horses out on the road; they simply followed the track. If one met a neighbor with machinery, the roadside was almost level with the track, so no problem; each farmer pulled out into the roadside grass a little, for a ways.

Meeting an eight row or larger machine on our narrow township roads is definitely a problem nowadays, especially at night. The 12, 16 and 24 row equipment has to be designed to fold up to allow traffic on farm to market roads, keeping farm machinery engineers busy. The fantastic prices for the new gigantic farm machines of today have created a vicious circle; one has to rent or buy more land to justify the cost of the equipment. Isn't progress Wonderful?"

Quaday's Quotes (Reprinted with permission from RR Quaday) Faribault County Register Monday May 22, 2000

211

I viewed crops from 2000 until 2010. It was part of my *Quaday's Quotes* feature articles, and the Editor of the Faribault County Register always went along and took photos. I started crop viewing when I was 80 years old and continued for 10 years. Crop viewing was done in late August and I would make a prediction in my article regarding the average yield per acre for both corn and soybeans, in Faribault County, of that year's harvest. In the ten years I did crop viewing and average yields per acre forecasting, I never missed the average yield by more than one bushel per acre.

Personal conversation with RR Quaday, 02.03.2011

Corn

Southern Minnesota is part of the Corn Belt, a region of the Midwest where corn has, since the 1850s, been the predominant crop, replacing the native tall grasses. By 1950, 99% of the corn was grown from hybrids. Most corn is fed to livestock, especially hogs and poultry, but recently a significant portion has been used in the production of ethanol. As of 2008, the top four corn-producing states were Iowa, Illinois, Nebraska, and Minnesota, together accounting for more than half of the corn grown in the United States.

The region is characterized by relatively level land and deep, fertile soils, high in organic matter. The area is also known for a lifestyle based on ownership of family farms, with supporting small towns and powerful farm organizations that lobbied to obtain higher prices. In the era from 1860 to 1982, new agricultural technology transformed the Corn Belt from a mixed crop-and-livestock farming area to a highly specialized cash-grain farming area. Vice President Henry A. Wallace, a politician and pioneer of hybrid seeds, declared in 1956 that the Corn Belt developed the "most productive agricultural civilization the world has ever seen."

While the landscape was greatly modified, the family farm evolved as well. Its acreage doubled, as farmers bought out their neighbors (who then moved to nearby towns). After 1970, increased crop and meat production required an export outlet, but global recessions and a strong dollar reduced exports, depressed prices below the costs of production, and created serious problems even for the best farm managers.

Horse Power And Corn Planting

"With the advent of hybrid corn, the seed corn companies began doing all the germination testing and grading for size that farmers formerly did with the open pollinated varieties planted from their own seed. My Dad always had some basins of dirt ready to test his home grown seed for germination. In our old farmhouse out on River Road we had two windows in the entry, with southern exposure. By the first of April the sun coming into this area simulated growing conditions outside about a month later. The farmers of the 20s and 30s used several of the open pollinated varieties; the only ones I remember are Reid Yellow Dent, and Murdoch. If one got a good stand (15,000 plants per acre was the very best), and the weather co-operated, the best fields would yield between 50 and 70 bushels per acre.

With the advent of herbicides, power checking and drilling of corn with consequent higher stands, came into use. I had quite a time convincing my Dad that more plants made more corn, and to prove my point I planted 10 acres of corn with wire check, right beside a power checked 10 acres. In the fall we filled two slat cribs; one from each ten acre patch, which when shelled showed a different yield of nearly 100 bushels in favor of the power check. After that little episode, Dad went along with all the "new" ideas in agriculture, which were coming in thick and fast at that time. After farming for 3 years on my own, I attended the School of Agriculture in St Paul one winter. I'm sure I learned much more while spending my own hard earned money than I would have before having "Hands On" experience in farming. Many of the facts learned were later proved incorrect, but I used much of the basics I learned all through my farming career. If nothing else, it taught me not to be afraid to try new methods of operation."

CORN TALK Monthly newsletter for corn producers who are members of Minnesota Corn Growers Association Vol 14, No. 5, June, 1994

Wire Check Corn Planting

"I heard rumors of some farmer over near Fairmont, who had 100 acres of corn planted on March 15. If true, that would be nearly two months earlier than we began planting corn out on River Road Farm. When I planted corn with a team of horses and a two row planter, we never started planting until May 5. In those days we planted with a wire check, which means that we had a wire strung across the field with notches (lumps) on it, that tripped a mechanism on the planter, dropping three or four kernels in a hill behind an opener, or shoe. A wheel (Packer) concluded the operation, with just enough pressure to make a firm seed base.

The wire trips were 40 or 42 inches apart, to correspond with the width of the row. The row width was determined by the width of a horse's behind, and ended at 40 inches. The driver had to get off the planter at each end of the field, pull up the stake, move it over 120 inches, and stomp it down firmly enough to withstand the pull of a rose bush root, or some other obstruction hanging on the wire. Sometimes these things would pull up the stake and one would have to retrace to the other end and reset the stake. It was an art to be able to set the stakes every time, with the same tension on the wire, so one could cultivate either lengthwise or crosswise without cultivating out too much corn. Please remember that this was before herbicide, so the weeds had to be cultivated out.

Nearly every farmer milked at least a few cows, so the farmer had to rise at 4 am, do his chores, harness the team, load up the seed wagon and have breakfast, before getting to the field. At noon, he had to unhitch the team and drive them home to feed and water them; after dinner, he'd hitch up and go again until chore time, which varied according to how many cows he had to milk. After caring for his team, he fed the hogs, milked the cows, separated the cream (the separator was turned by hand), had supper and went to bed, usually around 10 pm. If he had a fast team of horses, he would have planted about 20 acres of corn that day. The soil was still young and rich enough that one did not have to fertilize commercially. The manure from the farm livestock kept up the tilth of the soil.

We thought we were in Heaven when we developed a tractor hitch on the old planter, and didn't have to put up with the foibles of a team of horses. The advent of herbicides and commercial fertilizer (dry), in a planter attachment, put more work back into planting but did away with the pesky wire; making it about a standoff. The cultivating became easier with the elimination of crossing. The four-row planter cut our field work in half, so we could go fishing on opening day. Soon that pleasure was taken away, because we had to rent more land and raise more corn to pay the bills. We were still heavy in the livestock program, so we had to plant still faster, so we bought an eight-row planter with fertilizer, insecticide and herbicide attachments. This again made heavy work for corn planting so we went to liquid fertilizer, with a pump doing the work. The invention of the "Terragator" with a 50-foot boom, made the planter attachments obsolete but it cost money to hire these monsters, so I used them sparingly.

When I quit farming in 1982, the more progressive farmers were already buying 12-row and 16-row planters which were wonderful in dry springs, but not yet practical in wet years. The biggest planter, cultivator and combine I owned was the eight-row machine. We had gone from the team and two rows to the tractor and eight rows in 44 years of farming. The progress has accelerated since then, so that one must farm a couple thousand acres just to keep the front gate open. I don't believe I could go into farming again without going back to school for 10 years to catch up with progress. The crops raised now are far superior in yield and quality to what we raised 30 or 40 years ago.

The meat, poultry, and vegetables produced are much better, even though some organic activists complain and boycott it."

Quaday's Quotes (Reprinted with permission from RR Quaday) Faribault County Register Monday April 24, 2000

Quaday's Qorn

"The bay horses were our corn planting team as they were light and fast, capable of planting twenty acres per day. One had to be moving right along pulling the stakes and stretching the wire on each end of the field. We owned a John Deere two row planter with our next door neighbors, the Wehseners. The partnership worked well, as one farmer would be working up the ground while the other planted. Our young farmers today would throw up their hands in horror at the thought of jumping off the planter at each end of the field to pull up and reset the stakes, which held the notched wire. A good team and a careful farmer could have what we called a "perfect check," if he never broke the wire and the stakes held. Sometimes rosebush roots would get caught in the buttons, pulling the stakes or breaking the wire. This always happened on the far end of the field, so one would have to walk eighty or more rods to make the needed repair. Before herbicides, the wire check method of planting enabled one to cross cultivate the hills of corn. On the best farms, one could drop four kernels to a hill, but many farmers set their planters for three kernels, hence producing bigger ears which were much easier to pick by hand in the fall.

My Mother was always glad to get the seed corn out of the house in the spring. We had "Corn Trees" with finishing nails driven in half way on six by six timbers. The butt ends of the best ears of corn are stuck on the nails. This method dried the corn through the winter and the ears were care-

215

fully shelled by hand, and graded to some extent to fit the planter plates. Needless to say, this system would not be too practical if one was to plant a thousand acres."

CORN TALK Monthly newsletter for corn producers who are members of the Minnesota Corn Growers Association Vol. 14, No. 4, April, 1994

Those Early Corn Cribs - Each Unique In Design

"In 1938, when I started up farming on my own, a great share of the corn grown in Minnesota was still picked by hand. Our farm was no exception. We had progressed to the point that we had a four wheeled trailer made out of a Model T Ford chassis, which made a lower target for throwing the ears of corn. It also made for a smoother ride home from our Jo Daviess 80 acres, 2 ½ miles from the home farm. There was one stretch of cross road, still mud at that time, which was really rough riding after the ruts and lumps froze. We would pick a load of ear corn at home, shovel it into the crib, eat lunch, and pick over at the 80 in the afternoon. The horses, who had good picking while hauling the trailer, always made it home on a trot, as we had no way to water them on the bare 80.

Some of the better pickers could throw out over 100 bushels a day, but after milking ten cows by hand and doing the other chores, I never made more than 90 bushels. I always did the milking right after supper, then scooped off the corn wagon by moon or lantern light. Days like this were not

1939 Corn Crib Oak Ridge Farm

conducive to all night partying or attending dances. There were only two mechanical corn pickers in our whole neighborhood, both single rows, and they were plagued with a lot of breakdowns. One good reason I raised sweet corn and peas for Green Giant was that I didn't have so much corn to husk by hand in the fall. I can truthfully say that I lived during the evolution of corn production; picking corn by hand and scooping it off, and combining with an eight row L Gleaner; hauling with a team and wagon, to trucks and auger elevation in two 5,000 bushel bins. What a change!

One pitfall that I avoided was building an expensive corn crib shortly before we went to shelling and combining. I designed and built a slat and pole crib for easy filling, used it quite a few years, then used the poles for a machine shed. Very little ever went to waste on our farm. Neva used to say, "This is a high producing farm; anything that does not pull its weight gets traded off or junked, so I raised nine children." During the time we were raising our family, obstetric care and hospitals were relatively cheap compared to the present costs. I'd hate to start raising a family of nine under the present circumstances pertaining to farming, with the low farm prices and high priced input.

1952 Corn Crib River Road Farm

This corn crib was built in 1952 and designed for easy filling. I made a trap door opening every six feet on the high side. I filled it without hardly any hand work in the crib. I fell off the slippery roof twice in one day, spraining my ankle the second time. The floor was two feet off the ground so we had no rat or mice problems. I could shove the hammer mill feeder under the crib for easy grinding for feeding the steers. The high side faced south, so we never shelled anything but No. 2 corn. The posts and planks were all treated with penta and creosote. I used the corn crib from 1952 until 1966, when we changed operations to shelling in the field. The posts and lumber were all perfect when we took it apart, so we used the posts for framing the machine shed."

Dick Hears The Corn Grow

"In the fall of 1950, Neva and I went to Ashland, OR, to visit Mary (Neva's sister) and Harvey Sorenson. They had six boys, the oldest of which was Harvey Jr. at age 12. He begged to come back to MN to live on the farm, and with Charlie at age 10 we figured they would make great companions. They were.

Harvey had never been on a farm, so he could be talked into anything farm related. He had a voracious appetite so we would pass the food clear around the table before we passed it to him, because he would empty the remaining food onto his plate. We had four children at the time, Charlie, Kay, Joan and Mary, who was three. Harvey, as he emptied the bowls onto his plate said, "Gee, Aunt Neva, you're the best cook, except my mom."

1950 Harvey Sorenson With Charles, Kay, Joan & Mary Quaday

Neva had a big garden, we milked cows, and raised 100 head of hogs, so there were chores to be shared by all. We had Bull and Canadian thistles that needed hoeing, and the boys would sneak their fishing poles along when they set out to tackle the thistles.

One hot, moist evening in July we were sitting on the screen porch reading and talking and I made the remark that this was the kind of evening one could hear the corn grow. Harvey, having been tricked so often with farm stories, was very skeptical and remarked, "I'd like to hear that," so off we went to the corn field across the road. Neva and our kids, who were just as unbelieving, joined Harvey and I.

Once in the field, I told them they had to squat down and be perfectly quiet. On my signal, no one even breathed for a short period of time and wonder of wonders, a person could hear the stock segments pushing up, with a slight squeaking noise. This restored Harvey's faith in the stories I had told him about farming.

I had a Model B Allis-Chalmers tractor at that time with a small manure spreader to match, so once the oats were shocked the boys were delegated to start cleaning out the straw shed used mostly for a lambing shelter. They were supposed to back the spreader into the shed so they would have easy going to haul the loads out.

One morning, after returning home from getting the buttermilk, I saw them running full bore out of the shed. I hurried to see what had happened. They had driven into the shed, and the exhaust pipe had passed under a bumble bee nest with the throttle wide open, stirring up the bees. The Allis had only a straight exhaust pipe and when they departed, leaving the tractor running wide open with only a foot of clearance, it didn't take very long before the smoke was rolling out.

I feared for my straw shed and tractor, and ran quickly into the shed and cut the switch. Thankfully I was in time. That evening I sprayed the bee nest with kerosene and fly spray, so they could continue the job the next morning.

Shortly after this episode, Neva vowed to fill Harvey up to the point of no more food. She fixed sweet corn on the cob, fried chicken with mashed potatoes with gravy and apple pie for dessert. When Harvey turned down her apple pie, everyone cheered. When he flew out on the plane from Minneapolis he vowed to come back the following year, but it has taken 40 years for him to return for a visit."

Quaday's Quotes-partial (Reprinted with permission from RR Quaday) Faribault County Register Monday August 19, 1991

Quaday Builds Furnace For Drying Corn

"Among the more innovative ideas to cut costs around our River Road Farm were the two large steel furnaces which we had built for drying corn. Harold Schwiess of Sherburn built them for us. Mike, my youngest son, and I stopped at his factory to discuss the project in July, 1983. We told him what we wanted and how it had to fit into the propane burners so that we could switch back to burning propane through the night.

In October, Harold phoned to tell us that he had the first experimental burner ready. We had a concrete level base all set up; we hauled it on our truck and unloaded it with our tractor loader.

1992 Corn Dryer Designed by Dick & Mike Quaday

Dimensions: firepot four feet by five feet and the door was three feet by two and one half feet. It was lined with fire brick with the fan mounted on top of the plenum. The propane burner stayed where it was in the wind tunnel, ready to be turned on in case of cold weather.

When the Dutch Elm plague swept through the Corn Belt, we lost hundreds of large American and red elm trees. They stood, stark and ugly, all through our woodlands. We could run them through the corn burner with a minimum of hand work by wafering them in two foot wide round chunks. These we loaded onto a snow bucket on our Allis Chalmers loader, loading them at ground level and rolling them into the firepot, off the loader.

If we did it just right, the 600 pound wafers rolled into the fire rather easily onto a bed of coals. This supplied six or seven hours of heat. Another touch was added later by Mike when he hooked up a dripper to feed used oil into the firepot, enhancing the heat from the wood.

The first worked so good, we decided to put in another, with a larger door.

We found that wet wood did not work well with the draft originally built into the door so to get more draft and more heat we simply opened the door according to the moisture content of the wood.

In 1983, the corn crop was fairly high moisture and the propane cost was proportionately high, so we figured that the burners paid for themselves in less than two years.

In 1984, cold weather caught up with us before the last bin was dry so we waited until the temperature went down to below zero, started up the fan, and froze the corn solid until spring. As soon as some warm, dry weather came we started up the burner and fan, and finished the drying process.

Harold Pitcher had several piles of used oak and walnut posts too short to put in the ground, which just fit into the firepots. These and a couple of dead Chinese Elm trees finished the job. We never hauled anything but No. 2 corn to Frank Brothers Elevator from this cheap drying method so it figured to be a great cost saver."

Quaday's Quotes-partial (Reprinted with permission from RR Quaday) Faribault County Register Monday August 31, 1992

In 1966 my corn won the Faribault County Corn Growers Contest, sponsored by the Frank Brother's Elevator.

Oats

The Minnesota tallgrass prairie has almost exclusively been converted into one of the most intensive crop producing areas in North America. States formerly with landcover in native tallgrass prairie such as Iowa, Illinois, Minnesota, Wisconsin, Nebraska, and Missouri have become known for their highly productive soils and the strength of their agricultural industries.

The region's fertile soil combined with the steel plow has made it possible for farmers to produce abundant harvests of cereal crops, such as corn, wheat, and oats. The region was soon known as the nation's "breadbasket." Oats were originally grown as feed for horses, but now are an important part of the cereal products on grocery shelves all over the world.

1944 William Quaday 105 Bu Oats

It Was Rough Farming In 1938

"The trouble really started in earnest in early August, when we began to cut our oats crop with our Deering binder, pulled with the three horses. It was a 5-foot swather, with canvasses running the grain up and over the bull wheel and down to the knotter, which tied the straw with binder twine made by prisoners in Sandstone. The binder was ground-driven with a steel wheel with traction cleats to keep it from sliding and a heavy steel chain

222

running from large sprocket-to-small sprocket, which speeded up the tying operation. Usually, the only trouble the driver had while operating the team and binder was having the canvasses plug up with weeds or green straw--or the knotter not functioning properly, dropping loose straw on the bundle carrier and stringing loose straw on the ground. The carrier was dumped by the binder operator--four bundles in windrows, so the shockers could pick up and set up two bundles at a time in the shock. This gave the shocker a balanced load; much easier on the back.

The trouble with the 1938 harvest was having a good crop with heavy straw, especially through the wet spots where the bull wheel would slide, rather than kick out a bundle. This would plug the sickle, making the driver back up the horses and take a new start, possibly with a crack of the lines on their backside to gain a bit more speed on the binder. Sometimes it worked. Later, after I built a tractor-hitch on the binder, I could just speed up the tractor for a ways and stay out of trouble. I invented a rig to run the bundle carrier from the tractor seat, eliminating the necessity of the farm wife riding all day on the rough binder seat, which was steel (no air cushion, either). Dad always had a tanned sheep hide on the seat.

The shocked grain was not meant to stay in the shock very long in wet weather, but that is what happened that year. The butts of the bundles sat in mud for a couple of weeks too long before we could thresh, and it turned into manure, and the shocks had to be upset for a few hours of drying before they would go through the thresh machine, even though the oats were dry enough to store.

Most of the farmers raised a few acres of flax that year, and the small grain had to be finished before the flax run could start. It was near the middle of September before the flax was all threshed. We were lucky to ever get it done, because the minute we had the flax threshed, the rains began in earnest; with three and four inches a week."

Quaday's Quotes - partial (Reprinted with permission from RR Quaday) Faribault County Register Monday August 30, 2010

1947 Dick Quaday Shocking Oats

Hay
Both Old And New Ways To Make Hay

"The task of making hay has changed as much or more than any other farm work in the 80 years since I was introduced to hay on the River Road Farm. At age seven I was ordered to climb into the hayrack and drive our small bay team, stop at each haycock and walk around on the hay to tromp it down, so Dad could pitch the hay onto the rack with his three tined fork. At that time in farm history, the hay was all put up loose on top of two sling ropes spread across the rack. We always used three slings on each load. The team of horses was taken off the wagon and hooked on the rope on the other side of the barn. A system of pulleys pulled the sling full of loose hay to a catch mechanism at the top of the barn, which tripped, letting the sling full of hay slide back in the barn where the mow man wanted it.

The guy in the haymow would do his best to keep loose hay slings leveled out for easy pitching down the chute for winter feeding of the cows. If too many loads of hay were put up in one afternoon, we simply waited until the next morning when it was cooler in the loft to spread out and level the hay.

It was still hot up there, but not much over 100 degrees, unlike the 130 degrees it reached the previous day. It was much easier than pitching every forkful of hay on the rack and pitching every forkful into the barn and carrying it to the back. When the barn was full, we stacked the rest of the crop outdoors. The outdoors hay was fed to the young stock and dry cows. When I was helping with the haying, the first few years we had all long grass hay, but after about four years we switched to alfalfa for the milk cows.

When the baling machines first came out, they cost a tidy sum. To spread out the cost, a farmer would bale his neighbors' crops for so much a bale. It took a bigger crew but made the task much easier and faster. The crew consisted of a tractor operator, one or two men on the bale wagon, one man to put the bales in the elevator and two or three good men in the barn. The temperature in the barn was still 130 degrees, so there was a lot of sweating going on. During World War II, my crew was two old men in the barn, one 86 and one 83, so I didn't dare put too many bales in the elevator too fast.

When I went to Montana in 1950, the ranchers were still stacking loose hay (grass) shoved into the stacker with a buck rake on the front of a tractor. They scoffed at me when I told them they would be baling hay with twine string in a year or two."

Quaday's Quotes-partial (Reprinted with permission from RR Quaday) Faribault County Register Monday August 4, 2008

Baling Hay Was Hot Work On The River Road

"If there ever was a time on our River Road Farm when four things had to be done on the same day, it happened when the first cutting of alfalfa started to bloom.

In order to preserve the maximum protein content of the hay, it should be cut at one third bloom stage. This was the time when one should be cultivating corn the first time. It was also the time when the soybean planting should be finished in the low ground where it was too wet earlier.

At about this time, the early peas were ready to can, and Green Giant was mighty fussy concerning the harvest at perfect tenderometer reading, which was between 90 and 110. The minute the peas were off, we always worked up the ground and drilled in a crop of early soybeans; many times the highest paid on the farm.

At the age of nine, I was deemed old enough to drive the horses on the hay wagon from one hay pile to the next. Dad never did own a hay loader, so it was all three-tine pitch forks for us.

The load of hay was divided into three slings--ropes which cradled the loose hay--that were pulled up into the barn with a team of horses. The next morning before it got too hot up in the barn, we had to go up in the loft and pull these slings of hay apart and level the previous day's production.

I forgot to mention that the teamster also had the job of tromping the hay down on the load so one could get more tons on each rack full. If the hay was just a shade green, Dad always spread a few handfuls of loose salt into the hay to keep it from heating too much.

On a 90 degree day, if the hay was heating just a little bit, the temperature in the loft could easily get to 115 to 120 degrees. The bet-

1960 Wm and Dick Quaday Haying

226

ter one pulled the slings of hay apart and leveled it, the less likely the barn would burn down. Almost every year some farmer in the area would hurry the haying just a bit too much and spontaneous combustion would start the barn on fire.

This method of handling hay all became obsolete with the advent of the pickup baler which picked up the hay from the windrow, pressed it into bales or blocks which one could stack on the wagons or flatbeds, thus hauling many more tons of hay.

It also saved room in the haymow besides being much easier to move out for winter feeding. After cracking a few floor joists in the barn, we realized more posts were needed if one was going to drop a sling full of bales from the top of the barn.

When the Olson Fork, sometimes called the pigeon claw, was invented, we did away with the slings and pulled in 12 bales at a time, making the job up in the loft much easier.

1960 Dick Quaday Using Olson Fork

Later still, we purchased a conveyer which moved the hay back into the far end of the barn. We used a Kelly Ryan elevator to move the hay up to the conveyer so un-loading from the rack became a technical job.

The bales had to be dropped into the elevator on edge because the tray was not wide enough for a bale. Other, higher priced elevators could handle the bales laid flat. My job was to get the bales from the wagon onto the elevator and up in the barn.

We always hired our baling

227

done custom with the cost running around 12 cents a bale, loaded on the rack. Fred Greimann baled with a Case wire tie machine for a few years. When twine tie balers came in we hired, at various times, Orville Stensland, Arnie Mensing, Don and Marcus Guerber, John Oelke, Rudy Cyphers and Harvey Warner. I liked the square bales best because I built the sheep feed bunks so that four bales just filled each bunk. We had a minimum of waste.

Many feeders now use the large, round bales weighing nearly a ton each which are handled hydraulically, with no hand work at all. I hung up my scoop shovel and bale hook before they became the popular way to make hay.

One thing I learned during my 46 years of making hay…there is always an easier way."

Quaday's Quotes (Reprinted with permission from RR Quaday) Faribault County Register Monday June 8, 1992

Dick Goes Industrial With DeHy

"In the fall of 1963, things hadn't been going too well in the farming business at my place, so I was looking around for some kind of supplemental income.

This was about the same time that a group of businessmen in Blue Earth were starting up a new business known as DeHy Inc. It was an alfalfa drying and pelleting plant, located on 14 Street in south Blue Earth. Harry Marks, a long time friend, was one of the directors of the corporation. I had let it be known that I would be available for some part-time work while talking to Hank Kuyper, who was also a director.

One day Harry came out to our River Road Farm, and we discussed the alfalfa plant and possible employment for me in the field part of the operation. They had purchased two field choppers and one had already been delivered. We looked it over and I allowed an opinion, "It looks like it might work." We made a deal, and work it did.

Arney Prescher, a farmer living near Delavan, was hired to work the opposite shift. He proved to be an excellent operator besides being a nice guy to work with. We broke in the new machine and later on, another one just about like it the second summer. These field choppers did the job very well under most conditions but were very susceptible to damage from rocks, and didn't handle wet pocket gopher mounds at all.

They did have a quick hydraulic which would keep one out of trouble if the operator saw the obstacles in time. These machines were made somewhere in Ohio, and Hank Kuyper, who ran the Massey Harris agency at the time, ordered the parts. Merrit Peterson, who worked as a mechanic, helped us out on repairs too difficult for Arney and I to handle.

The late Ted Wiederholt was superintendent of operations all the while I worked there (two and one half years). Herb Hanson signed on as field supervisor the second year. When the plant was operating full speed we had to move from farm to farm at night quite often. Having worked some for Green Giant, I knew how easy it was to get into the wrong field, or even the wrong farm during the night.

I always had the bosses draw me a map of the fields to be chopped so if I got in the wrong place, we could figure out who screwed up. The installation of CB radios midway in the second year made things work much smoother and saved a lot of time.

I'm rather proud of the fact that I farmed for 46 years without ever tipping over any trucks, pickups, or machinery. One evening near the time for Arney to take over, I was chopping on Harry Mark's 80 over north of Bass Lake. The field had a flat bottom and a flat top and in between was a very steep hill. I had been chopping half a load on the hillside and finishing up on the top near the driveway. Being in a hurry to fill the truck which I would drive in, I took one more swath on the steep part of the hill.

Things went okay until the drive wheel on the high side rolled over a pocket gopher mound with a round rock in it. The rock rolled under the big wheel raising it in the air nearly three feet. The fully loaded machine hung there for what seemed to me minutes, before bouncing about five more times, each a little lower. When it finally came to rest, I drew a very deep breath and cramped the chopper down the hill the shortest way to level land, not giving one whoop about the hay I was running over. I was too shook up to even lower the header and chop my way down.

In July of the third year, I had been chopping hay over on Stauffer's place by Winnebago through most of the night. I finished there about 3 am and started back to the plant, towing the "gas buggy" full of diesel fuel. I had cultivated most of the previous day and driving down 169 was so easy, I dozed off. When I jarred awake, I was rolling over a gutter on the wrong side of the road north of the Golf Course. I decided right then and there that 12 hours for me, made too long a day.

A few days later the late Chuck Neuhalfen, who was my gas man for many years, told me the home place three miles south of us was up for rent. We made a deal and Neva and I took a two week vacation before I started to plow the Neuhalfen place. This started a period when we rented more land, and it was a great feeling to be working just for us again."

Quaday's Quotes (Reprinted with permission from RR Quaday) Faribault County Register Monday December 16, 1991

Soybeans

In recent decades soybeans have grown in importance. The U.S. produces 40% of the world crop. On our River Road Farm crops were rotated between corn, soybeans, peas and alfalfa to control weeds and pesticides and replenish the nitrogen in the soil.

Dick Tells Yarns of Soybean Harvests in the 30s

"As our county heads into the soybean harvest, with very spotty yields at best, I'm reminded of the first years that soybeans were grown here. During the late 1930s we planted a few acres of the new 'wonder crop' spreading seed on top of the ground with a box seeder.

Herbicides had not yet been developed and weeds did not present a real problem because of the late seeding. The first crop was cut with a six-foot Deering binder, shocked up like oats, and stacked for cattle feed when the bundles got dry. The beans were still green when we cut them, much as a lot of this year's crop. They were a high protein feed with the green leaves and stocks making good roughage needed for ruminants.

The mice hadn't seen this new crop either, and were very experimental with building nests in the stacks the first year. They knew a good thing when it came their way, though, and moved in en masse the second year. That time we let about half the beans get yellow before cutting, and again cut and shocked the other half green. The whole bean after turning yellow and mature was not as good as roughage feed for ruminants.

We let all the beans get ripe the third year and cut them with a six-foot Deering mower. In the morning when the beans had dew on, we raked them into small piles. O.J. Wendt, who had a Huber threshing machine, took out nearly all the concaves and we pitched the loose beans into the hopper with the dividing board removed. At low cylinder speeds, this proved satisfactory. They were not cracked too much if one threshed them before they got too dry.

The main problem with that method was the amount of work involved. Pitching the loose beans with a pitch fork was heavy, exasperating work, as the vines all stuck together in the raked up piles. Pulling the vines apart at the thresh machine was another nightmare, so everyone was ripe for a new method of soybean harvest when the small combine was invented.

Yields of 15 to 30 bushels per acre were typical of that era. What seems so simple today was really a wonderful invention back about 1950. My 8-row Gleaner would have swallowed the little three-footer and never even stopped to burp if they appeared in the same field today."

Quaday's Quotes (Reprinted with permission from RR Quaday) Faribault County Register Monday October 7, 1991

Dick Bemoans Battle Against Weeds

Weeds
I hope that I will never see
A Button Weed as tall as me
And nestled down among my beans
A Nightshade creeps, and on them leans.
In among my corn stalks tall
The Creeping Jenny wraps them all.
My pea field stretches, lush and green,
There thistles, also, can be seen.
Farming would be fun, you know
If only crops, not weeds, would grow.

Quaday's Quotes -partial (Reprinted with permission from RR Quaday) Faribault County Register Monday May 4, 1992

Peas

Minnesota is the United States' largest producer of sugar beets, sweet corn, and green peas for processing.

Harvesting Peas With Horses

"It is 4 am on the Bill Quaday farm. I am 10 years old. Dad is shaking John and I awake.

"Get the cow in, we've got to haul peas at 6 o'clock."

Thus began a day in my youth, out on our River Road Farm in early July, 1930. After the milking and separating was done, the horses had to be curried and harnessed. We hitched one team to the surrey, led the other, and after loading up the neck yokes and eveners in the surrey, we set off for our Jo Daviess "80."

The peas were usually raised on the 80 because it was right on the road to the viner, and was one less crop to haul home to the River Road Farm. The soil there was a bit lighter and more suited for peas.

The pea vines were loaded onto flatbed Army-type wagons with a long tongue horse assembly. The vines were mowed by a specially built harvester with a platform behind the sickle and a rotating set of rakes which shoved the vines off in bunches. The vines were loaded onto the wagons by field hands with pitch forks. These fellows were husky men of all descriptions. Some were "road agents," out-of-work laborers from anywhere, U.S.A., who rode the railroad cars to where the work was being done. We called them "bums" and they were an interesting lot, with stories about the places they had worked and folks they had met in their travels.

The drivers in the field had to stand up on the wagons without support, start the team up when needed, and be able to stop them before they got too far ahead--no small task for a 10-year-old. If one went too far before the pitchers caught up, some guys would give us "what for" in no uncertain terms. The vines were always wet and heavy early in the morning and sloshed against our legs, getting us wet to the knees and making us shiver. By 7 am the first load was on the way to the viner, McClosky, two miles north. Dad pulled the loads to the viner with our Model A Ford. Emil

Henke had made a sturdy trailer hitch and a crooked clevis hooked the wagon tongue neck yoke iron to the Ford.

Promptly at 8 am we all piled into and around the Ford and headed home for breakfast, one on each fender and two hanging on the running board. Safety didn't count in those days--just anything to get the job done. The farm wives always fed the field workers during pea harvest, threshing, sweet corn picking, and all strenuous hand jobs requiring heavy meals to keep their strength up. At that time, the viner was run by the Tillia Brothers' steam engine 24 hours a day. The four Tillias lived and farmed right across the road so they could take turns running the steamer. Ed McClosky was the viner superintendent and the viner was on their land. They also raised peas.

The workers on the viner were more of the same, tough individuals who had been everywhere and done everything. There was always some farmwife who had time and wanted to make a few extra bucks, who would cook for the viner crew. Most of the crew were partial to alcohol, rationalizing that a steady diet of whiskey staved off the "summer complaint," which ran rampant where many men of all descriptions all drank out of the same cream can and used the same dipper and cup. Some of the threshing crews had the same philosophy, but our run was a bunch of tea-totalers.

The pea vines were pitched into a huge machine which shelled the peas, running them into boxes at the bottom and running the vines up into a stack for winter animal feed. It was a good system; nothing was wasted. Manpower was cheap in those days, with top wages running about 15 cents an hour for field and viner laborers. The whole process was rather scary, at least for a ten-year-old who had never been farther away from home than Elmore. It was interesting, too, getting acquainted with these travelers and hearing their stories about faraway places. It was our first knowledge of what alcohol did when imbibed, and how it affected different people in different ways.

The crews that Mother fed all knew her reputation against alcohol and were very careful to not offend her by coming to meals inebriated.

One of the true "characters" who worked for us through the years was "Iron Horse Red," a red-haired Irishman whose last name I never did hear, but who was a friend for life at our house. Mom knew he drank but, in his case, didn't care because he was Irish. My sheltered young life."

Quaday's Quotes (Reprinted with permission from RR Quaday) Faribault County Register Monday July 16, 2001

The summer of 1938

"Our summer, so far, has had to be classified as wet, causing a lot of lawn mowing every few days. It reminds me of the summer of 1938, the year I started farming in partnership with my Dad. The first part of the summer was just beautiful, with moderate temperatures and rain when it was needed for the crops. The pea crop was good but toward the end of the late pea harvest the weather cycle changed and the last few fields were mudded out, leaving huge ruts in the fields. The peas were cut with a windrower pulled with three horses. It had two arms which rotated on a platform behind the sickle, shoving off a fork-full of vines every three feet. Yes, they were still loaded on trucks or flat-bed army wagons at that time, and hauled to a viner which shelled the peas, running them into boxes which were trucked in and dumped onto a moving belt for inspection before canning."

Quaday's Quotes - partial (Reprinted with permission from RR Quaday) Faribault County Register Monday August 30, 2010

In 1903 the Green Giant Company was founded in Le Sueur, MN, as the Minnesota Valley Canning Company. The company processed vegetables grown throughout

1930s Green Giant Canning Factory

the Le Sueur, Blue Earth and Minnesota River valleys, including the sweet corn and peas grown on the Quaday River Road Farm for 44 years.

Today, the "Jolly Green Giant®" is the third most recognized advertising icon of the 20th century, behind Ronald McDonald and the Marlboro Man. A 55-foot statue of the Giant stands in Blue Earth, MN, paying homage to his birthplace. Just about every member of the Dick Quaday family worked in the Green Giant canning factory in Blue Earth, at one time or another.

The Quaday Family And The Canning Factory

"In my earliest years I, being the "caboose," youngest member of the Bill Quaday household, got to listen in on a great many earnest discussions between Mother and Dad. Mother's sewing room was actually situated in one corner of the downstairs bedroom, where I did my napping and sleeping. She did most of her serious sewing at night, when she could concentrate on it and not have too many interruptions. After the milking was done Dad would read for awhile, then come and discuss the main topics of interest at the time with Mother before going upstairs to bed. If they were talking over something of interest to me I would pretend to be asleep, and many times hear a whole story unfold before drifting off to sleep.

In the middle 1920s, the big topic before the farmers of the area was a canning factory, which was being built in Blue Earth to help the farmers diversify their crops and provide employment for residents of the City. I believe the original name was something like Blue Earth Co-op Cannery. Anyway, the local farmers and townspeople bought shares to raise money to get it in operation. Dad bought 500 shares in the original operation costing, I believe, two dollars a share. Many problems plagued the first management and predictably, the stock price went to near zero.

In the fall of 1926, my oldest brother, Carl, was a junior in Blue Earth High School, and started beating the drums for a car of his own. Dad, as usual, was short of cash. My uncle, Rudolph Baum, was a car salesman for the D.D. Murphy Ford Agency on South Main Street. The three of them worked out a deal so Carl got a new 1926 Ford Roadster with Dan Murphy getting the shares of stock, which Dad considered worthless. Mr. Murphy already owned quite a number of shares and was trying to maintain the price and keep the factory going. He owned a few farms at that time and would later buy more in Faribault County.

Dad still contracted peas and sweet corn production with the canning factory, and one by one, the family became involved with it through the years. My sister, Marie, worked there through the summers to make college money. My brother, John, pitched peas and drove truck for college money.

My own involvement came at an early age, driving a team in the field on a flatbed pea wagon. These were wagons bought from Army surplus, I think, and they were driven through the field between rows of cut and windrowed peas. They first tried to cut them with a mower with a swather attachment, but peas were a juicy, tangled mass of vines at harvest time and contained a great deal of moisture, so the mowers always plugged up. Labor was plentiful and cheap at that time, so they hired a "Bum," the name for all transient workers in those days, to walk along behind the mowers with a pitch fork, raking the pea vines back so the mower could cut instead of pull. It was a killing job, so everyone took his turn walking and pitching onto the wagons.

I had heard so many stories about "Bums" that just being in the field with about eight of them scared me half to death. We started at 4 am, while it was only just light. Many of these transients had put in long days in the field for a period of weeks. Some of them were alcoholics and lived from one job to the next, always on the move. It seemed to me that they were constantly angry about something, and the language sometimes got to be profanely obscene. So when they got the chance to have a bit of authority, even over a scared, scrawny 8-year-old teamster, it made them feel better.

A year later, International Harvester came out with a mower with a platform and rotating arms to shove the pea vines off in rows and bunches. This made the pitcher's job much easier, but still heavy, grueling work.

The group of pitchers which treated me the best and actually made me feel important was five local men from the Third Ward in Blue Earth. They were not like the other transients. They were good men: Curt and Walt Fezler, and Ray, Don, and Ted Lamont. They always had some kind of cheerful banter and seemed to have a certain amount of fun, even with the mosquitoes, heat, and sweat, that went with the job. The "Jolly" part of Green Giant came much later, and that's another story."

Quaday's Quotes (Reprinted with permission from RR Quaday) Faribault County Register Monday February 18, 1991

Canning Crew Did Top Notch Work

"One beautiful warm night shortly after Labor Day, I donned my yellow hard hat, picked up a new hair net, and headed for the empty can department of the local Green Giant Canning Factory. I was scarcely inside, when Roger Malwitz walked by, gave me a knowing look, and remarked, "I thought it was about time for you to show up."

Every year since moving to the house in Blue Earth, I have managed to put in a few nights in the employ of Green Giant. For two years I worked in the so-called automatic husker department. These wonderful machines sometimes need human help getting the ears of corn husked, so that the cutters and sorters can do their work down on the belt. This part of the operation too closely resembled farming, so the next year I applied for the de-palletizer job, in which the empty cans are moved onto the can line using a lift truck and a hydraulic machine that pushes a row of cans onto the line. The can department is normally run with a crew of five; the lift truck operator, two hydraulic machine operators, and two floor men, who strip the plastic covers off the pallets, do the paperwork and shove full pallets down the rollers into the machine.

1992 Green Giant Crew

After Labor Day when the high school and college kids go back to school, it is usually easy to get employment at Green Giant. I would not dream of competing for employment there when the kids need the money for school and college. I work only nights, because I could not take the heat of the day in the summer.

I thoroughly enjoyed getting into working condition one more time. It is a great way to pick up a bit of gambling money, a sport which I enjoy even more."

Quaday's Quotes - partial (Reprinted with permission from RR Quaday) Faribault County Register Monday November 23, 1992

The Orchard

Before 1868, only crab apples grew reliably in Minnesota. American Indians in the area harvested other crops, but they did not grow apples. Apples have had a rocky history in Minnesota.

The famous 19th-century editor and politician Horace Greeley, perhaps best remembered for the quotation "Go West, young man. Go West and grow up with the country," is reported to have warned an audience in 1860 not to bother going to Minnesota, because it was impossible to grow apples there. This disparaging remark was not far from the truth. The Minnesota climate and soil were a hard sell. Early white settlers to Minnesota tried to grow apples using seeds and seedlings from their former homes to the east and the south, but their plants died, usually because of the region's harsh winters.

All that changed, however, when the apple-loving and apple-breeding Peter Gideon arrived on the scene. On his property near Excelsior, Gideon tested thousands of seedlings. By 1868, he had come up with the mother of all Minnesota commercial-quality apples, the Wealthy.

The Wealthy apple was the earliest apple to thrive in the Minnesota climate. Beyond his employment at the state farm, Gideon never made any money from the Wealthy apple. However, his apple made commercial fruit growing possible in Minnesota, and it was the most profitable apple in the Northwest for decades, contributing to the livelihood of many other people. The Wealthy apple also was the parent of other successful Minnesota apples, such as the Haralson, which was developed at the Minnesota Horticulture Research Center in 1922. It is named after Charles Haralson, superintendent of the University of Minnesota Fruit Breeding Farm.

The Haralson is medium-sized and has a round-conic shape. It has a red color and large, moderately conspicuous dots. Haralson apples are crisp and juicy, having a tart flavor. They are good for eating, cooking, and are an excellent choice for pies. The skin is medium-tough, and the stem is medium. The tree is hardy and vigorous, but relatively small. It has a strongly developed central leader and wide-angled lateral branches. The flowers bloom late, and the fruit ripens in early October.

On the Home Place, across the road from the farm buildings, was an apple orchard with many different varieties, some of which ripened early in the summer and others later so that we had a plentiful supply of fruit from July until October or until it froze. Usually there were so many apples that, in order to keep the ground clean under the trees, we picked up the "windfalls" and fed them to the hogs and sheep. In order to make the best possible use of the abundance, Mother fixed apples in every imaginable way: sauce, pie, jelly, apple butter, apple cake, dried apples, fried apples, baked apples, apple salad, pickles and probably others which I have forgotten. In spite of eating such a quantity, I never got tired of them, and apples, in whatever form, are still one of my favorite foods.

Dad liked all kinds of fruit and had planted plum trees, grape vines, and a cherry tree--all of which produced abundantly. The only problem with the cherry tree was that the birds liked the cherries just as much as we did and started sampling them even before they were ripe enough to pick. In order to stop this thievery, Dad bought a huge piece of mosquito netting and put it over the whole tree, which worked quite well until the tree grew so big that covering it was out of the question. So the birds finally won the war.

Taken from Overture to Anderson Unfinished Symphony, 1914-1942, written by Marie Anderson.

Growing Fruit On Our Grain Farm

"There was a time way back in the 1920s when my parents had finished putting up all the new buildings on their farm after moving back from Long Beach, CA, when they could settle back and relax. They did actually rebuild the 'Old Pitcher Place' out on River Road, building a new house, barn, hog house, chicken house and pump house. The barn was built first because it had to house the milk cows and four work horses, the basic elements of any farm in those days. The hog house and chicken house were next and, of course, the new house was last because that was not a money maker. My Mother's uncle by marriage, Charley Quantz, was a carpenter by trade so he was hired to put up all the new buildings.

Dad had plenty of cash to buy the 80-acres from Wesley Pitcher, after selling his 40-acre orange orchard in Long Beach. He rebuilt with state-of-the-art buildings at that period, after the First World War. Lumber was cheap and of excellent quality, because the big lumber companies had more or less cleaned out the old growth forests in WI and MN, and moved their equipment west to Idaho, Oregon, and Washington. The dimension lumber (2x4's, 2x6's, and big beams) were all 18 feet, as was the drop siding and the roof boards. The shingles were all No.1 cedar, at $1 a square, and lasted 50 years. The buildings all had pitch enough so the snow melted and ran off, and the hail very seldom did any damage.

The new three story farm house only cost $4,000, including labor. Mr. Quantz did it all alone in one summer, finishing the inside trim in golden oak, which Dad sanded and varnished himself during the winter months. In the Depression 1930s, Charley Quantz moved his family to Chicago to find work. He was a fast worker and a good craftsman so he had plenty of work there, as the Chicago area was rapidly expanding with many immigrants from Europe settling there at that time. He detested labor unions, saying all they did was slow a man down and collect union dues without doing any work.

Due to my Dad's experience working one year in a nursery in CA, he planted a great variety of fruit trees and several kinds of grapes, some of which prospered here and some did not due to the severe MN winters. The 24-tree apple orchard all survived and some of the plum trees did well, but the compass cherries and the concord grapes lasted only three or four years. The well-planned orchard had nine or ten varieties of apples, from mid-summer to winter-keeping apples. The Strawberry Crabs were ready to eat by the time the oats were ripe to cut and shock. The Duchess followed, with the Okabena, the Wealthy, the Banana Crabs and the Melinda in spaced succession. We always wrapped the Winter's Jewel and the North-western Greenings, storing them in bulk in our attic stairway hall where the temperature was just right without freezing. We had good apples to eat with popcorn all winter.

There was an early variety of grapes that somehow escaped the trellis that was built for it and climbed into an accidental clump of plum trees. I say accidental plum trees, because they grew into a sold mass from some seeds thrown out by previous occupants of the farm. It was quite a job picking the grapes because the plum trees had long, sharp thorns and the trees grew quite tall. Both the plums and the grapes were good tasting fruit, so we harvested every bit. I'm sure my Mother detested plum and grape season as our pockets in our overalls and jeans were always full of the fruit, and some inevitably got crushed while climbing over fences or chasing cattle. That was cattle herding time, by the way, because the pastures were drying up in mid-summer.

During harvest and threshing time we always had a good supply of fresh fruit to carry around in our pockets for between-meal snacks. Being the youngest boy in the family was wonderful, in some ways. After raising two boys ahead of me, the folks realized that everyone was much happier if they would let me do my own thing. The garden, after planting, turned into my plot of misery. It fell to me to weed and space the carrots and seed onions, mainly because Mother's eyes (she always wore glasses) were not good enough, she said, to distinguish between the tiny seedlings of carrots and onions. Once it was discovered that I was able--though unwilling--to do these hand-and-knee operations, they became my responsibility until I was judged old enough for field work.

I have always liked carrots, but never cared that much for onions ever since."

Quaday's Quotes (Reprinted with permission from RR Quaday) Faribault County Register Monday July 13, 2009

Apple Orchard Varieties

"With the first hint of a September morn, my Dad always began preparations for the picking and storing of what he called the winter apple crop. He planted 24 apple trees, with staggered maturity so we would have apples all summer with 'keeping' varieties. These late-maturing apples we wrapped in white tissue and packed them in crates, just the way he had learned to do in California. He sprayed the orchard three times during the summer for a variety of moths, worms, and scab, with a very potent poisonous material, now taken off the market because of the environmentalists outcry.

Kids from town always stopped to rob a few apples to eat on their trips out to the swinging bridge, and usually on the way back too. We ate thousands of apples through the summer and actually all year long, with no ill effects; all four of us are going strong at 79 to near 90. Many times through the

241

years, when we meet folks around the state who find out we are from Blue Earth, they tell us they used to steal apples out of our orchard and they were the best apples!

We had Strawberry Crabs for pickling and early summer eating. We had Duchess and Okabena for pies and mid-summer eating. We had Wealthy apples to can for apple sauce and apple butter, or jelly. We had Winter's Jewel for early winter use and Northwestern Greenings for late winter and spring use. The favorite apple of all us kids was the Malinda, of which we had two trees. They were so sweet that the worms and bugs of all kinds like them best too. When we were going to District 104 school, we used water from a clear water spring down below the big hill, in back of the Sailor farmhouse. The spring was probably one of the reasons Abel Sailor homesteaded that particular farm, as it was still the best tasting water in the neighborhood 60 years later.

His son, Perry, had planted a large orchard out south of the house and we stole a few apples every time we carried water through the orchard. Why did the stolen apples always taste better? One of Perry's trees survived until Neva and I bought the farm in 1942; fortunately, it was the favorite kind of apple.

Perry was afraid that the government would take his apple sauce during the First World War, so he cut a trap door in the living room of the farmhouse and stored the family's canned apple sauce in the crawl space, with the door covered by a braided rug. The first spring we lived on the Sailor place, I planted a 12-tree orchard; all grew but one.

The old tree that Perry planted survived even longer than our plantings. But a windstorm split it and ruined it shortly after the other trees died. A fence and a thick hedge row more or less kept the apple stealing kids out of that orchard.

We always planted a potato and melon patch down by the Blue Earth River during the Great Depression drought. The sandy loam soil was ideal for both crops, and the water table was high enough even then, to produce big scab free potatoes and luscious muskmelons and watermelons. We hid the patch in the corn field so marauding town kids would not find them, but they sometimes did anyway. The bad part was they didn't just steal the melons, they trashed the patch so it was ruined for the summer."

Quaday's Quotes (Reprinted with permission from RR Quaday) Faribault County Register Monday October 11, 1999

Apple Orchard Was Childhood Delight

"We had a great variety of apples for sauces and pickles that were cooked and processed and put into glass jars. Kids on their way to the Swinging Bridge would stop and swipe a few coming and going. When I bought the home farm from the folks, I fenced in the orchard and pastured two sheep bucks there through the summer. This made it a hazard to the timid kids planning to swipe apples on their hikes on River Road.

Our children formulated games to play among the trees, which anyone could climb very easily. These games involved the buck sheep, and getting into a tree before getting bumped in the behind.

By the time I owned the orchard we had mature apple trees, and we hauled truck loads of apples up north to sell. I would sell the apples door to door, and buy cheap lumber to build needed machinery sheds on the farm place. I sold apples in the Long Prairie area, and stayed with Herb and Ruth Klinder. Ruth is Neva's older sister. We would sneak in a day of fishing at Lake Beauty, which adjoined Herb's pasture.

Dad helped me pick apples and rode with me to Grand Forks, ND, where we stayed with my brother, John. We sold door to door in the poorer areas of town where they would buy the apples by the bushels, while in the rich sections they wanted enough for a pie or two. At Grand Forks, I got the idea that we could drive back with a load of potatoes. We headed to Ada, where we drove in the fields and loaded 100 pound bags of potatoes into the truck. Everything went fine until I tried to use my brakes going down the hills. The brakes had failed on my old truck, so time was spent at the local garage to get them fixed. By the time we got home it was bean combining time so I wholesaled the potatoes to Les Krusemark, who ran the Red Owl store in Blue Earth."

Quaday's Quotes-partial (Reprinted with permission from RR Quaday) Faribault County Register Monday, September 10, 1990

Social Life

William Quaday's family--two sisters, three brothers and their families--all lived either in Blue Earth or on farms nearby. Grandpa (Charles) Quaday lived with one of his daughters until he was in his eighties. So for many years, on his birthday as well as on Thanksgiving, Christmas and New Years, we had family gatherings. All contributed to the meal and the families changed off hosting the get-togethers.

The country school was the center for many community activities. In October, at Halloween time there was often a carnival with all the traditional "fun things" (bobbing for apples, fish pond, fortune-telling and numerous other ways of getting money out of those attending). After that we started preparing for the Christmas program--a big event held in the evening with all the kids taking part in the plays, recitations and songs and then exchanging gifts afterwards. Of course, "Teacher" got the most gifts!

One of the "happenings" in our school each year was the peanut shower. On a day agreed upon by the kids, everyone brought a big bag of peanuts in the shell. At a signal from one of the big boys (usually during a dull math class), everybody grabbed the bag of peanuts which they had sneaked into their desks and threw the contents a handful at a time at the teacher. In order to shelter her face from the deluge (some of the boys could throw with a lot of force), she usually turned her back to us and waited until it was over. Then everybody rushed up to the front of the room and grabbed as many peanuts off the floor as they could and we munched on peanuts for the rest of the day. After it was all over we had to sweep up the shells, but even that was fun after such an exciting day.

A few times we had "spell-downs" held in the evening with the whole neighborhood attending. Two leaders chose sides from among those who wanted to participate and the teacher read words from a list she had made, starting with easy ones. Contestants took turns spelling the words, alternating from one side to the other. If someone misspelled a word, he (she) had to sit down and the next in line tried to spell it. Sometimes as many as five or six went down on the same word. The contest was over when only one person was left standing.

In January or February, when things were getting a little dull, there might be a basket social. Each woman or girl who came was supposed to pack a basket with goodies and decorate it in the best style she could manage. Somebody volunteered to be auctioneer and the men were urged to bid on each basket as it was presented. Usually the gals tipped off the particular male whom they wanted to buy their basket as to which one it was and, if a particular girl was especially popular, and two or three men started bidding on her basket, the price could go up and up until all but one ran out of money. After all the baskets were sold, the men found the girls whose baskets they had bought and the couples ate the contents. This was fun for most but for a shy or unattractive girl it must have been a nightmare.

Taken from Overture to Anderson Unfinished Symphony, 1914-1942, written by Marie Anderson.

Basket Socials Brought Out The Boys

"A great deal of the social life of farm folks who populated the Corn Belt in the early days revolved around the rural schools and country churches. The school building was usually located near the center of the district so children wouldn't have to walk too far on the muddy or snow covered roads.

1933 Marie Quaday Teacher at District 104

District 104, where I attended my first seven grades, was built much closer to Blue Earth, probably because "Grandpa Dobson" donated the land on which it was built. This location served the rural community well because the farmers could drop their children off at school, then proceed to town for cream and egg delivery.

Miss Marie Quaday (my sister) was a teacher in 1933 in District 104.

In the "era of the horse," distance meant much more than it does now. The Neuhalfen Place lay

246

at the extreme southern end of 104, with 80 acres of the Murphy Place also lying in the district. The location provided a two edged sword in later years, because most of the farmers lived on the north end, and petitioned into the Blue Earth system.

The spelling bee with the "Basket Socials" after the contest proved to be the major attraction to the young people. For instance, if a young farmer or hired man was "sparking" a young lady living in the district and was rather public about it, there were boys in the area who would make him pay dearly for the privilege of lunching with her. In those days it seemed an auctioneer was available to "cry the sale." This was a fun way to raise money for school books, repairs and even a new building.

Sometimes the young men got carried away with the bidding and the well decorated basket brought more than the suitor had planned on paying. Then, just possibly, there could be a fight outside after the festivities inside were over. The young husbands had a hard time bidding on their wives' baskets.

Of course one had to know which basket belonged to whom and the less attractive girls got to be adept in the decorating, sometimes copying other girls' works of art to confuse the bidders. With fewer farmers farming more land, the rural schools and churches lost memberships to the point that the spelling bee, with the added basket social attraction, became obsolete. It took quite a number of spellers and basket packers to create the atmosphere necessary for success, financially, as well as socially.

The last basket social I attended occurred after an evening of "500" at the old K.C. Hall on 7th and Main Street in Blue Earth, with Carl Wessels crying the sale. I paid $25 for Grace Murphy's beautifully decorated basket, a nearly unheard of sum at that time, with the proceeds going to the building of SS Peter and Paul School.

I believe the year was 1945. Nearly 100 people crowded into the upstairs of the "King Building" which stood on the southwest corner of the intersection.

I wonder if this old tradition would be novel enough to attract young people today."

Quaday's Quotes-partial (Reprinted with permission from RR Quaday) Faribault County Register Monday February 24, 1992

Charivari or Shivaree, (also called "rough music") is the term for a French folk custom in which the community gave a noisy, discordant mock serenade, also pounding on pots and pans, at the home of newlyweds. This type of social custom arose independently in many rural village societies, for instance also in England, Italy, Wales or Germany, and was brought with the immigrants to America. Though it evolved in various forms, the custom was familiar to most farmers and rural communities, and helped to welcome newcomers to the neighborhood.

Shivaree Custom Fades Into History

"One of the quaint customs practiced in the early days here in farm country and through the Corn Belt area was the welcoming, about a month after a wedding, of the bride and groom into their new neighborhood. It may or may not have been of French origin. Anyway, the name sounds French: Charivari-pronounced shivaree. It was always meant to be a surprise, although the young couple knew it was going to happen sooner or later. It was just a 12-gauge shotgun or two.

Neva and I were married in January, so along after the middle of February we began to expect the inevitable shivaree. She was a very popular girl, and I had a few friends too. We dreaded the affair because we were living with my parents out on River Road, until we could get possession of the farm next door. The house was large, but like a good many of the houses of that period, had many small rooms and was not built to accommodate a crowd. My folks retired upstairs giving us the run of the house, with 15 or 16 guys and gals. We did find enough chairs and filled two rooms. I did smoke a cigar once in awhile at that time, and we always needed to have some on hand when my brother, Carl, visited. He smoked or chewed cigars continually.

I passed out cigars to the boys, and wonder of wonders, everyone smoked whether they had ever smoked cigars or not. In 10 minutes the house was blue inside. At about 10 pm, I suggested heading for Jack's Sport Shop where Neva had worked evenings. I financed malts for everyone and the party went on until closing time. Thankfully no one got sick; they must have been smart enough to not inhale the smoke from the White Owl cigars. I was selling milk to the Sport Shop at the time, so got a bit of a discount on the malts. They only cost $.15 each at that time, full price. These neighborhood affairs were always fun, but our neighborhood only had about three more before the custom faded into history in our area. I understand the shivaree is still very popular in parts of Iowa and the Dakotas.

As long as I'm bringing back old times, I might as well put in a bit about our honeymoon. After Roy Dobson at Motor Inn steamed off the Limburger cheese from the manifold on my new Chevy, we drove to Minneapolis. We stayed at The Andrews Hotel and commuted out to the University Farm where Farm and Home Week was in session. I had the pleasure of introducing Neva to a lot of my friends, who still attended school there. I knew most of the kids there, having attended the previous year. The weather was just grand all week, so we went to Como Park and the zoo one day. I took in a couple of sessions and Neva hit a couple of home economic lectures."

Quaday's Quotes-partial (Reprinted with permission from RR Quaday) Faribault County Register Monday March 2, 2009

Riverview Community Club Began in 1930

"The neighborhood on the River Road and the square mile to the west, for most of my life, was a very congenial area. We had our own school district, with the schoolhouse standing just south of the Terry Classon Driveway.

About 1927, O.J. Wendt and his father bought a new Case threshing machine, plus a new Heider tractor to pull the thresher. These were gas tractors rated at 40 hp. The Case machine was a 26-inch cylinder, which could keep two bundle pitchers busy if the grain was dry and conditions right.

The people in the threshing run kept track of the hours worked at each farm. At the end of the season O.J. hosted a meeting with lunch and free ice cream for the families. At that time, the hours of work were tallied up and the big farmers paid the smaller operators for the overtime at the rate of 25 cents an hour for man, team, rack and fork. The idea was to get the threshing bill paid, which at that time was about one half cent a bushel.

In 1930, Mrs. Walter Plocker, Ida Ristau, Julia Wehsener, Helen Wendt and my Mother, Lorena Quaday, got together on the party telephone line and decided to form a social club. The club had bylaws and good parliamentary procedure for meetings. Officers were elected at the annual meeting in January and the club met the third Friday of every month. Meetings were held in the homes as most of the farm houses could handle a crowd of 25-40 people, kids and all.

249

After much discussion, the name "Riverview Community Club" emerged. After the business meeting, a lunch was served. We usually had some program, sometimes instrumental, sometimes special songs sung by our own members. Poems were read and anyone who went on a trip gave a travelogue. We had song books for group singing, and a set of traveling trays and silverware which went from house to house.

The club quartet had many different members through the years, with some excellent choir singers, like Julia Wehsener, O.J. Wendt, Herb Schwen, Fred Paschke and at times Helen Wendt and Julia's sister, Melva Johnson. The Wehsener twins, Jean and Joan, played violins and sometimes a neighborhood hired man played a mouth organ or guitar.

We had an unwritten rule that the club would never cross the Blue Earth River, which was supposed to keep the membership down to a manageable crowd.

Sometimes the youngsters got rambunctious. I remember when we had the housewarming on the old Sailor Place, I had to pick up many canned goods which fell off the shelves in the basement from the activity among the kids out in the kitchen. I put three more oak brace posts in the basement under the kitchen before the next club meeting."

Quaday's Quotes -partial (Reprinted with permission from RR Quaday) Faribault County Register Monday July 23, 1990

Reunion Of Riverview Community Club

"The Riverview Community Club held its 70th Christmas Potluck supper at the First National Bank Party Room on Sunday, December 2. Twenty-two members enjoyed delicious salads, bars, cakes and cookies for dessert. John and Rosie Plocker, along with Neva and I, did the chores.

Two couples host the Christmas Party, the Springtime Eat-Out, and a fall wiener roast. When the Club was formed, we met every month in farm homes. The meetings were held on the third Friday of the month, barring snow storms and sickness.

The first meeting was held at the home of Walter and Hilda Plocker, in mid-January, 1930. The families attending were Walter and Julia Wehsener, my parents, William and Lorena Quaday, Fred and Emma Paschke, Gust and

Ida Ristau, Oliver and Helen Wendt, Mr. and Mrs. Tom Collins, Bill and Forrest Johnson's folks, and Frank Willmert, a bachelor. The Johnsons were never in our threshing run so sadly, I don't remember their names. Frank Willmert actually had the best deal of the neighborhood, as he never had to serve or entertain the club.

When everyone showed up with about 40 arriving in team and bobsled, it made quite a houseful. We purchased trays and cups for lunch, songbooks for group singing, and took turns forming programs that were limited to half an hour. If some member took a trip or witnessed some extraordinary event, they were obligated to report and have a show-and-tell at the next meeting. At that time, farm help was cheap and plentiful, so several of the families had a hired man at least part of the time. The hired men were invited to attend and if any of them had special talents, such as singing or playing a musical instrument, they were expected to perform for the club.

Herb Schwen, who owned land in "the square" and his wife Minnie, attended some meetings. When he did, he was part of a quartet. Herb sang tenor, O.J. Wendt sang bass, Julia Wehsener sang alto, and Helen Wendt sang soprano. They sang together at the Evangelical Church and were very good. Fred Paschke had a bass voice and sometimes sang humorous solos to the delight of all the youngsters in the club. The Wehsener twins, Jean and Joan, played violas and were drafted for the program quite often. Sometimes games were played if no one had a program--but never card games. Certain events became annual, such as the "Oyster Stew," which was always held in November at someone's farm who had a dairy herd.

The Club Picnic was always held in June, the first few years at the Swinging Bridge, and later at the Faribault County Fairgrounds.

The Club membership was limited early on to the "The Square," the square miles surrounding the Country School District 104 The schoolhouse stood where Terry Classon's driveway ends up on River Road. The School meetings, held in late May or June, were also an interesting bit of country living at that time in history, but that's another story. The election of the school board involved much politicking some years, with some of the renters trying to get on the board, and land owners trying to keep them off. All was forgiven or forgotten by early June, when the school picnic was held at the Swinging Bridge.

If memory serves me correctly, Lester Paschke, John Plocker, Don Wendt, Dick Paschke, and I are the only charter members of the Riverview Community Club. Lester dropped out upon moving to Delavan and Don moved to Zumbrota, leaving John, Dick Paschke, and me as the only active "Old-timers" in the club. I believe several hundred people have belonged to the club through the years while living in or close to "The Square." One original rule pertained to moving across the Blue Earth River. If a family left the farm, and moved to Blue Earth, their membership was terminated forthwith.

When my folks and Walter Plocker moved to town, the membership tried to abrogate the rule. Dad, who had always enjoyed the visits with the neighbors as much as anyone said, "Nope, a rule's a rule," and promptly resigned his membership much to Mother's chagrin. When we had club at our place, they did come out and had a great time, "Just like old times," Mother said."

Quaday's Quotes (Reprinted with permission from RR Quaday) Faribault County Register Monday December 17, 2001

Card Playing
Dick Picks Up "Tools Of The Devil"

"Card playing was not on my parents' agenda for activities. In fact, my Mother went so far as to call a deck of playing cards, "Tools of the Devil." I never paid much attention to such pastimes in my youth. However, my sister, Marie, came home from Winona Teachers College in the mid 30s and she brought home a deck of "Tools of the Devil." She introduced us kids to a game called Honeymoon Bridge. We played the game when Mother was not around, and as I recall, the honeymoon part meant the game required two people to play. I don't think Dad cared much one way or the other, but he did give Mother moral support when she tried to save our souls."

Quaday's Quotes-partial (Reprinted with permission from RR Quaday) Faribault County Register Monday February, 11 1991

When I moved to town, I had three jobs: driving cars and pick-ups for delivery, or exchange for the L & M Motors for 20 years, working the 'Corn Pack' for Pillsbury Green Giant at night for three years, and writing weekly "Quotes" columns for The Faribault County Register. For personal jobs, I did our yard work, and took care of Neva. Our Penny-ante Poker Club played on Tuesdays and Thursdays during the winter months.

2004 Poker Game

Bowling

Dutch Colonists brought bowling to America in the 17th century. The game consisted of nine pins set in a triangle. It was regularly played in an area of New York City still known as 'Bowling Green'.

In 1841, Connecticut banned "bowling at the game of ninepins" because of widespread gambling. Other states followed suit. It is popularly believed that today's game of tenpins was devised to circumvent the laws against the game of ninepins. An outdoor game for most of its history, indoor bowling became popular in the mid-nineteenth century after the introduction of indoor lanes in New York in 1840.

Bowling became very popular over the years in America, developing into one of the biggest betting games. In 1920, the Prohibition law led to an increase in bowling as proprietors discovered that patrons wanted to bowl, even if they couldn't drink.

In 1951, the America Machine and Foundry Company purchased patents to eliminate the "pinboy", a person responsible for setting up the pins, and added an automatic "pinspotter" in 1952. After these innovations in the sport, media embraced bowling by the 50s and NBC had "Championship Bowling," the first airing of network coverage of bowling. Bowling for Dollars and several others followed. The sport of bowling grew and grew because of all the media attention. Most small towns in rural areas had bowling alleys that supported leagues from the surrounding communities.

He Set The Pins On Saturday Nights

"One of the favorite winter sports of the Blue Earth area during most of my adult life has been bowling. The first bowling alley that I recall was owned by the late Mr. Burt Rorman, and was located under his pool hall where Double Play is now operating. His brother, Bill, operated the alleys for him during the winter, when he wasn't selling popcorn and gardening out south of town.

The way I was introduced to the sport was through setting pins before automatic spotters were introduced locally. I think we were paid five cents a line at that time. There was intense competition for pin setting jobs, except on Saturday and Sunday nights. It seemed that the most powerful guys in the area would come to bowl on those nights. Some would load up on a few beers before coming down to bowl, which would make them feel more powerful, and they would show off by throwing the bowling balls with greater velocity, scattering pins high and wide. One had to be pretty agile to dodge pins when Ed Tomche or Morris Hanson bowled. By far the hardest thrower I can remember was Club Evans, and I have a scar on my left leg to remember him by.

Usually, I would make enough money over the weekend to pay for my bowling on Tuesday, which was National League Night. The first team I bowled on was "Guckeen," with Bud Okerson as captain. Morris Hanson, Ralph Ficken, Junior Long, and I were the regulars. You might say we made our mark on the game. There was a hole over one of the alleys where Mr. Hanson really lofted the ball once. Many years later when I bowled on Breen's team, our captain John Breen, made his mark on Ankeny's Alleys by putting a disgusted foot through one wall when he missed a spare.

Through the second World War, I believe Alf Ludtke owned the alleys under the pool hall, with his brother, Fred, operating them while Alf was in the service. Later, when Clayton Ankeny had made his mark in the poultry business, he built an alley where the present Ankeny Furniture now operates. This was an ultra modern alley for its day with automatic pin spotters and 16 alleys. I bowled on several different teams during the time Clayton and his sons, Wayne and Wendell, operated the alleys, which Wayne sold to a South Dakota firm some years ago. The Knights of Columbus sponsored a team for many years, and I bowled with them on Tuesday night.

1962 Blue Earth City Bowling Champs

Later, I bowled for Ankeny's Recreation team. It was on this team that we won the National League Championship, and in the City Championship bowl off, the Rev. Herman Knoll, needing only five pins to clinch the tourney, threw his first ball in the gutter and picked up four pins on the second and we were just that--second.

When I bowled on the Knights of Columbus team, the State Council started up a State K.C. Tournament. I think I bowled in every one up until last year, when I had to watch my boys carry on the family tradition, because of a two week hospital stay at Rochester. John Breen and I were always partners in the singles and doubles, getting in the money every year, one way or another. The last year John bowled, he had a very gimpy knee, which really ruined his game. In the doubles, I was just as bad as John, so we got a good sportsmanship award, which actually is a booby prize. The years on Breen's team are a story in themselves, and I'll bring that up some other time."

Quaday's Quotes (Reprinted with permission from RR Quaday) Faribault County Register Monday December 3, 1990

I belonged to the Knights of Columbus Council 1836 (KC) in Blue Earth for many years, elected to all the local official offices. I was elected to the District Knight of Columbus as a District Deputy, which represented the communities of Wells, Easton, Albert Lea, and Blue Earth for four years. I was the State KC Charities Commissioner for eight years, and also participated on the State Student Loan Board, as Vice Chairman and Scribe for eight years. We offered college loans to qualified students who were sons or daughters of KC members, that ranged from five thousand dollars to two hundred-fifty thousand dollars. I was elected as a delegate to the International Knights of Columbus Convention held in Denver, CO. I wrote monthly articles for the state paper for eight years.

I won second place in the KC State Bowling Tournament and also won first place in the KC State Officers Bowling Tournament, with a total of six hundred twenty seven pins, with no handicap.

1985 KC State Bowling Tournament

After 20 Years, Dick Decides Not To File For Re-Election To KC Student Loan Board

"At the May 17th Knights of Columbus State Convention, I wore two hats; while attending as a member of the State Student Loan Board, I was also a delegate for our local K.C. Council 1836. It was quite an emotional three days for me because, after about 20 years in State Office I decided not to file for re-election to the Student Loan Fund Board. It has been a great learning experience for me; my job was writing an article each month for the State K.C. Council periodical, about the workings of the Student Loan Board.

In addition, I, along with two other members, reviewed the student applications for loans. This was all done by mail to avoid expensive meetings and to save time, as driving to and from meetings usually killed a day. Richard Smith at the Blue Earth Post Office, always checked to see that I had the next address on the envelope containing the applications, so it wouldn't come back to me after paying the postage.

The flurry of activity in my later years of Knights of Columbus membership began when my good friend, Jim Doerr, nominated me for District Deputy for District 35, encompassing the Albert Lea, Wells, Easton, and Blue Earth Councils. The term of office is four years and it is a rewarding job with many interesting public relations contacts. I really enjoyed attending council functions in the other Catholic parishes. Wells always had a big feed after installation of their officers, and Albert Lea put on a steak fry after theirs. Blue Earth usually had a potluck supper following their installation. We had the biggest district meeting ever held in our district at Easton, with a pork chop dinner and state officers on the program. Our Lady of Mount Carmel Church was filled to capacity. Tom Warmka was Grand Knight at the time, and really put a great deal of effort into it.

My next state job was on the State Charities Commission, a unique group of men who met three times each year to arrange the distribution of $50,000 to various charitable organizations around the state, from Blue Earth to International Falls. We had four categories: church, community, education, and one time others. I thought when elected to the position, that it would be great fun and a breeze to give away that much money. It turned out to take much thought and consideration to the allocations of funds while trying to keep it geologically fair. I had a wonderful group of fellows to work with, and we had many a brainstorming session while deciding which applicants got the money and how much. The gifts ranged from a water heater for the Blue Earth Senior Center to a meat slicer for the Bird Island School. I served two three-year terms, after being appointed to fill out two years of another member's term.

Finally, I had a chance to serve on the Student Loan Board, which was the position I had always wanted after helping to vote it in at the 1958 State Convention. I put my name in the hat when a member moved out of state. There were three applicants for the position, and with six members, each voting for their favorite friend, the vote went two-two-and two for three votes. Archie Rauzi, State Deputy at the time, anticipating just such a dead-lock, sent a proxy tie-breaker vote for me and I was in. Again, I worked with a grand group of Knights. This turned out to be a very ambitious and forward thinking board. The first money allocated for loans was $5,000 from the State Council in 1959.

From this humble beginning, the funds grew to $500,000 by 1985. We hatched the idea of a Million Dollar Drive, as some students had to wait in line until we had enough money to fund them. The drive was a great success with help from the State Bishops, many Parish Priests, nearly all the Councils in the State, and many private donations.

In less than 1 ½ years, the funds grew to well over a million dollars, all of which is on loan to college students at the present time. I have loved being a part of this group of men who have such a far reaching, beneficial effect on our youth of college age. I also feel that, after eight years on the Board, it is time for younger members to carry the ball, thus bringing in new ideas and new methods of operation. The program, I'm sure, will carry on and get bigger and better."

Quaday's Quotes (Reprinted with permission from RR Quaday) Faribault County Register Monday June 24, 1996

Fishing

Minnesota's license plate reads 'Land of 10,000 Lakes' and while most of these lakes are in the northern part of the state, the Minnesota River Country region has a fair number too, providing excellent fishing opportunities for its settlers.

Fishing History

"My dad and my grandfather both loved to go fishing, in the Blue Earth River or any number of Fairmont area lakes. My bachelor uncle, Jule, was an avid fisherman, driving his topless Model T Ford to Lake Imogene or East Chain quite often through the summer. The limits in those days consisted of how many fish one wanted to clean.

There were no refrigerators yet, so it wasn't too smart to catch more than could be eaten in a couple of days, or kept alive. The bullheads of the Fairmont chain of lakes lived very well in the stock tanks. They cleaned out the green algae that grew in the tanks, and one could have fish for breakfast any time.

Most of my early fishing experiences happened in the Blue Earth River, where my brother, John, and I spent many lazy days catching shiners and small bullheads. Very seldom did one catch a fish of any size, the way we did it. Our equipment consisted of a ten foot willow pole, fifteen feet of cheap line, a hook, a bobber, and a small bolt or nut for a sinker. Occasionally one would catch a carp, and the fight would be on. They were wary, indeed, and didn't bite too well on worms, which was all we used for river fishing.

The river was so polluted in those times, that it is a wonder we lived through fish consumption from there. Everyone had cows along both sides of the river and through the summer, the cows always stood in the river to cool off and escape the flies and mosquitoes.

I do remember getting deathly sick from some large suckers caught too near the Rendering Plant, which dumped raw sewage into the river as did the Cities of Blue Earth and Elmore. We could safely eat fish caught or speared in the river in winter time, when freezing temperatures cut down on the bacteria count. We must have been tough to ingest all the add-ons that came with river fish. When the settlers first came to Minnesota, the streams were clear and unpolluted, teeming with Northern and Walleye Pike. The small lakes held plentiful supplies of Bluegills and Crappies, even Brown's Lake named for the Brown Family, which owned the land surrounding the small lake.

By the time I began to fish, the Pike populations had been seriously depleted by over-fishing and indiscriminate spearing in our area. The old Germans called the Northern Pike 'Pickerel', but I never found out why.

I didn't get introduced to real fishing until after Neva and I were married and her uncle, Walt Willis, talked me into going up North to fish Leech Lake and Winnebegoshish, for Walleye and Northern Pike. Once I had caught a few of these lunkers, I was hooked for life and went fishing at least once a year for the big ones on the big lakes.

In recent years, after the small towns along the Blue Earth River installed treatment plants and the Canning and Rendering factories corrected their dumping of raw sewage, our local river fish are once again fit to eat. In fact, they may be better than lake fish, which have a buildup of mercury, of which the river water moves too fast to become loaded. Several local fishermen have told me that if one goes to the right hole, Walleyes are plentiful and safe to eat. Some of these Pike reach the weight of four or five pounds, and that makes good sized fillets.

On the Minnesota River, north of Mankato, one can see Iowa cars and pickups parked along the Hwy 169 corridor. These folks come up to fish for catfish, which come up the river to spawn in early June, usually just after the spring flood. Filleted catfish, deep fried in beer batter, are delicious as southerners have long known. In fact, they raise catfish in captive ponds, feed them some of our corn and soybeans, and serve them in restaurants as a southern delicacy for a big price. Dad caught many catfish just below our River Road Farm in early June, weighing three to six pounds. He used frogs for bait. Unless one fillets catfish, it is difficult to fry them really done without a trip in the oven for a finishing touch. Beer batter was not available in the Quaday domicile because of my Mother's aversion for anything alcoholic."

Quaday's Quotes (Reprinted with permission from RR Quaday) Faribault County Register Monday June 14, 1999

Dick Recalls Fishing Trips With His Buddies

"I can remember one fishing trip to East Chain when I was very small, with Grandpa Charley Quaday. He took along a pitch fork, with which he went below the dam and scooped out five- and six-pound "Pickerel," the German name for Northern Pike.

On another trip to the East Chain of Lakes, we fished for bullheads out of a flat bottom boat. Grandpa Charley, Uncle Jule, Dad, and Charley Leath, a brother-in-law from IL and I filled the boat. We rowed out to about 9 feet deep water in a stiff wind and fished for a couple of hours. The wind became a gale, and forced our boat into a rocky shoreline.

With no life preservers we were actually in great danger, but I was too young to realize it. Jule and Charley Leath jumped out of the boat and held it from being dashed against the rocks. Dad swam ashore with me and carried me up the high bank and back around the lake for two to three miles. That was my first experience with rough water, and I was grateful it was a smaller lake.

My oldest son Charlie, Neva's uncle Walt Willis, and I were fishing up on Lake Winnebegoshish on a launch off Denny's Resort. We had a guide named Clyde running the boat and he decided to go across the lake to the place where the Mississippi River runs into the lake. We had fished for a little over an hour when a squall blew in from the east. In a short time the lake turned into a churning maelstrom, with waves five feet high rolling under us. It was raining cats and dogs, and Clyde headed his launch into the wind and we plowed clear across the lake with the windshield wiper trying bravely to help us see ahead. Everyone crowded under the canopy making the launch too heavy in the front so the boat could not plane, and we struggled against the wind and waves for the 12 miles back to the resort. My main concern was for Charlie and Uncle Walt, who had recently experienced hip replacement, so he was not real steady on his feet."

Quaday's Quotes-partial (Reprinted with permission from RR Quaday) Faribault County Register Monday June 24, 1991

Fishing Up North

"Nodaks Resort was our destination up north for fishing when Neva and I went to Bena, MN, to Lake Winnebegoshish.

After some vacations at this resort Neva decided she would rather do something else, so my fishing buddy became her uncle, Walter Willis. He was born and raised in fishing country and knew all about fishing and hunting.

1992 Nodak Lodge Fishing Trip

Walt and his wife, Eleanor, sort of worked together for the common good as they later bought a cabin on Lake Shamineau. Walt came to our place for pheasant hunting, accompanied by their three children.

1962 Original Willis Cabin Lake Shamineau

Prior to their cabin purchase, Walt and I fished a few years on Winne and Leech Lake. My oldest son, Charlie, took over as a fishing partner when Walt retired to San Diego.

Walt Willis used to go fishing at North Star Camp on Leech Lake when it was too windy for Winnie. It was only six miles south of Bena. We'd rent a row boat, row out about five blocks, anchor, and fish with minnows and spinners. The nastier the weather got, the better the fishing."

Quaday's Quotes-Partial (Reprinted with permission from RR Quaday) Faribault County Register Monday, July 2, 1990

Quaday Shares Memories Of Uncle Walt

"The first time I met Neva's Uncle, Walt Willis, he was on the night shift at the Great Northern Railroad Yards in Staples, MN. Her aunt, Eleanore, worked for the Retirement Home, also in Staples. When you get right down to it, farmers and railroad men do not have a lot in common for conversation. In our case, though, we found many things of common interest to converse over through the years. Walt was an avid fisherman and did his level best to teach me the best way to success in the fishing game. Eleanore and Neva got on well; Neva had spent summers at their place when they lived in Motley, MN.

Walt loved hunting almost as much as fishing and was an excellent shot. When we had pheasants, the Willis family came to our place for a few days or a weekend during the season. When I got the crops in I always got in a few days of fishing, early in the season when fishing was good. Later on, when the weather warmed up, the whole family would get in a weekend at Walt's lake (Lake Shamineau, south of Motley). It is a beautiful, sand bottomed, spring fed lake, with very clear water and few if any rough fish. The hard sandy bottom made it a great swimming lake for children, with few drop-off places to worry the mothers.

1962 Eleanor & Walt Willis Lake Shamineau

The first couple of years we went to Shamineau we rented cabins on the west end of the lake. The Willis family soon got tired of this arrangement and purchased a cabin on Pike Point, in the southwest portion of the lake.

When Walt bought a new boat or motor, I'd have to try it out; when I bought a new tractor or combine Walt would give it the once over. We hunted pheasants together, until the raccoons got so thick there were no pheasants to hunt in our area.

We fished together until Walt's retirement, at which time he moved to San Diego. When the fishing was poor on Lake Shamineau, we fished on Winnebegoshish at Bena and fished the Mississippi River for walleyes. Sometimes we drove down to the Federal Dam six miles south of Bena and fished on Leech Lake.

I remember the 6th of June, 1950, when we fished out of North Star Camp up in Portage Bay on Leech. It was so cold, we put on all the clothes we had along, including our pajamas. We had a piece of canvas along to cover our legs and feet. We rented a rowboat and rowed out about three blocks from shore and still-fished with a spinner and minnow. The walleyes bit steadily until we had our limit. It was hours by the fire before we stopped shivering."

Quaday's Quotes (Reprinted with permission from RR Quaday) Faribault County Register Monday May 24, 1993

Fishing Lake Sylvia With Charlie and Steven

"The first weekend in June has always been my time to head for the lake and a fishing trip. This year is no exception, and Friday morning found me on my way up to Lake Sylvia, halfway between Annandale and Kimball. After 50 years of fishing Rainey, Winnebegoshish and Leech, Sylvia is small and tame. It was featured in the sports section as a good Northern Pike Lake, but I think the writer exaggerated just a little. It is a clear water lake, and one can see clearly at about ten feet deep.

One can fish much later at night with some degree of success, than either Leech or Winnie. Sylvia is not a Walleye lake, but as I arrived before Charlie and Steve, I tried a little casting from shore. Sure enough, I pulled in a ten inch Walleye, a great deal too small to keep. I told the boys when they pulled up, "There's at least one Walleye out in your lake, because I threw him back to grow up."

As soon as we could unpack, we put out in Charlie's 15 foot run-about to try our luck. His cabin, or rather, house, is located only 40 yards from a point which juts out into the lake with a drop-off on one side. This is as productive an area as any on either side of the Twin Lakes, as it is sometimes called.

I fished with leeches and the boys used minnows. It wasn't five minutes before we caught a keeper Northern and was very lucky to land him, as Northerns many times will cut off an invisible leader such as I was using and get free. A steel leader about three inches long, is actually standard equipment for Northern fishing. I didn't expect to catch any big enough to cut the nylon leader and hooked him in the lip, so he didn't have the chance. Bass are plentiful and fun to catch in Sylvia, some of which reach three to five pounds. They put up just about as much fight as Northerns and will usually surface trying to shake out the hook, many times succeeding. Northerns, on the other hand, will traditionally dive deep trying to wind the line into the weeds to get enough slack to spit out the hook.

We caught fish every time we went out, but after the first flurry I did not do very well. I was using a fly rod, which is actually for sunfish or crappies, and has much too sensitive a tip to set the hook properly on bigger fish. Charlie and his youngest son, Steven, are both good fishermen, getting a good share of their bites in the boat. I used up all my leeches without doing any catching and had to go to minnows without much better luck.

We fished Monday evening, but the biting was light and the catching was poor. It was a wonderful day to be out on the lake and the sunset was gorgeous. That was just before the mosquitoes took over, with the distinctive whine so common in northern Minnesota at this time of year. We had planned to fish on Tuesday morning but it was raining, so I packed up and headed for home. I did bring home a few filleted Bass and Northerns."

Quaday's Quotes -partial (Reprinted with permission from RR Quaday) Faribault County Register Monday June 28, 1999

County Fairs
County Fair And 4-H Projects Offer Endless Learning Opportunities

"The Faribault County Fair, which has a rich tradition for exhibitions of quality produce through the years, begins today at the fairgrounds in Blue Earth. Neva and I have many fond memories concerning 4-H Club work with our children: preparing records, last minute preparations and the climax of it all, the proud showing of the livestock or project at the County Fair.

No one could have been greener than Neva and I, when we enrolled our oldest son Charlie in the Jo Daviess 4-H Club. We need not have worried.

1955 4-H Joan & Charles Quaday Sheep Project

The adult leaders of the Jo Daviess Club at that time had many years of experience ahead of us and were eager to help new-comers into the world of 4-H. Lucille Nelson, Madeline Ehrich, Alice Winters, and Club President Duane Murphy nursed us along through the first two years, until we got our feet on the sawdust of the livestock ring and pens. The club always held a tour of all the projects enrolled for the fair, usually a week or ten days ahead of the fair.

There were more livestock projects in that club than are now enrolled in the County, I believe. When our nine kids were all in 4-H, we had nearly enough to run our own private fair. Each child had at least three projects, ranging from bread baking to sewing, soil demonstrations, hog, lamb, and beef animals. It seemed no time at all until Neva and I were designated leaders for projects. Sometimes we learned right along with the children, but we didn't risk telling them.

266

Our county was one of the top ten, with extension agents striving to be sent here. We have had many well organized and knowledgeable county agents through the years. One always remembers the best and most thorough teachers. I remember C.G. Gaylord, who was county agent when our children started 4-H. Fred Giesler, Jim Johnson, Harlan Johnsrud, Mr. Williams, all come to mind, and of course Hank Bollum, who was assistant agent for a number of years before being promoted.

Jim Johnson was a fairly cocky young agent, not too long out of college, who prided himself as a cattle judge. We were raising hundreds of hogs and feeding quite a few steers at the time he was here. I'm sure I was just as cocky about my abilities as a cattle judge. The inevitable happened with a case of beer being bet on Charlie's Shorthorn steer. There never was a more carefully weighed steer in the history of the fair, with the end result being a free case of beer for me, which Jim had to buy for being three pounds further off than I."

Quaday's Quotes (Reprinted with permission from RR Quaday) Faribault County Register Monday July 25, 1994

1955 Jim Johnson County Agent

Dick Recalls Some Great Old County Fairs; Dick's Family Was Involved In 4-H Fair Activities

"When I see signs advertising for the Faribault County Fair it always brings back memories of our children in the Jo Daviess 4-H Club. All of our kids participated in 4-H as soon as they were old enough to pick a project to do, and to keep the records necessary to enter the fair competition. Neva and I were 4-H project leaders for 24 years, she in sewing and me in caring for livestock. We hoped for blue ribbons, but competition beyond the County Fair was not a particular goal. We preferred the auction process, where local merchants bid for the purchase of the animals for advertising, paying a premium price which the kids saved for their college educations. One year Charlie, Kay and Joan traveled with me to Havre, MT, and my friend Steve Boyce helped them pick out blue ribbon calves for the next year's fair.

One year Pauline showed a pig we raised that was good enough to compete beyond the county to the JR Livestock Show, where she placed for a blue ribbon. She had to keep the pig's weight down and yet keep the animal lean, so she spent many hours walking her pig and feeding him acorns and grass.

1966 Pauline Swine 4-H Project

My oldest boy, Charlie, worked up a demonstration on soil compaction in 1952-53 that took him to the state fair where he earned a blue ribbon. When we asked our children later in their lives what they had gained from 4-H, they all said the demonstrations given in front of the club and their friends and accepting constructive criticism.

All six girls raised barrows, steers, baked bread, and sewed aprons and dresses. Kay gave a demonstration that took her to the state fair on "bread baking." Jim and Mike were heavy in the beef projects with both heifers and steers. They also showed hogs, with market barrows and pens of three."

Quaday's Quotes-partials (Reprinted with permission from RR Quaday) Faribault County Register Monday July 15 and July 22, 1991

Quaday, Halligan Rule As Fair's Outstanding Senior Citizens

"When it comes to outstanding achievement, Blue Earth's Dick Quaday and Evelyn Halligan sit at the head of a crowded table. Both were recently recognized and crowned as king and queen, during the Faribault County Fair, as the county's Outstanding Senior Citizens.

Quaday believes the honor is one of the highlights of his life and he was shocked to receive it. The retired farmer has been active in SS Peter and Paul Catholic Church, serving on the Board of Directors, in the choir and in other areas. He has also been an active member of the Knights of Columbus for more than 50 years, serving as District Director, working on the Charitable Commission, the State Student Loan Committee, and as one of the state convention organizers. Besides being an active fund raiser, Quaday served as the Blue Earth Township Treasurer for many years, as well as an honorary member of the Future Farmers of America. Dick was also a 4-H leader,

Quaday still writes a weekly column in the Faribault County Register. He and his wife, Neva, have nine children. This year's winners move on to compete at the Minnesota State Fair during Senior Citizens Day."

Faribault County Register - By Editor 1996. Kyle J. MacArthur

Travel

During our life together, Neva and I have traveled through forty-five of our fifty states. International travel included trips to Canada, Mexico, the Caribbean Islands, and briefly, in Central Venezuela, the Caracas, and Aruba, South America. In 1950, we took our first trip west to Montana, Dakotas, Idaho, Washington, Oregon, California, Nevada, Utah, Wyoming, Colorado, and Nebraska. We stopped in Havre, Montana to see Steve Boyce at his ranch.

Incident Profoundly Influenced Thinking

"The story begins long before 1950 in a little town called Motley, MN. Neva's Mother, the late LaRue Fischer, was born in Motley to the John Newcomb family. John ran the heating plant at the local school, after being a boiler operator for the area sawmill for many years.

LaRue's closest friend was Sadie Haymaker, whose family ran the Motley newspaper. The girls grew up together, graduated from high school and went off to different colleges; LaRue to nursing school, and Sadie to teacher's college. They corresponded without seeing each other for 25 years. LaRue met her future husband, Helmuth Fischer, in a hospital in Fargo, ND, where he was a patient with frozen feet. They married and leased a farm in Valley City, ND. Farming was a productive first year; then three

1950 Helmuth and LaRue Fischer

years of drought broke the Fischers, just like the rest of all the other farmers.

The Fischers came back to Minnesota Lake and Helmuth, being a smart and handy mechanic, went to work for his brother-in-law, G. A. Beske, in the John Deere agency. The family lived and prospered in MN Lake and later in Blue Earth, until the second World War. At that time Helmuth heard of high wages in the Kaiser Ship Yard at Portland, OR. He went there and instantly became a pipe welder, which was the most skilled class because every weld had to be perfect. He sent for LaRue and she also became a welder in the shipyard. They built all the tankers to haul crude oil from the Middle East to the US.

In the meantime, Sadie graduated from college and hearing there was a teacher's shortage out West, sent her resume to Havre, MT. She bought passage on the Great Northern Railroad for an interview. When she stepped off the train, a young Irish cowboy named Steve Boyce had finished loading a car-load of horses, which his father had sold to the Army.

The Boyce Ranch at that time raised horses and with seven sons of tough Irish blood, broke them to ride or drive, whichever fit the horse.

Steve saw Sadie and immediately staked his claim, saying, "That's my girl." The rest is history. They were married and went ranching, but times were hard on the ranchers and worse on the farms, with drought and the onset of the Great Depression. The horse business dried up during the sleeping sickness epidemic of the 1930s.

The Boyce Ranch was sold to the Henderson Brothers and Steve went to work for the government trapping wolves, which were ravaging the sheep industry of northern MT.

The couple had seven children to feed and clothe, so a steady income had to be maintained. After six years of trapping, Steve had worked himself out of a job, so he and Sadie bought a ranch in the Bear Paw Mountain area, 27 miles south of Havre, MT. Steve was a good cattleman, and cattle prices were on the way up, so the deal was a success right from the start. He was nearly 60 years young when his ranching career for himself began.

He was on good terms with the Indians on the Rocky Boy Reservation, hiring help and leasing grazing land from them.

When LaRue went west to work in the shipyards, she wrote Sadie that she would be coming through Havre on the railroad and would like to visit. After 25 years, the relationship between the two girls was re-established."

Quaday's Quotes-Partial (Reprinted with permission of RR Quaday) Faribault County Register Monday, May 28, 1990

Stop To Say "Hello" Was Three-Day Stay

"LaRue Fischer was heading for the Swan Island Kaiser Shipyard and stopped off at Havre, MT, to see her old girl-hood chum, Sadie Boyce, who lived on a cattle ranch.

In typical MT style, Steve Boyce said he would take her back to the train after, "He showed her the ranch." The "hello" turned into a three day stay.

LaRue continued on to Portland and welded her way through the war and when it was over, Helmuth and LaRue came back to Minnesota Lake to work into retirement.

Neva's sister, Mary, loved Oregon and her husband, Harvey, got a job welding sawmill burners and heavy logging equipment, so they settled in Ashland, OR.

In 1950, Neva and I hadn't had a vacation since our wedding so we decided to visit Mary and Harvey in Oregon. Her mother told us, "Now when you go west, you stop and say "Hello" to Steve and Sadie." She knew what would happen, of course, but didn't tell us what to expect at Havre.

We had no idea of the vast distances one must travel to get any place out West, so we blithely made a date to meet the Boyces at The Havre Hotel on a certain day in late August, at 6 pm.

We stayed at my brother, John's place in Grand Forks overnight (no money), and set out for Havre at 6 am. We stopped for Mass at Devil's Lake, ND, at nine and drove west, averaging 90 miles per hour between towns. There was no speed limit out west then, thankfully, and we gained an hour or two because of time zones. Anyway, we pulled into The Havre Hotel nearly an hour late after covering 975 miles, besides going to church.

Neva's sister, Gloria and her eight year old son, Roger, were traveling with us. My oldest son, Charles, was along too.

On the way out to the ranch, we had to stop and open seven gates between ranches. The cattle gate had not yet come into existence. These were barb wire, pole and stretch gates, easy for a rancher but tough for a soft handed kid.

Gloria asked Steve's youngest son, Mickey, who was with us, "How far is it out to the farm?" Mickey's reply, "We're not farmers, we're ranchers," very indignantly.

It was dry time yet in August, so the dust on the mud road blew into the car. There was no air conditioning yet in 1950. I had a new 1950 straight eight Buick Special with a low center of gravity, which did not adapt well to Montana high centered roads (if you didn't ride the sides you tore your pan off).

There were no telephones and no electric lights in ranch country yet, so that night after a huge supper we played Whist by lamplight.

The next morning before breakfast, three of the Boyce boys and another guest, Big Hans from Minneapolis, and I got into a football game. The boys were supposed to milk the four cows at that time, but the breakfast

1950 Neva Quaday on horse 'Big Enough' in MT

273

gong caught us still playing football.

Gloria's boy, Roger, would center the ball, then get the heck out of the way, hopefully before annihilation. Hans could block two kids and I'd run over the other one for two easy touchdowns.

The boys had three bodies and soon learned to do it the easy way by passing over the top of Big Hans. The score ended in a tie, with everyone having a battle scar or two. One time Roger didn't quite make it out of the center, but he survived.

After breakfast, Sadie asked one of the boys, "Where is the milk?" Then I found out how high sheep buyers are rated in cattle country.

Steve said, "I need the boys up at the upper ranch for the hay crew." I still milked 10 cows at home by hand then, so I was drafted to milk the four ranch cows which I had never seen in a corral with no ties (I was used to stanchions).

This survived, Steve said he was going to "Show us the ranch."

The boys, Roger and Charlie, were already given a horse and saddle to struggle with, and Mickey stayed with them "so nobody gets killed."

The upper ranch was out of chow, so Steve, Neva, and the food got into the cab of the pickup. Two hay hands and I were relegated to the box outside. We drove 27 miles up and around mountains and were still on Steve's Ranch. Again I'm out of space and will have to continue next week."

Quaday's Quotes (Reprinted with permission from RR Quaday) Faribault County Register Monday, June 4, 1990

Casinos

Neva and I enjoy our Casino trips together. We frequent the Mystic Lake Indian Casino, when weather permits, for a free Monday night hotel and breakfast buffet on Tuesday morning, along with free Bingo. We play often, and I have to say, we have lost very little cash, for the amount of fun we have had.

Dick Recalls First Trip To Las Vegas

"Neva and I have spent a number of our wedding anniversaries in Las Vegas, beginning some 40 years ago, with mixed results. The first time we saw Las Vegas was 1950, and at that time it was just a typically western cow town with the exception of the gambling, without which it would have been mighty poor financially. This year, we hit town a couple of weeks late but that only made for better weather, and this year it was absolutely perfect.

We arrived in Vegas on Saturday night, after walking many miles in airports at each end. The day was lengthened two hours by U.S. time zone changes. Time for bed, right? So, the first thing we did after checking in at The Jockey Club, a time-share apartment and a Christmas present from Pauline and Merlyn, our daughter and son-in-law, was to hoof it over to Bally's Casino.

We played 5 cent machines, with Neva doing well enough to finance me, as I couldn't make mine function for profit. After we had been up for about 18 hours, at 12:30 pm Pacific Time, we decided we had enough and walked home on sidewalks still thick with gamblers.

We had breakfast at home most mornings, but took advantage of the special $1.69 breakfast at The Union Plaza. The buffets in the big hotels cost between $5 and $6, and have every kind of food in the world--all you can eat. I loaded up on several of the buffets, but still lost 3 pounds from all the walking we did.

On Tuesday, we bought a bus package to the Golden Nugget in Laughlin, NV, down the Colorado River from Vegas about 100 miles. Laughlin was started by a Minnesota man and has grown even faster than Vegas. There are seven or eight huge casinos, located across from Bullhead City on the Colorado River, and every one of them was filled to capacity. There, the slot machines were much more liberal in payouts, and that was one of the few days I broke even."

Quaday's Quotes-partial (reprinted with permission from RR Quaday) Faribault County Register Monday February 26, 1996

Why Do We Go There?

"Ho-Hum--Another birthday come and gone. Neva and I celebrated my 84th by heading to Mystic Lake Casino for a bit of slot machine activity. Outside it was sunny, warm and beautiful; inside it was cold, dark and gloomy. So why do we go there?

There are many reasons why we and millions of other folks attend casinos. The first for Neva and me is that it is one vacation from a mostly humdrum existence, now that we are into old age.

I guess 84 years does qualify me as an old-timer. There is an aura of excitement which comes with the possibility of winning some money that has always stirred my inner being. Casino gambling is one activity that we both enjoy.

The people who run those places do go over-board to attract elderly men and women, many of whom are divorced or widowed and have a bundle of insurance dollars to spend on something. They no longer need material possessions like furniture, fancy clothes, kitchen equipment or a brand new automobile every year. They would rather live comfortably with the things they are used to than break in new equipment and have more do-dads to hang on the wall or store in a dresser drawer. We have told our children, "We do not want any more things; our walls are full of pictures and our closets and dressers are full.

We like gambling cash." They oblige."

Quaday's Quotes-partial (Reprinted with permission from RR Quaday) Faribault County Register Monday September 27, 2004

Dick and Neva Find New Way To Celebrate 66 Years Together

"On the occasion of our 50th Wedding Anniversary, we celebrated for about a month with various clubs, family and friends. Lots of Hoopla!

Since then sixteen anniversaries have come and gone without much partying, with the affair only lasting one or at least two days. This year we decided that, giving our age is in the middle 80s and some year could be our last, we would go the extra mile and squeeze in a little more fun than we had other years. We did! The gambling establishment of the Prior Lake-Shakopee area known as Mystic Lake sends us a few free-bees, especially in winter, to attract us to their diggings hoping we will bring money.

Our anniversary fell on Saturday this year but we don't really like to go there on Saturday, so we decided to partake of their offers on Tuesday, when

1992 50th Wedding Celebration

they cater to elderly folks 55 and up. On Tuesday morning they run two buffet breakfasts; one early and another at 9:30, with a free Bingo following the buffet. The breakfasts are an all-you-can-eat affair, with a fine array of muskmelon, pineapple, honeydew, rolls of all descriptions, waffles, fried potatoes, scrambled eggs, sausage links, bacon, corned beef hash, biscuits and gravy, bananas, orange juice, coffee and soft drinks. I have hardly ever been known to turn down a free handout, especially if it is things I like.

We sometimes play Bingo in the afternoon before starting home. Last year I won what they call the pull tab game, with $100 in cash and $150 in pull tabs. I have never bought nor won any pull tabs before, so didn't know what to look for. I was hastily pulling them open and throwing them in the waste basket. Neva was helping me open them. She had won the game once before and knew what to look for. She told me to look for a line going through the figures, and showed me one. I hastily combed my waste basket for the discards, finding $272 that I had missed. Speaking of pull tabs, the casino sent us a coupon, which, if I bought $10 worth of tabs I got $5 in tabs free. In my ten dollar tab I had a $2 one. In my free tabs I had a $200 one.

I guess I could call myself a lucky gambler. Neva and I agreed on one thing many years ago; if we go gambling, we go together. We would each start with a hundred dollar bill, and if we doubled it we went home. If we lost it, we went home."

Quaday's Quotes- Partial (Reprinted with permission from RR Quaday) Faribault County Register Monday January 28, 2008

Our 68th Anniversary Celebration

"Once every year a married couple celebrates their wedding anniversary, especially if it is a long and happy marriage. Neva and I just finished celebrating our 68th wedding anniversary of wedded bliss.

It began with a fun party at St Luke's, with Arnold and Beatrice Mensing, and Lester and Eulah Paschke, old friends and neighbors from when we lived out at River Road Farm. We try to remember birthdays and anniversaries with coffee and cake or cookies, as we three couples are the last members of our neighborhood "500" card club of 45 years in the Blue Earth area. We then used our free night at Mystic Lake on Monday night, so we could enjoy the free old-timer breakfast on Tuesday January 19, our anniversary day. We drove in a dense, but spotty fog. The trees and shrubs were just gorgeous with frost. We sit at the same table with friends we have made over time and one of the ladies, hearing it was our anniversary, offered to list it on the announcements at the free bingo game. We had to stand up and receive quite a round of whistles, whoops and applause.

When we got out on the road again, the sun came out in patches and the frost came alive with picture-perfect scenery the rest of the way. Neva put on some of the country CDs from the 50s and 60s--before country became polluted with rock and roll. Just as the sun burst forth a male balladeer with a guitar sang "It's Such a Pretty Day Today." Everything was perfectly timed and it all came together, bringing tears to my eyes. I am quite an emotional guy, so I cry at weddings, funerals and other emotional events.

After that song, a great favorite of mine played, "Pick Me Up On Your Way Down." The music back then had simple, straight forward words you could understand and the lyrics included love, laughter, rainy days, pickup trucks, sorry and human nature in general, including accidents and death.

On Monday afternoon we suffered through a bingo game with no luck and played slots for a couple of hours. At about 5 pm, when we usually have supper at home, we drifted to the Minnehaha Café for soup and ice cream.

After supper Neva wanted to play another bingo game, but I had had enough frustration there, so I tried to find some paying slot machines. Neva came up empty at bingo and I didn't find much to crow about until after 11 pm. We decided to call it a day at 1 am. Tuesday, after breakfast, we started for home. It was a great anniversary celebration. Just the two of us and our financial outlay was not much more than it would have cost to take in a show and pay restaurant fare at a posh dinner theater. We had our type of a good time!"

Quaday's Quotes -partial (Reprinted with permission from RR Quaday) Faribault County Register Monday February 1, 2010

An Anniversary Spent At The Slot Machines

"As I type this "Quotes," Neva and I just returned from Mystic Lake Casino, where we went to celebrate our 69th wedding anniversary. We were up on Tuesday morning at 6 am, on the road by 7 am, and unloaded our suitcase at the hotel at 8:30 am.

We inserted a $10 bill each, with no profitable results. At 9:30 am we lined up for the free breakfast buffet, followed by a free bingo game for folks older than 55 years of age. We have qualified for quite a number of years, and with a gold Mystic Lake Club Card, we receive three sheets with three games on them.

We ate heartily on honeydew and muskmelons, scrambled eggs, bacon, diced fried potatoes, sausages, biscuits and gravy, waffles, rolls and coffee. We didn't win bingo. At 11 am we attacked the slots again, stopping only for a 5 pm supper of soup and a sandwich, followed by ice cream--for which we paid, getting a discount of 15 percent for being a Club member. Neva was having terrible luck so I suggested we stop for supper, telling her things might improve after taking a break. They did.

We each took $300 along, fully expecting to come home either broke or badly bent. I had been cruising along rather well early in the afternoon, but things had begun to sour by supper time. We talked it over and decided to keep going full bore and if we went broke, we would save enough money for breakfast and just watch a movie, people-watch or retire for the night a bit early. At our age who knows how many more anniversaries we'll celebrate, so we wanted to do it up right. We did.

We still had a number of machines to try after supper and, sure enough, we found several which were in a paying mood. We play nothing but 2-cent machines, but of course, if you designate enough two cents it runs into higher figures, like fifty 2-centers make a dollar.

Some machines don't play less than fifty 2-centers, so the public is actually tricked into playing a dollar a poke. At about 10 pm, Neva let out a yell. She had hit a bonus of 50 free games, which doubles the payouts. While in the bonus 50 freebies, she hit the bonus again, so she had hundreds of free games all multiplied times four on any wins.

Almost all the modern slots pay out with paper slips which one can cash at a cashier window; or if one is in a hurry, at an automatic cash machine. There are ATM's all over the place, too. They make it so easy to blow your money.

About five minutes later, I hit the bonus five coins on my machine. We were playing side by side then, but I had to be satisfied with less than half as much as Neva cashed in. We played on, cashing in smaller tickets and going up and down until 1 am, and then called it a day.

Upon hearing that we were celebrating our 69th anniversary, our waitress at the Minnehaha Café who we always ask for when we have supper, brought a tremendous frosted cupcake for us which we shared at bedtime--free, of course. It was thoughtful of her and it was good.

I don't know whether we would be called VIP customers or not but they treat us very well, especially when we win money; they always congratulate us.

We seldom go in the winter unless we have some big deal to celebrate. I suppose some folks would consider us addicts, but we hardly qualify for that title. The same people who figure us addicted gamblers probably spend as much, or more, on hunting, fishing equipment, golf, whiskey, cigarettes, high-priced cars or a show place at the lake. We both enjoy playing bingo and slot machines and, occasionally, get a pretty good payoff. One does not win any jackpots on the other playthings. It is our thing, and fun for us.

The streets and sidewalks have been so icy and full of snow all winter so far this year, that it has been risky to go out walking and some days almost too cold to keep up our walking exercises. It has been a long winter already and it is only half over. I still do my exercise routine every day before breakfast, no matter where we are or what is going on. It only takes a half hour and they tell us it is necessary for old people to get a certain amount of exercise to ward off heart trouble and the many other maladies that slow old people down. My blood pressure is still perfect and I haven't gained a pound since high school graduation, so it must be working. We try our best to stay in shape and enjoy life as we go along."

Quaday's Quotes (Reprinted with permission from RR Quaday) Faribault County Register Monday January 31, 2011

Iowa-Style Holiday Impresses Dick

"On about the 1st of June, we were invited to Soldier, Iowa, to spend the 4th of July weekend with Jim and Elsie Kalskett.

I always like to drive through the Corn Belt in two or three directions just to look over the crops.

We met our daughter, Peg and Craig and the kids, at Humbolt and traveled together to Soldier. The trip was uneventful, except for a serious, four ambulance accident west of Rockwell City. Had we not stopped in Humboldt for ice cream, it could have very easily been us in one of the mercy vehicles.

All the young people were primed for a trip to an Indian Casino about 30 miles away on No. 29. It has never taken much arm twisting to include Neva and me in such a venture, so accompanied by Elsie, Craig and Peg, and Gary and Diane Kalskett, we set off in Gary's van.

The place was too crowded to swing one's arms about but a good time was had by all, especially Neva, who hauled out a little Indian money.

On the way home, we began to see some lightning in the distance. Sure enough we woke up to a nice shower which they had been praying for. The crops were as good as I've ever seen but the hill country of southwestern Iowa needed a shower to keep them progressing.

The sound of meadowlarks woke me about 5:30 am, a sound I have nearly forgotten. There is much pasture land in the area and killdeers were everywhere.

After a sumptuous feast for breakfast, Jim and Elsie gave us a guided tour of parts of three counties. We saw Pisgah, Iowa, where C.W. (Cash) McCall made the famous commercial at The Old Home Fill'er Up, and Keep On Truckn' Cafe, with Mavis Davis, the waitress, pouring him a hot cup of coffee. The cafe is still there but we didn't see Mavis. The film had McCall driving a semi load of white chickens. The town is located at the edge of The Loess Hills (pronounced Loss). These hills were never leveled by glaciers and in some places are very steep, with Murray Hill high enough for hang-gliding. The soil is very exotic with the only other soil like it in China.

We drove on out of the hills toward the Missouri River, a distance of about 40 miles. We drove through River Sioux and Little Sioux, the location of Abe's Place, a water hole where the River Rats and the Hillbillies danced, drank and fought in the old days.

All of Jim and Elsie's six children live within 40 miles of home except Craig, who lives near Leland, Iowa. They all own farm land or work in farm related occupations. Besides farming, Gary Kalskett, works in a hospital in Denison. Gary and Diane hosted the 4th celebration, with a feed bunk full of food (a 16 foot bunk FULL of food), gallons of lemonade and coffee, and the gol-blamdest picnic table I have ever seen.

One of Craig's neighbors made it and loans it all over the area. It is near 20 feet long and mounts on wheels so it can be pulled around with a pickup. The wheels are de-mountable and there is a jack on each end which raises it to put the wheels back on for transit. I think around 30 people sat around it without crowding.

After dark, Gary treated us to fireworks comparable to the old 4th celebrations at our fairgrounds. Right on cue, a shower started to form in the west and the fireworks against the storm clouds with interspersed lightning made a memorable display. Many uninvited people parked along the road to watch.

As we were packing for home, a bobwhite serenaded us under our window, a sound I hadn't heard since leaving the farm. They are usually very timid but this one walked around in the open spaces as though he owned the place."

Quaday's Quotes-partial (Reprinted with permission from RR Quaday) Faribault County Register Monday July 20, 1992

Breakfast Club
Breakfast Club Brunch and Old Friends

"One day in the middle of March Neva was feeling okay and decided that she should be hosting a brunch for our Thursday Breakfast Club, which has been in operation for twenty years or more. We have had a few extra events through the years but, by-and-large, it has been breakfast at Country Kitchen every Thursday morning at 9 am.

Larry Trenary demonstrated his cooking abilities with a brisket supper once and Margaret demonstrated her new remote control vacuum cleaner one evening.

The Club actually formed with Ralph and Dorothy Ficken and Neva and I having an occasional breakfast at the Country Kitchen, with the Thursday date becoming regular over time. When the Trenary's retired they moved in across the street from Fickens, and with both families working a long time for Green Giant and we as long time growers, it was a natural.

The Richard Christiansons moved into the neighborhood and were invited to join us a few years later. As time went on, the Fickens and the Christiansons developed health problems, ended up in St Luke's and passed to their reward. Ray Wigern and Donna Nelson lived next door to the Christiansons and were invited to come along and became long-time members. Larry and Jeanne Larkin live across the street and asked to join the crowd when they saw how much fun we had. When Lonnie and Janine Skaar moved to Blue Earth from Britt, Iowa, Lonnie being a Grant School buddy of Larry Trenary, and his wife Janine, were asked to come along and join the fun. When we all make it on Thursday's now, we fill up two tables at Country Kitchen. Lawrence and Bea Wolf were the last to move into the South Nicollet area and, with a long time Green Giant connection they fit right in with us.

The management of Country Kitchen is very glad to have a steady local flow of breakfast patrons and treat us very well, helping us to celebrate birthdays and wedding anniversaries. Neva mentioned the brunch plans at one of our Quaday Family parties and daughter, Jeanette, who is now a famous chef at

Eden Prairie Schools, volunteered to come and cook and serve the brunch if it was scheduled after school was over in June. The offer was eagerly accepted and when our other girls, Kay Husfeldt and Mary Stoffel, heard the plans they wanted to join the fun. In the meantime, daughter Pauline Siem's job at the Faribault County Library was terminated, so she wanted in also. That made quite a kitchen crew. They bought and prepared all the food and came to Blue Earth on Wednesday, having an old time slumber party at the Super 8.

They were bright and early and had a feast of eggs and sausage bake, an original concoction of Jeanette's (delicious). An apple, grape, and celery salad was made by Kay, who also made the breakfast caramel rolls. I don't remember who made the coffee cake, but it too was delicious. Mary, who doesn't care to be a cook, helped pay for the materials and Neva made the coffee. It was a very successful meal, all served in grand style by our three daughters. Pauline was there but had to go to work, so she missed out on most of the fun. Seating around the big dining room table, which expands to seat twelve, with linen table cloth, cloth napkins, all of Neva's fancy china and serving dishes, was quite a sight. Of course pictures had to be taken of the event, which will most likely be one of a kind in our mansion. The remark of our guests, "The girls are having just as much fun as we are." They had their own private table out in the kitchen, with the same menu."

Quaday's Quotes -partial (Reprinted with permission from RR Quaday) Faribault County Register Monday June 28, 2010

Neva Celebrates Eighty Years

"An 80th Birthday only comes around once and Neva hadn't even had a birthday 'party' yet, so it was high time to get it done. Our six daughters have a get-together at Jeanette's Lake Sylvia home on the anniversary of Kay's liver transplant in July. This year they hatched the idea of an 80th birthday party for their mother. They called me, asking what I thought about the idea.

My reply, "I'm all for it, but it will have to be kept quiet because she won't want it."

We agreed that we would not tell her until all arrangements were made and the invitations out. I nearly let it out myself when typing up addresses of relatives and friends living at a distance by leaving the Christmas cards out on my basement desk overnight. Neva walks by there 20 times a day but she never noticed them.

On a trip to Minneapolis for a doctor's appointment, I told her we had better go shopping for a new outfit for the birthday party. The thought of a new fall suit made the party sound much better and I spotted one in the Roseville Mall that looked like her color. Wonder of wonders--it fit like a glove. She usually has to have alterations which she does herself. It is the type of suit that she will wear for many years because she liked it and it is not a trendy style; very conservative. All the daughters approved my taste and agreed it was just meant for Neva.

I wanted her to have a dozen red roses from me to display at her entrance table near the card bowl. I was a bit hesitant to order them because of an event that my rancher friend, Steve Boyce, had told me about many years ago. He owned a matched team of black Percheron mares, large draft horses which he used for ranch winter feeding of cattle. They were perfect in every detail and big enough for heavy work. One day, a stranger came to the ranch looking for directions to a neighbor's ranch. He saw the team and asked how much Steve would take for them. Steve, who was several times a millionaire by then, said he didn't want to sell them. The stranger persisted, so Steve put an exorbitant price (for that time in 1950) of $1000.

The gentleman whipped out his checkbook and wrote out a $1000 check. When Steve and Sadie were married back in the 1930s he didn't have money to buy her an engagement ring, so that's what he decided to do with the $1000. He presented her with the expensive ring and it was such a shock, she fainted away. They were nearly 70 years old at the time and he was afraid she had a heart attack. Steve said he would never do that again. "I darn near lost her," was his comment on the matter.

Neva has always been a lover of flowers, flower gardens and center pieces with flowers. I, on the other hand, don't appreciate flowers because of my pollen allergies. I have always told her that, if it didn't produce corn or a pod of soybeans, what good was it?

So I, after hearing about shocking an aged wife with an unexpected gift, was somewhat worried about the roses. It is the very first time that I ever bought flowers for Neva. Thankfully, roses don't spew pollen all over the

285

Neva's 80th Birthday Celebration

room so they didn't set off a sneezing binge for me while the party was rolling, and I got to mingle and visit with all the guests. I guess nothing I do shocks Neva anymore.

The party was a huge success. All our children came with all but three of our grandchildren.

My oldest brother, Carl and his wife, Mildred, came with his son Duane. My sister, Marie, came with her oldest daughter Carol and husband John. All of Neva's side of the family--her sister Gloria and her three children: LaRue Staloch, Shirlee Stevens and Paul Harris with his wife, Zee. Silvin and Joyce Pribyl from Owatonna, old Knights of Columbus friends came to help celebrate. Many of our children's friends from school days came. A special Mass at SS Peter and Paul's Church followed the party. Father Ozburn and Father Brown each wrote a letter for Father Troffler to read.

It only happens once, so we did it up right."

Quaday's Quotes (Reprinted with permission from RR Quaday) Faribault County Register Monday November 2, 2004

The Lost Art Of Ballroom Dancing

"In my youth, dancing was a very popular entertainment. Local bands, including Whoopee John, all had their fan followings wherever they played.

At high school parties and Proms, dancing in the gym and live dance music were always provided. In those days the young man took a firm hold of his dance partner to keep her from falling, since she was perched on spike heels. Anyway, it always seemed so much fun to get one's arm around someone else's girl. It was a great way to meet the opposite sex, and many couples who could dance well together were later married.

Bancroft, IA, Bass Lake, Lakota, IA, and Interlaken Ballroom in Fairmont were the Dance Halls of the time.

Two weeks ago my oldest daughter, Kay and her new husband Larry Husfeldt, held a wedding dance at the Lake Marion Ballroom. Larry's son, Doug, plays drums in a rock band, so we danced to some modern music.

The dances today are so different from the old waltzes, fox trots and polkas that were so popular in my generation. This was the first time I had been to the Lake Marion Ballroom and I was impressed. Since Neva had her back surgery she doesn't dance, but she certainly enjoys the music, and has a good time watching the kids do their thing on the dance floor. Larry and Kay's home is just across the road from the Lake Marion Ballroom and Supper Club. I have no idea exactly why the big ballrooms have disappeared, but they certainly have."

Quaday's Quotes (Reprinted with permission from RR Quaday) Faribault County Register Monday November 2, 2004

Lost Jacket May Soon Be Found

"Strange things do happen sometimes when the Quaday family gets together. In mid-April our daughter Mary's stepson, Tom, was on his way to the Bush War in Iraq and had one week at Jim and Mary's before shipping out. They threw a party so the relatives could see Tom off. It was darn cold that day so we all wore winter jackets. I rode up to Isanti with our son Jim, and his son, Nico. They had it hot in the car so I took my jacket off and carried it to the party. I thought it would be held out in their big machine shed where we would have plenty of room but it would be cold. They had it in their garage and with two heaters, it was hot.

We all threw our hats and jackets on a big table until it was time to go. I grabbed a jacket of the same material as mine, threw it in the car, and when I got home, hung it in the back of our hall closet. On Thanksgiving Day, I reached back in the closet, grabbed my jacket and put it on. It felt different somehow. I looked down and saw a Corvette logo on the pocket. It fit me perfectly so I knew it had to be our son-in-law's, Larry Husfeldt's. He is a Corvette enthusiast and about my size. I wore it up to Kay and Larry's for dinner, showing off my nice jacket. He said he went to go home after Tom's party and the only coat left wasn't his, so he left it there. I figured he would have my jacket at their place in Brownton. No such luck!

They are coming to Blue Earth for the Quaday Family Christmas party early in December, so I can get it then. A week later I remembered to call Mary, getting her answering machine. She called back the next morning and Neva answered the phone, telling her about the mix up. Mary had almost given my jacket to the Salvation Army and was going to do so the very next day. Kay was going to order Larry a new Corvette jacket the day after Thanksgiving. Hopefully, at our annual Christmas party, everything will be straightened out with the jackets. Nobody hurt, but of course winter will be nearly half over with two guys freezing away the first half."

Quaday's Quotes-partial (Reprinted with permission from RR Quaday) Faribault County Register Monday December 10, 2007

288

Quaday's Quotes

Semi-Retirement

In 1982, we retired from active farming and rented the farm to Mike, our youngest son. We agreed on a stock partnership. He cash rented all the land I had farmed, but the landlords raised the rent. We were under the President Ronald Reagan administration, and his policies nearly broke half of the young, upcoming farmers. Mike started his farming operation with sixty thousand in equity, and in two years he was one-hundred sixty thousand in debt.

1985 River Road Farm Auction

In January of 1985, we were forced into a farm auction where the machinery brought ten thousand dollars more than the estimate by the auctioneer. I had washed all the windows on all the trucks, the tractors, and the combines the day before the auction. It helped. The day after the sale I was so tired I was out in my station wagon, heading to town for breakfast, before I realized I hadn't shaved, brushed my teeth or cleaned up yet.

I had worked two years for Mike, and worked harder for him than I did for myself, wanting so badly for him to succeed.

River House

Neva and I made an agreement before we began to build the River House; she did the blue prints and the inside of the house. I did the outside, garage and landscaping. Neva forgot to allow for the chimney, so we had to redraw the prints to allow the chimney to go up through the center ridge, to avoid getting smoked out from the fireplace. She had one entry door opening the wrong way, so we adjusted that error and we tripled the insulation in the attic.

Building Home Was Enjoyable

"In May of 1978, Gus Katzke stopped by the house inquiring about a corner of our pasture that he liked, to build a home on the Blue Earth River bank. My youngest son, Mike, was getting serious with an Iowa farm girl and wanted to farm. Neva and I had been thinking of remodeling the farmhouse on the Home Place, but put it on hold until we found out what the young couple had in mind.

My decision to Gus after thinking about our situation was an easy, "No, Neva and I are going to use that piece of land for our new home." Gus's comeback was, "Dick, two houses will look better than one." So we made a deal.

1980 River Road House

We went to Minnesota Lake, Neva's home town, to talk to Nordaas North American Homes. They showed us some of their houses and they looked well built to me, so we discussed price.

We wanted a modest, no frills house. Since we owned our lot and we sold a lot to Gus, financing was streamlined as much as possible.

The Nordaas office force was very professional and knew their business well, so the blueprints didn't need much changing.

We hired Jerome Wiltse to dig the basement and haul the clay into my cattle yard which needed fill badly. Neva's nephew, Paul Harris from

290

Minnesota Lake, had a crew of block layers, so we hired him to set up the foundation. The only variation from other basements was that I wanted to do the tiling myself. Charlie and Mike helped me dig and we put one string around the foundation, just above the footing. We put two more strings under the basement floor, with another running to a drain under each stall into the garage.

Our extra work paid off, since we had a downpour the first year we lived in the house, and not one drop of water in our basement."

Quaday's Quotes-partial (Reprinted with permission from RR Quaday) Faribault County Register Monday January 4, 1993

Our neighbor next door to the River House was Gus Katzke. He was sure our retaining wall was on his lot, so he hired a surveyor to prove his point, but the property lines were correct. I refused to pay the surveyor's bill. Gus's dog ran all over our wet driveway concrete, so that had to be replaced at his expense. When things settled down, Gus and I decided to change one acre parcels to square up our lots; I gave him forty feet by the road to square his driveway.

Retirement

In 1986, Neva and I moved into 218 West fifth Street on Mother's Day. We had a huge remodeling job ahead of us. We remodeled the kitchen, installed a new fuse box, carpeted and paper/painted the living room, replaced the linoleum in the bathrooms, sanded and varnished all the woodwork, and rebuilt the basement shower and laundry room. Our children bought me a set of new golf clubs and stock in the Minn-Iowa Golf Club. We had a foursome, Lester Paschke, Don Guerber, Weldon Willette, and later Raymond Frey, who played regularly until I had shoulder and hip problems in 1997, and had to quit.

Dick Takes Readers On A Tour Of His Home

"We are going to tour our home at 218 West 5th Street in Blue Earth.

It is the fourth home that Neva and I have owned and lived in. We have come full circle, having owned the Sailor Place on River Road, which was a primitive structure at best, to the Oak Ridge Farm house (the Home Place), to a new home on the banks of the Blue Earth River, to our "Town House."

291

When Mike sold out from farming, we tired of looking at the empty farm buildings on my home farm, so we decided to sell the River House and move into Blue Earth.

Having been born and raised on the Home Farm, which my Dad always called Oak Ridge Farm because of the abundance of oak trees along the river, I was very apprehensive about moving to town. I feared I would get bored and have too much idle time.

It hasn't turned out that way. Neva and I have been so busy since we moved to town I wonder how I had time to farm.

1992 Blue Earth 'Town House'

Our present house is in the older part of town. We purchased it from the Jerome Wiltse Estate. Kitty Fletcher was our realtor. Jerome had done all the expensive things to make the old house livable, with the added exterior feature of new windows and shutters.

Neva supervised the re-decorating and changed the floor plan. She also bought new oak kitchen cabinets and incorporated a new shower and laundry room in the basement. New carpet in the living room and bedrooms and new linoleum in the kitchen, with all new wall paper, brightened up the interior.

The beautifully carved staircase was never changed and is a silent reminder of the age of the house. The basement contains a stove, sink and refrigerator, bar, pool table, and poker table. Our color TV, daybed, and two Lazy Boy chairs complete the comfort zone, where we read and Neva does her fancy work, while watching TV.

Blue Earth House Living Room

We have a few trophies of our farming days, such as the Frank Brothers' corn production 1st prize yield of 185 bushels per acre (sounds small now, but came in 1966, with 40-inch rows). Also we have an "I Love Lamb" miniature statue for my many years of lamb production and feeding.

This last Christmas, Kay and Larry had a WD Allis Chalmers Tractor built for me to remind me of the old money makers of which I owned five (every time I traded one off I missed it so much around the farm, that I bought another one). It is completely made of different kinds of wood, built perfectly to scale; a real work of art, without a nail or screw in it.

I have several Knights of Columbus trophies: one for outstanding District Deputy, a Family of the Year Award, a first place trophy for bowling at the State K.C. Tournament (this award for State Officers only).

I have a Blue Earth City League trophy for bowling one pin from a perfect game in league bowling in 1964.

Three Charles Russell prints of the early days in Montana grace our living room wall. Uncle Jule's Hamilton Railroad watch, under glass, adorns a buffet table.

I mounted the 4th Degree Swords of D.D. Murphy and his two 4th Degree sons, Vincent and Cyril, all Charter Members of our Knights of Columbus Council 1836. This I did after joining the 4th Degree (Patriotism), of the Knights of Columbus. These swords date back to around 1920. A different style is used now.

Baby photos and graduation photos of our nine children adorn the "L" wall of our basement, with grandchildren (16) pictured on the east wall next to an aerial photo of our River Road Farm."

Quaday's Quotes-partial (Reprinted with permission from RR Quaday) Faribault County Register Monday March 8, 1993

Poetry
Poetry and Farming

"The meaning of the word "Poetry" apparently has taken a drastic change since I took grammar, English and literature in Blue Earth High School in the mid-thirties. The beautiful words of Shelly, Keats, and Browning were written in various rhythms, and with a little poetic license, they rhymed. At that time, this form of literature was called poetry. To me, poetry could easily be put to music in a way to sound pleasant, even to one uneducated in music. Things do change through the years, and the poetry of our present day is simply a collection of beautifully descriptive words assembled on a paper. It does not rhyme and it is not verse. To me, it is a hybrid, developed from both prose and poetry and like the proverbial "mule," has its good and bad characteristics. As a poet, I have always considered myself to be in the strictly "corny" category.

One should always do what one likes best, so I've thrived on telling stories and composing essays, which are sometimes sarcastic, sometimes critical, and hopefully, interesting. I must say that anyone who has been praised in "Quotes," has darn well earned it. That old Scotsman, Robert Burns, was a poet and a farmer; historically, a much better poet than farmer. I have always leaned towards being a better farmer than poet, with a longing to be good at both. My critics and detractors would probably put me into the "mediocre" class of farming, poetry and prose, but if they read the stuff I wrote, and ate the food I produced while farming out on River Road, I would be satisfied.

Many years ago when I was young, in love, in farming, and independent, I would sometimes compose a silly song or some corny poetry, while doing some routine task which did not require strict attention to the business at hand. A few weeks ago, Neva was cleaning out drawers and throwing junk accumulated through the years. She came across a poem that I had written many years ago in one of my more exuberant moods, and long before farming out on our River Road Farm had become a business, and somewhat of a drag. I noticed an ad in a periodical about a poetry contest sponsored by The National Library of Poetry, located in Owings Mills, Maryland. While in a lighthearted mood I thought, "What the heck can I lose?" Only one $.32 stamp went into the investment category, "What can I lose?" Very shortly back came a reply praising my verse rhythm. Being of a suspicious nature, I immediately thought "scam" as they would publish my poem in an anthology book, which would be in print soon. The book would cost me $43. I was a semi-finalist in the contest which had a $1000 first prize.

Our River Road Farm

The buildings are white
The fields are green
It's the prettiest farm
I've ever seen.

The Blue Earth River
Deep and Wide
Runs silent, past
The eastern side.

I vow our farm
Will never see
A button weed
As tall as me.

This farm of ours
Has raised our nine
All healthy as
The tallest pine.

Our blue black earth
Which named our town
Produces crops
Of world renown.

Now, really, what would you expect from an old dirt farmer?"

Quaday's Quotes- partial (reprinted with permission from RR Quaday) Faribault County Register
Monday January 29, 1996

This is one I wrote when we were at the end of our farming career.

Old Farmer's Retirement Rhyme

"I ain't ever
Gonna farm no more
No early mornin'
Or late night chore.

No early spring mortgage
Due March first
No hot mow work
Dying of thirst.

My corn is all picked
My hay is all made
I can watch farmers work
Sitting in the shade.

My cows are all milked
The hogs are all fed
So now I can spend
More time in bed."

Quaday's Quotes -partial (Reprinted with permission from RR Quaday) Faribault County Register
Monday September 7, 1998

An Old Age Ditty

The setting sun
Is quite like me
An old, bent tree
Is more like me
One day, of course
I'll planted be
I'll never make
One hundred three
And that is young yet
For a tree.

June 17, 1971

Pa's 90 Years

The birth was number one
For Charles and Pauline
When Pa was born in '81
By a lamp of kerosene.

Times were hard
Life was a battle
Pa's earliest job
Was herding cattle.

Plenty of work
And not much school
The Blue Earth River
Was Pa's swimming pool.

When fodder was shocked
And grain was in stacks
It was off to the woods
With the saw and the ax.

When Charley lost an arm
In a horse power rig
Then Will did the work
And he wasn't very big.

297

He tipped the scale at one hundred thirty five
Five feet ten from head to toe
Very strong and lightning quick
With boxing gloves he was pretty slick.

When Pa was twenty five
He met a school marm
He decided to marry
And keep her from harm.

Four kids came along
One at a time
Three boys and a girl
Brought them joy sublime.

On Pa's farm
The Bible was read
Every morning
Before the stock was fed.

In '31 Pa paid the taxes
Said the politicians are fickle
That old Herbert Hoover
Just got our last nickel.

Times were tough
We were losing the farm
Pa played basketball and hurt his arm
He was about ready to holler enough.

When Grandpa said "Let's go to Californ"
Away they went and Pa was reborn
Came back and farmed fifteen more years
Made lots of money and had no fears.

For sixty years
Some time he'd take
At ten and at three
For a coffee break.

When sixty five Ma said let's quit
We've done our share

Let's rest a bit
and for each other care.

Life didn't get him down
Nor did he get poor
The twenty years in town
At 415 South Moore.

My Life

I always was a sickly child
Tended by Mother, so tender and mild

In my teens, the Lord said "Grow"
Our River Road fields, He said "Sow"

I married Neva, a wonderful girl
Our love produced a family of nine
All healthy as the tallest pine.

And when our farming days were done
We felt that battle had been won.

Then, instead of raising oats
I spent 21 years at writing "Quotes"

When the Lord said "Time to Rest"
Whatever I've done, I've done my best.

Minnesota

Minnesota Minnesota,
Land of plenty, Land of chance
Gets so cold there, in the winter
That you need six pairs of pants.

Tis the land of tall Norwegians
Ole, Oscar, Nels, and Hans
When the music starts a playin'
Oh! How those tall boys can dance.

Gets so hot there, in the summer
Burns your skin, and makes you sweat
If you feel like going swimming
Lots of lakes there to get wet.

Tis the land of farms, and mining
Mines are North, and farming South
Farms alive, and saws a whining
Crops thrive, without a drought.

Tis the land of tall pines forests
Full of rabbits, herd of deer
Lots of hunters, out a hunting
Every Fall, with weather clear.

River Colorado

Mighty River
Flowing down from the mountains

Mighty River
Running out to the sea

The sun on your rapids
Makes your white water glisten

The mighty Colorado
She charms you and me.

When men tried to tame you
With dams made of concrete

Your billion gallons of water
Raised millions of acres of wheat.

You make electric power
By turning giant turbines

You light the teaming cities
And water California's vines.

Corn Talk

In April of 1994, I was introduced as a 'New Feature' for the Minnesota Corn Growers State newspaper, *Corn Talk*, by the Editor Mr. Tom McGraw of Buffalo Lake. He owned and managed a crop monitoring and soil testing business, covering local counties and a five state area. In his column he wrote, "I am happy to offer you, the readers of *Corn Talk*, a subtle change of pace for our monthly publication. Dick Quaday, a retired farmer from Blue Earth, writes of his farming years in a storybook fashion. I think you will find his columns featured in *Corn Talk* not only reminiscent to the old timer, but also gratifying to the younger farmer. Times have changed, and Dick specifically remembers farming as it was in his day." *Corn Talk* will feature Quaday's Qorn from time to time, printing his stories of the trials and experiences of the early farming days in Southern Minnesota.

Quaday's Quotes

"*Quaday's Quotes* was instigated in November of 1989, at a conference between Rich Glennie, who was the Editor of the Blue Earth Post Register; Ms Linda Adams, who was the business manager of the paper, and myself. The column began as an old-timers column, telling stories about my life and times as a farmer, living out on River Road for seven decades, starting in 1920. After a few issues I was given a free rein to state my opinions about past and present events, as I saw them. I have tried to write about things which would interest both young and old people of our farming area, projecting a farmer's viewpoint. The feature articles were requested by Rob Nolte, who succeeded Rich as the Editor of the Faribault County Register, which changed from a bi-weekly publication to a weekly paper.

My literary efforts were so well received that I was asked to syndicate Quotes but I declined, mainly because of the extra research involved. I wanted to have fun doing a column; when it became work I said, I'd stop right there. My hope is to leave a start of a Quaday Family Journal, which some of my children or grand children will someday carry on. This is my reason for delegating Kay Husfeldt to make up books of "Quotes" columns for our nine children. I feel that there is adequate talent coming along to carry on and possibly enlarge upon my literary efforts.
Danke Schön, German for "Thank You,"
Dick Quaday"

Quaday's Quotes-Partial (Reprinted with permission from RR Quaday) Faribault County Register, 1989

FOCUS
ON THE PEOPLE
MONDAY, AUGUST 16, 1999

DEB
O'BRIEN
City Clerk -Frost & Bricelyn

DICK
QUADAY
Local Columnist

Richard Quaday Local Columnist

For twenty years and two months I have been writing "Quotes" for The Faribault County Register. I have never missed a week, nor have I ever missed the nine o'clock Monday morning deadline. I have enjoyed writing every column and my weekly twenty minute conferences with the managing Editor at the time. I have outlasted six editors: Rich Glennie, Leonard Kranzdorf, Rob Nolte, Joe Moss, Kyle McArthur and currently Chuck Hunt, who freely publishes the nasty letters to the editor, for my opinions of politics and other issues. Many letters arrive when I write a Democratic opinion of the middle-east situation and the history of politics in our area. I have written many scoops (opinions) on national issues, before they are talked about on National TV and in publications. I offered my opinion on the quagmire Wars in the middle-east and things that would happen in the Reagan and Bush administrations, and my predictions usually came to be true.

A Little Stir Makes Life Interesting

"It has been my life-long ambition to make enough of a stir to keep my life interesting.

When writing and composing, I always prided myself on being an amateur. There are no aspirations in my little Olympia to gain professional status. Different people are interested in different sections of a weekly paper such as our Faribault County Register.

My sister, Marie, who went to college until she was 60 and has a masters' degree in about everything, spent a weekend with us recently. She was very interested when told I was now a writer of sort. After reading through most of Quotes, she said " I saw one error in grammar in one column. You wrote Neva and I where it should have been Neva and me." Such a small amount of criticism from her, I consider a great accomplishment.

My daughter, Mary, who is still going to college at the age of 42, stopped by on her way from Iowa to the Twin Cities, read a few of my efforts and proclaimed: "Hmmm, not bad."

This type of remark from true intellectuals, I consider high praise. In summing up my ideas and thoughts on the matter, I personally am happy to see that we are being read."

Quaday's Quotes partial (Reprinted with permission from RR Quaday) Faribault County Register Monday September 24, 1990

Quaday Quits His Quotes Column

"Next week's Faribault County Register will be different--something will be missing. For the first time in more than 20 years, the Register will not contain a *Quaday's Quotes* column.

Dick Quaday, our featured columnist, has decided it might be time to hang it up. You can read his final column, where he wraps up some loose ends, and bids his fond farewell to his readers, below.

He and I both want our readers to know this was a mutual decision. Dick still feels he has some good columns left in him, and I think he is probably right. But, at age 90, he says it might be time to 'retire' from this job.

Dick tells me he has "worn out" six editors over the 20 years and three months that he wrote the column. He thought it was five. But, Register publisher Lori Nauman found out it was six. I guess one was here for a very short time, and Dick couldn't even remember the name.

He does remember that it was editor, Rich Glennie, now of Glencoe, who hired him. And, he remembers that he had to educate each editor after that, as to what his column was supposed to be about. That included getting a little upset when an editor would change a thing or two in the column, or argue over a point.

But, for the most part, his column was his own. Dick says he was always grateful that the Register printed his columns, and that the editors over the years were willing to let him pick his subjects and get away with a thing or two.

I'm amazed that he created an interesting column week after week. As someone who has tried to do the same thing over the past 35 years or so, I know it is difficult; sometimes even impossible. Sometimes the column just flows out; other times you just sit in front of the keyboard with no idea what to write about.

Richard Quaday Local Columnist

In my case, a computer screen is involved. In Dick's case, it is a typewriter keyboard. That's right, he had written all of his columns on an old manual typewriter.

He says that in all 20 years, he has only had to start over a column a couple of times. Otherwise, they just flowed out, with few changes needed. (Of course, the editor has sometimes worked a little magic later.)

Doing the math, Dick has written 1,130 columns since he first started. He says he has never missed a week. Well, there was that time that he was scheduled to have surgery in Rochester. He wrote the column at home before he left, but forgot to tell his wife Neva to deliver it to the Register--so there was one issue in which a column didn't appear.

Dick has upset a few people over the years, especially when he wrote about religion and politics. And, yes, there was the occasional reader who wondered why we kept running his opinions; or dropped their subscription in protest. The reason we ran them, of course, was for our readers to enjoy, whether they agreed with him or not.

Many have sent him notes over the years, asking him to keep writing forever. I guess that is not going to happen. How are we going to replace him? Well, you can't really replace a columnist with a similar type of column, as everyone has their own style.

We have chosen to start running a column by well-known writer, humorist and story teller, Al Batt.

We think our readers of the Register will enjoy his weekly column. So, starting next week, *Quaday's Quotes* comes to an end.

Dick thanked me and the Register for running his piece for 20 years. Actually, it is we who should say thanks.

Or should I say, "Danke Schön?"

Editor's Notebook by Chuck Hunt - partial; Faribault County Register Monday February 7, 2011

Dick Says Auf Wiedersehen To All His Readers

"This last issue of "Quotes" will be the hardest one that I have pounded out on my little Olympia Portable typewriter during the past 20 years and three months.

I have thoroughly enjoyed reporting my experiences, activities and opinions of various subjects, new and old. I have tried to keep the articles short enough so my readers can see the end from the beginning; then keep them interesting enough so that they finish reading the whole piece. I don't always finish up an article on the same subject on which I began. My English and grammar teachers do not recommend changing subjects, or changing the flow of thought in opinion pieces of this length. However, teachers are much better paid so they are entitled to their opinions.

My life for 90 years has been more or less an open book. I have tried to cover the old-time activities; what happened, why it happened and how it turned out. It is sometimes hard to remember the exact sequence of events as they occurred 40, 50, or 70 years ago, but the last few years it has become more difficult to remember what happened last week than the events of long ago. I'm told that this is perfectly normal for people after the age of 80, and older. The rudest shock comes when I've gone to the basement for some errand and have forgotten what I went for by the time I get there.

I profusely apologize if my political comments have offended any of my Republican friends, especially the lady who canceled her subscription to the Register because I thought the "Tea Party" would be a short-lived addition to the orthodox Republican Party. I would have cheerfully paid her subscription, but do not know her name or address.

Many of my best friends and about half of our children are rabid Republicans, which is fine with me as they are certainly entitled to their opinions, pro and con. We live in a free country, thankfully, and can think, worship and vote just as we darn please. If we should happen to differ in thought, word or deed from any speaker in public places--be it church, a theater or political meetings--I believe we should hear the speaker out without interruption, being courteous enough to let the speaker finish, then form our own opinions.

I thank all my readers who have sought to correct my diatribes with letters to the editor for their input, pro or con. I stress that my salary does not justify a great deal of research spent to shore up my opinions. I have, through the years, received encouraging letters urging me to continue writing on my chosen path, in a ratio of 10 for to one against. I freely admit that on occasion I have deliberately tried to stir up a little controversy when I ran out of things to write about. After all, one can get pretty bored just writing about the old days, and history about "The Great Depression" and how to avoid another one. We didn't listen very well, did we?

I'm sure our children have gotten tired of having their actions and activities turn up in "Quotes" for 20 years, but Neva and I are continually asked about them. So many of our friends had their children at the same age and after children grow up and scatter, it is hard to keep track of offspring as the generations go by. I know we ask about the progress in education, marriages, grandchildren, jobs and retirements of old friends. We are so grateful that all of our nine children are still alive and well and enjoying life, as we are--with another generation coming along, hale and hearty, getting educated and preparing for life's battles. We are so thankful that we did not have to raise our brood under the present situation, with everything so terribly expensive and so many obstacles to overcome for youngsters.

I hope my readers enjoyed my articles as much as I have enjoyed expressing my feelings about what had been, what is and what will come. I do feel that Neva and I have lived in a golden age when farming was a way of life, as well as a business. We always found a way to enjoy ourselves, even though times were hard and we had no money to spend for enjoyment. We were both Great Depression babies and learned to get along on very little and still have a lot of fun as we went along. We were in debt all of our farming life until we achieved the age of 60 plus. It was a relief to finally get our chin on the curb, have a few bucks to waste, build a new house, travel where we wanted and see what we wanted.

My thanks to the management of the Register for allowing me to write my opinions without interference and let me retire, with no pink slip, when I felt like it.

To all my faithful readers,
Danke Schön and Auf Wiedersehen,
Dick"

Quaday's Quotes (Reprinted with permission from RR Quaday) Faribault County Register Monday February 7, 2011

Dick and Neva Celebrate Their 70th Wedding Anniversary

1942 Richard & Neva Quaday Wedding

On January 19, 2012, our parents, Dick and Neva Quaday celebrated their 70th wedding anniversary. Farming for 70 years didn't hurt their health one bit.

Firm Believer In Love At First Sight

"I am a firm believer in 'love at first sight', in sharp contrast to the present system of courtship which involves five, 10 or 50 years, while raising a family before marriage, if there ever is a marriage.

On a full moon night in mid-August, Neva and I were introduced on Main Street in Blue Earth. My offer of a moonlight ride to Winnebago was promptly accepted, and off we went, cruising Highway 169—no speeding, just enjoying the cool night air. My car was not equipped with air conditioning.

This was 1942, and my car was not new. We cruised around a few blocks in Winnebago before starting for home. By then we were in love, so no hurry. Trying to be romantic I turned the lights off, which made no difference, with the moon so bright. It was a good thing we weren't in a hurry, because Ed Dickman's cows were all out in the road. We went between cows without hitting any for a while, and turned our lights back on before seeing any traffic.

We were married at Nine O'clock Mass in the chapel of SS Peter and Paul's Church, Jan. 19, with Father John Mich officiating. Our attendants were Gordon Siebert and Lauretta Warmka, who married a year later in Easton. We had seven guests who enjoyed a wedding breakfast at the apartment of Helmuth and LaRue Fischer, Neva's parents. Orval Paschke, a guest, had managed to coat the manifold on my car with Limburger cheese, which was steamed off for free, by Roy Dobson at the Motor Inn.

Upon hearing about the wedding, several of the elderly women relatives on both sides offered the opinion "That'll never last." On our wedding day the temperature was 48 degrees and there was no snow, much like 2012. We honeymooned at Farm and Home Week at the St Paul Campus, where Neva began to find out what she had gotten into. She was a city girl who said she would never marry a farmer. Seventy years later, we are still madly in love, as attested by our holding hands as we walk around town together. It is getting to the point that we both need the support about as much as the show of love!

Danke schön,
Dick"

Special to the Register (Reprinted with permission from RR Quaday) Faribault County Register Monday January 16, 2012

2009 Richard & Neva Quaday

Neva and Dick are still together in retirement in their 'town home', and have kept busy with their daily walks and driving everywhere they want to be. Mom cooks the meals, and Dad still appreciates her home cooking. They attend SS Peter and Paul Catholic Church regularly, and live in their own home without any outside assistance.

They celebrate all the family holidays. Mom sends cards on birthdays for children, grand- and great-grand children. They just became biological Great Grandparents for the seventh time on January 6, 2012.

Dad said in one of his columns that his hope was that the Quaday story would continue to be told by his children and grandchildren. We also hope that is the case. By no means does the end of this book signal the end of the saga.

It has been our privilege to present these words of down-home wisdom and common sense that we grew up with, and that have shaped our lives. We are so blessed that these two remarkable people not only brought us into this world, but instilled in us the qualities of honesty, integrity and old fashioned honor that helped to make this country great. Our wish is that you have enjoyed reading this story as much as we have enjoyed bringing it to you.

Danke Schön and Auf Wiedersehen,

The Richard & Neva Quaday family: Dick, Neva, Charles, Kathryn, Joan, Mary, Jeanette, James, Pauline, Margaret and Michael

2010 Quaday Family
Back row: Pauline, James, Jeanette, Mary, Joan, Kay, Charles
Front row: Margaret, Neva, Richard, Michael

14206413R00182

Made in the USA
Lexington, KY
15 March 2012